BEING HUMAN

BEING HUMAN

150 PRACTICES
TO MAKE IT EASIER

GINGER ROTHHAAS

The Library of Congress Cataloging-in-Publication Data
Names: Rothhaas, Ginger, author.
Title: Being Human: 150 Practices to Make it Easier / Ginger Rothhaas.
Description: First Edition.
Identifiers: IBSN 979-8-218-29799-2 (paperback)
Imprint: Walker & Rose

Cover and layout design by Olivia Feathers

To my loves: Rob, Chase, and Lauren. You fill my soul with love, joy, and fun. Thank you for your patience, grace, and love as we all continue to discover what it means to be human. I love being in human school with you.

To my parents: Bev and Jerry. Being your only child has been an honor and privilege. I love you and am so very grateful.

To you: Beloved reader. I hope these practices help make being human a little easier for you. We are having this human experience together. Let's make it a loving one.

TABLE OF CONTENTS

INTRODUCTION

In your hands, you hold a book of practices to help you make life a little easier. It is hard to be human and we are all trying to figure it out. There are a lot of great books on philosophy, theology, psychology, self-help, and caring for our bodies, but this is a book of tools – this is the how. In my library of books, I would flip to the exercises, wanting to cut to the chase and find solutions. I knew what I needed to do, I just didn't know how to get my brain there. This is a book of how.

Author Toni Morrison said: "If there's a book that you want to read, but it hasn't been written yet, then you must write it." This quote never left my mind after reading it for the first time. This is the book I was looking for. So here it is.

I need these 150 tools to help make being human a little easier. So I wrote this book for me, for my precious children Chase and Lauren, and for you. We are all on this human journey together, and I hope this helps us find our way forward.

I write like I talk, so you won't find a super polished technical book—but what you will find is a heartfelt invitation into finding a way to be a more loving person to yourself and others. I have led a successful coaching practice for almost ten years and tested these tools out on clients, my coaching team, my friends, and mostly in my own lived experience. Each of these has been a personal tool to help me. Some are inspired by brilliant people I have learned from; others are created by me in my desperate moments to get unstuck.

Names of my clients have been changed throughout this book; however, they know who they are and I am indebted to them for sharing their story with me and allowing me into their life. Most of my clients have been with me for many years and we continue to navigate life together with the help of these tools.

I want you to have this book on your nightstand or bookshelf and return to it as a quick reference. Let this be a companion in your human experience. I also encourage you to have human companions that help you get through life. I think we all need people to talk to – friends, family, doctors, therapists, teachers, and coaches. Find a loving person who can be neutral and help you find perspective and new ideas for moving forward. Don't hesitate to hire professionals to help you be human. And if a professional doesn't feel like the right fit, keep shopping for the right match. There are lots of great providers out there, so keep looking for the right one for you.

It is so cool that you and I get to be humans on this planet at the same time. We are souls here in human school together. I'm honored to be a student with you. We are all learning new things every day. This book is like me handing you my notes from the classes I've taken. I hope they help make your human school experience a little easier so you can have more fun!

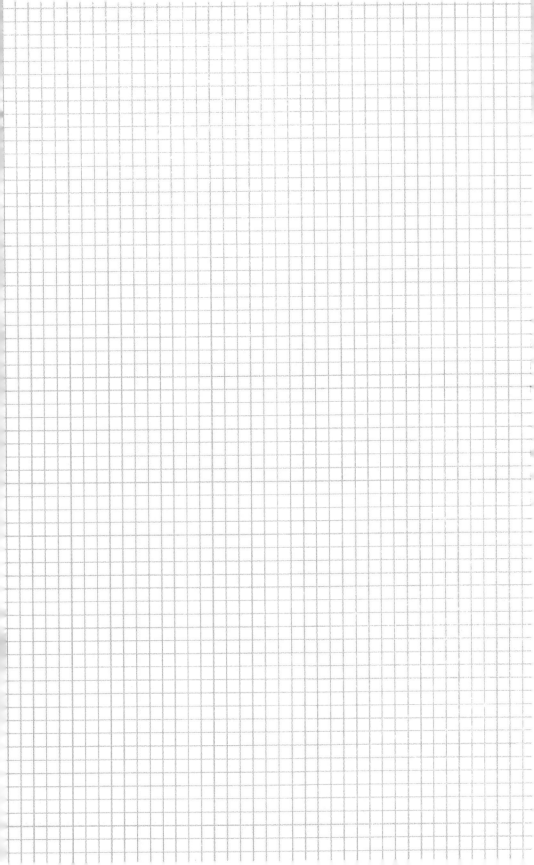

FEEL BETTER QUICK

As I was organizing my favorite tools that help me be human into this book, I noticed that there were some that I go to repeatedly for a quick fix. A few of these may seem obvious to you, like taking a deep breath, but I have included things in this section that almost always lead me to a better mindset, give me clarity, or help me calm my nervous system quickly.

Did you know zebras don't get ulcers? Can snow globes help our brains? Can you tell the difference between facts and stories? Can you believe the Target emblem reminds me of my priorities? Did you know that tears help us get rid of stress hormones? All these insights and more are found in this section.

Dog-ear your favorites, but then come back to this section periodically and try something new. These are great tools to help us feel better quick when life gets overwhelming.

BREATHE DEEP

A few years ago, I learned something really interesting while sitting on the sidelines of my son's baseball game. I was chatting with another parent, who happened to be a pulmonologist. He had just come back from a conference and was telling me about a talk he'd given about how we don't use the full capacity of our lungs, and how, because of that, we often don't take proper deep breaths.

I was intrigued—I certainly knew about the benefits of deep breathing, but had no idea that I might be doing it wrong. He shared with me that because we're often taught to have a tight core, we hold in our stomachs, which actually leads to shallow breathing and less oxygen—which, in turn, can exacerbate the physical effects of stress.

The goal of a deep breath is to fill both lungs with air and to do so, you have to start by completely relaxing your core. Then, place your hand at the bottom of your rib cage. As you inhale, picture your lungs inflating like balloons with the awareness that your lungs extend all the way down to where your hand is. During a truly deep breath, your ribs and belly will expand while your shoulders and chest remain still.

When teaching deep breathing exercises to children, you can place a stuffed animal on their tummy while they lie on their backs. With a deep breath, the animal will rise and fall (an adult can try this method too!).

Deep breathing is an important part of mindful breathing, which is when you focus on your breath to calm a racing mind and bring your attention back to the present. Any time you're feeling stressed or rushed, try just a few moments of mindful breathing, making sure to breathe all the way down to the bottom of your lungs.

After a few deep breaths, you'll notice a calming sensation wash over you as you inflate your entire lung space. Doing so will increase the oxygen flow to your brain, which leads to clearer thinking, calmer behaviors, and a release of stress—truly an expanding practice.

TRY THESE

1. Start by breathing as you normally do without yet focusing on deep breathing; just breathe with ease. On your inhale, focus on the word "inhale;" on your exhale, focus on the word "exhale." As you practice, these words can change to "in" and "out" or another pair of words that help you focus on your breath.

2. Once you feel comfortable enough to progress further, try following the path of air as it travels in through your nose, down your throat, and all the way into the bottom of your lungs. On an exhale, notice the air as it travels back up through your lungs, into the back of your throat, and out through your nose or mouth. Repeat this observation until you notice a sense of calm. Try practicing this exercise several times a week until it becomes second nature to you.

3. Throughout your day, just pause to notice your breathing. Spend a few moments matching the length of an inhale to the length of an exhale. In those few moments, your nervous system calms, you oxygenate your cells, and you can return to your task with renewed energy.

TAKE A SOUL STROLL

Many of us have a watch, phone, or fitness tracker that suggests we take 10,000 steps a day. Like so many things in our lives, this becomes a goal we're trying to reach, a measurement of success, without making us mindful of our intention or what we're really accomplishing.

In the past, I used walking only as a means to an end: either getting to a destination quickly or as a way to lose weight. One day, I heard about the idea of a "walking meditation" and I wanted to know more. I saw this quote, by the author and Buddhist monk Thich Nhat Hanh, and it stuck with me: "Walk as though you are kissing the earth with your feet."[1] Which definitely isn't just a mindless way to get steps in.

I hadn't considered walking as a form of meditation. But I noticed once I turned my walks into a meditation practice, I was calmer, could think more clearly, noticed a greater sense of gratitude, and felt more connected to nature.

No matter where you are—office building, parking lot, gym, city sidewalk, or nature trail—you can turn your steps into what I like to call a "soul stroll."

---

[1] Thich Nhat Hanh, *Peace is Every Step* (New York: Bantam, 1992).

Each time you take a step, be mindful of your movement and the present moment. This walking meditation is a way for you to tune into awareness, peace, and soul guidance. To deepen the experience further, you can even add breathing practices or a mantra. If I feel overwhelmed by a decision I need to make, I might take a walk and, on every exhale, say to myself: "I am taking a step forward."

Soul strolls can be life-changing as a calming mindful practice—and a healthy way to cope with stress. Moving your body triggers the release of endorphins and dopamine, also known as "feel-good hormones." The physical act alone will make you feel better.

As you walk, you can also ask yourself for wisdom. Is there something you're struggling with? See if you can be quiet enough to hear the answer of your soul.

TRY THESE

1. Allow at least 10 minutes today for a mindful soul stroll. Choose a place to walk that will be quiet and contain few distractions. Walk without headphones or conversation.

2. Try gently counting while you walk; begin with a relaxed pace. This is a walk to calm your nervous system and connect your mind, body, and soul. First, notice your right foot. Every time it lands, silently count that as a step until you reach a count of 10 (this might be your thinking: Right foot, 1. Left foot. Right foot, 2. Left foot.). When you reach 10, start over. Count in 10s as long as you need to quiet your mind and become more aware of your steps. Notice that your racing mind quiets as it can only concentrate on counting steps and not the worries of the

day (important reminder: you do not have to look at your feet to count your steps! It's always safer to look forward while you're walking.).

3. When you're ready for something different, try becoming mindful of your heel-toe movement. Without changing your stride, notice when your heel touches the earth, and when your toes touch the earth. Observe this heel-toe rhythm as long as you can to keep your thoughts calm and focused.

4. Now, try to lighten your steps. Walk gently on the earth. Notice if you were stepping heavily or with tension as you began your stroll. Think about floating as you walk and becoming lighter. Try to see if you can let go of stress in other parts of your body as well. Notice if your jaw is tight, relax your forehead, allow your shoulders to drop down, and let your arms swing at your sides.

5. After you feel more at peace and tuned into your body, connect with your soul. Ask yourself questions and see what your soul has to say in response. Feel gratitude for nature or things you see around you. Notice the miracles. Tune your soul into the present moment and identify what you can see, smell, taste, touch, or hear in this moment. Listen to the wisdom of your soul.

SHIFT "WHAT IF" TO "WHAT IS"

As human beings with access to 24/7 news coverage of global crises, pandemics, financial uncertainty, you name it, we spend a lot of time awfulizing: spiraling down a rabbit hole of "What if?" questions.

We can't help ourselves. There are a lot of moving parts in our lives and a lot of things that could go wrong. Somehow, we feel safer if we've considered every possible outcome and what potential devastation might lie ahead.

Awfulizing begins with fear, before our imagination turns it into a worst-case scenario very quickly. You might start with a fear like "the stock market is crashing" and spiral down from there:

- What if I lose everything I gained in the last five years?
- What if I can't retire as planned?
- What if the nation goes into a deep depression?
- What if my company has to close?
- What if I can't find another job?
- What if our lifestyle has to change drastically?
- What if I have to file bankruptcy?

Awfulizing can be toxic. When we are afraid, our amygdala—the "fight or flight" part of our brains—kicks into high gear, and cortisol floods our bodies, keeping us on high alert. This can be harmful to our sleep, relationships, productivity, and mental health.

We can stop the awfulizing and quiet that amygdala by shifting into the pre-frontal cortex, the calm and rational center of our brain. And we can do that by asking ourselves "What is?" questions instead.

When you notice you are spiraling deep down into the what-ifs, you can pull yourself out by asking:

- What is happening right here, right now?
- What is true?
- What is right?
- What is good?
- What is healthy?
- What is in this moment?
- What is likely to happen?
- What is his track record?
- What is she made of?
- What is our connection?
- What is real?

Asking "What is?" questions helps your brain feel safer, reminds you of the truth, and brings you back to the present moment. Remember, our big, beautiful brains are always trying to keep us safe. They love to imagine every scenario and add a disastrous twist or two.

But our job is to notice when this is happening and steer those beautiful brains back to a much safer place: the present. Coming back to what is true at this moment, right here, right now, is a lifeline for quieting our worries.

TRY THESE

Self-talk is a powerful tool to help our brain find calm and rational thinking. The moments you tell yourself you are fine link together into minutes, hours, days, weeks. When you notice that you are thinking about worst-case scenarios, try the following steps and self-talk prompts:

1. Look at factual data and ask yourself: "what is real?" Often, we start with a fact, then add imagined—and often sensationalized—outcomes. Filter through to find the real story by trying this self-talk: "I am only reading/watching [*a trusted source*] for updates, and I will be careful not to add a horrible story to the facts. When I catch myself asking 'what if something bad happens to me?,' I promise to also ask 'what if nothing bad happens to me?'"

2. Hold onto perspective and ask yourself: "what is likely to happen?" Remind yourself of the threats you have already feared and survived throughout your life— even when you weren't sure that you would. Remember that you will survive this one too. Try this self-talk: "[*your name*], remember when you did nuclear bomb drills at school and a nuclear bomb never hit? Remember when you thought you had eaten contaminated romaine, but you hadn't? You are afraid now too, but in the past, you've over-worried about things that never occurred. That is probably the case today."

3. Educate yourself and ask yourself: "what is true?" Determine three things you can do to help keep

yourself safe during the crisis. What do the experts say to do? What does research tell us? Once you have those three things, write them down. Your brain will then be satisfied that you have a plan and it will quiet the amygdala response to your fear. Then, try this self-talk: "[*your name*], you have done your homework on this crisis and you know what you need to know. Now, let's go do something that makes you feel peaceful and calm."

4. Assess your adrenaline addiction and ask yourself: "what is healthy?" Do you feel a high when you turn on the news and see a breaking story? Do you then feel a wave of fear after that initial excitement? You might be getting a chemical rush when you read about a new virus outbreak or a new development in a tragic story. This doesn't mean something is wrong with you; it just means you may need to wean yourself off from things that upset you. Try this self-talk: "[*your name*], you seem to like watching for updates, but I think you've had enough. This is harmful to your brain. What else could we do that seems exciting, but doesn't upset you as much?"

5. Stay in the present and ask yourself: "what is in this moment?" Deep breathing sends oxygen to your brain, allowing it to think more clearly. Take a deep breath, place your hand on your heart, and say to yourself, "[*your name*], in this moment, you are fine." Cycle through 3-7 deep breaths. When you place your hand on your heart, it causes a release of oxytocin, a hormone that makes you feel safe.

6. Practice gratitude and ask yourself: "what is good?" What we focus on grows. If you want more goodness in your life, focus on good things. List five things you are grateful for. Spend more time thinking about gratitude than worry. Try to imagine the best-case scenarios instead of the worst ones. This self-talk may help: "what if I stay healthy and virus-free? What if my immune system is as strong as it has ever been? What if the market rebounds tomorrow and stays there? What if this is my best year yet?"

STOP THE STORIES

If you feel anxious about something, it might help to understand facts versus stories. Many times, we feel anxious because we are using our imagination to create stories that are likely not true. We imagine what people are thinking. We imagine how people will react. We imagine what might happen. Our imaginations can lead us to worrying more than we need to.

Here is an example: I once worked with a client who was anxious about her daughter's upcoming wedding. In addition to worrying about all of the details, she was very nervous to see her ex-husband and his new wife. She was already feeling insecure about a lot of things, and then she went to her dress fitting two weeks before the wedding date. She panicked when she tried on the dress and it was tighter than she thought it would be.

We explored the facts and stories running through her brain during this experience. The fact was the dress was snug. The stories in her mind included: everyone is going to think I look disgusting, my ex will be glad we are divorced, people will think his new wife is much prettier than me, my daughter will be embarrassed by my appearance, people will talk about how tight my dress is. A snug dress turned into self-torture.

For many things in life, there are the facts, and then there are the stories we make up about those facts. With some awareness and practice we can learn to see just the facts and avoid the stories that cause us greater suffering.

Another example of this practice can be illustrated by the experience of a teen client. She and her boyfriend ended their relationship and months later, she was still obsessing over the fact that he was now talking to other girls. She asked for help getting her brain to settle down about the likelihood he would have a new girlfriend soon. We looked at the facts and the stories.

The fact was this boy posted pictures on social media with another girl. The stories included: he likes her more than he ever liked me, they have more fun together than we did, he thinks she is prettier than I am, he is happier now, everyone thinks she is better than me for him, they will be together forever, no one will ever love me. A photo turned into a self-deprecating attack.

We can learn to accept facts. But, when we imagine stories we only torture ourselves. It is the stories that cause the deep suffering, not the facts. Often when working with people, I find the stories my clients are imagining are more painful than the actual facts. Facts may hurt, but stories add a salty sting to the wound.

TRY THIS

Practice noticing a thought, considering the facts, then stopping yourself from creating stories around that fact. See if you can notice where the facts end and the stories begin. After noticing this a few times, you will begin to see that we often add unnecessary editorial stories onto many of our situations. Notice the facts, stop the stories.

CRY IT OUT

Crying is an essential part of the human experience. We cry when we are sad, stressed, relieved, happy, exhausted, in pain, angry, disappointed, surprised, empathetic, experiencing love, experiencing loss, laughing really hard, and while cutting onions.

Interestingly, scientific research on crying is hard to find, but here are a few fun facts:

- The Hebrew Bible refers to crying as one's heart melting.
- We are told Jesus wept. So did a lot of biblical characters.
- Babies communicate with us through crying.
- Voltaire called tears "the silent language of grief."
- Poets, philosophers, and Shakespeare have written a lot about tears and broken hearts.
- Danish scientist Niels Stensen discovered the lacrimal gland as the physical source of tears and noted their purpose was to keep the eye moist.
- More recently, the stress chemicals cortisol and adrenaline have been found in tears, which means stress literally leaves our bodies when we cry.

Michael Trimble, a behavioral neurologist at University College London, said:

The same neuronal areas of the brain are activated by seeing someone emotionally aroused as being emotionally aroused oneself. There must have been some point in time, evolutionarily, when the tear became something that automatically set off empathy and compassion in another. Actually being able to cry emotionally, and being able to respond to that, is a very important part of being human.[2]

Crying is good for us; it helps us develop more empathy and compassion. Crying signals that you need support. Think about how babies cry to get their needs met. They are signaling that they need support from their care-givers. Crying is communication—to another person and to ourselves.

Crying can help us bond to one another. It invites us into deeper conversations, increased awareness, and more meaningful lives. So let's stop apologizing for tears. Instead, let them be a signal to pay attention to our own souls and the souls of people around us.

TRY THIS

Explore giving yourself permission to cry. Find a safe place alone or safe people to cry with. Free of judgment. Free of expectations. Free of responsibilities. Release what you have been holding in. Let music, movies, memories, or the beauty of nature help you. Some clients tell me that my counseling office is their safe place to cry—so hire a professional if you have to.

When something brings tears to your eyes, embrace it, feel it, stay in that moment. Something really big is happening (when it isn't onions and maybe even when it is). See tears as an invitation to be fully human. Tears signal feelings that deserve loving attention. Love yourself through your tears and be fully present for someone else's

---

[2] Mandy Oaklander, "The Science of Crying," *Time*, March 2016. Retrieved from https://libguides.heidelberg.edu/chicago/article#:~:text=Footnote%2FEndnote,necessary)%2C%22%20page%20cited.

tears. You don't have to fix anything, just listen. Crying is communication from the soul. Let's all compassionately pay attention to our souls and our need to cry.

DRAW YOUR CIRCLES

I see a lot of women who think they need to be all things to all people, all the time. We so often think we need to take care of everyone, and if we don't, we're failing. It's important for us to pause and determine which relationships need the most attention right now.

Many clients I meet with are overwhelmed by the feeling that they need to take care of everyone. One woman I worked with was in the process of choosing an assisted living facility for her hospitalized mother, her daughter was about to graduate high school and had a party to plan, and on top of it all, her husband was in the process of starting his own business. Emotionally exhausted, she wasn't eating or sleeping—she was on the verge of collapse.

Together, we used a tool I call "Drawing Your Circles" to help determine where her focus needed to be right then, and to help her triage the needs of others in order to better take care of herself.

We started with a big circle, then drew three more inside that circle, each smaller than the one before. Inside the smallest one, in the center, we wrote her name. She was priority one: she had to eat, sleep, and do everything else that was necessary to keep herself healthy. In the next circle, we put her mother; that felt like the relationship with the most pressing needs at the moment. In the next circle, we put her graduating daughter, whose needs weren't as pressing—her party could include last-minute decorations and pizza, which were both perfectly fine. Finally, in the largest circle, we put her husband and other children, who at the moment, didn't have any pressing needs and would be just fine if her attention went elsewhere.

She'd also mentioned a few friends she was afraid she was ignoring; she felt like she was dropping the ball on texting them. I was able to show her that while they were important to her, they were actually a few rings out from anyone else who needed attention right then. They could wait and would understand why she was slow to respond.

Drawing your circles can help provide clarity as you set priorities, make commitments, consider whose opinion counts, and decide how best to focus your energy on those most important to you. It helps you determine who needs you the most right now and who can wait, so that you don't try to help everyone and burn yourself out in the process.

The circles will change as needs are met for some and new needs arise for others; just because someone is further out right now doesn't mean they're not important, and doesn't mean you won't have the time or energy to focus on them later. People move in and out of our circles as needs change.

Everyone in your life is important to you, but this tool can help you remember where to focus your energy right at this moment.

TRY THIS

On a piece of paper, start by drawing a small circle. Put your name in that circle, since it's important that you take care of yourself first. You can include others along with you, but take care not to overwhelm yourself with too many. Be realistic about who may not need as much care as you think, so that you don't end up overextending yourself.

Draw a second, larger circle surrounding it, continuing to add more circles and names as you determine who's in each one. Consider who you care about the most, whose presence you value in your life, whose opinions matter the most, and who primarily receives your love and attention—and offers it back. The circles might include a partner, children, immediate family, dear friends, coworkers, extended family, or others.

RETURN TO NEUTRAL

Everything is neutral until we label it as good or bad. We give meaning to things, circumstances, behaviors, decisions, and outcomes. Without us giving something meaning, it just is what it is.

A rainy day, for example, is just water falling from the sky until I decide that it is inconvenient to get wet today or that it is good for the grass. Rain is neutral until I label it good or bad. It is going to rain, no matter what I think about it.

Broccoli is just broccoli, but some of us think it is bad and some think it is good. Broccoli will continue to exist, no matter our preferences.

It is mind-blowing to realize everything is neutral until we have an opinion about it.

Think about something you think is bad. See if you can see it as neutral. It just is what it is until you give it your assessment, opinion, or editorial. Now bring to your mind something you think is good. Again, it just is what it is until you label it good. Can you see something as neutral and resist the urge to assess it?

Our brain likes labeling things to keep us safe. Our inner protector (our amygdala deep in our brain) keeps us safe and alive and it likes rules: blueberries are good, red berries are bad. That labeling will keep me safe if I am lost in the woods, but it doesn't leave room for nuance. Yes, red berries in the woods might be dangerous, but raspberries are red and they are safe and delicious, as are strawberries. We have to stretch our brains away from their tendencies to label things. Labeling everything as good or bad, right or wrong, limits our human experience.

There is a big fun world out there to explore and be curious about if you can see things again as neutral.

And this perspective can help us in the areas we tend to judge ourselves. A messy kitchen is neutral until I editorialize that I shouldn't go to bed with a messy kitchen. Some of you are reading this thinking: going to bed with a messy kitchen is awful. Some of you are thinking: leave it until morning and go to bed, no big deal. Work with your own brain to see if you can stretch it out a bit to see the messy kitchen as neutral.

I think it is fun to experiment with this and it always blows my mind when I realize how much I'm labeling everything around me.

William Shakespeare wrote: "There is nothing either good or bad, but thinking makes it so."[3] I'm always amazed at the timelessness of Shakespeare's commentary on human behaviors—he was teaching us about the power of our thoughts over 400 years ago.

Everything is neutral. Take a deep breath and let that sink in.

---

[3] *The Tragedy of Hamlet, Prince of Denmark*. (London: The Folio Society, 1954). 2.2. References are to act and scene.

TRY THIS

That thing you think is ugly, that thing you think is beautiful, that thing you can't believe people would do, those clothes kids are wearing today, that trashy TV show, that pet peeve you have, those wrinkles, that cellulite, the way those people spend their time—all of it is neutral, absolutely neutral. Can you let yourself return to neutral without judging those things?

See if you can get to neutral with other religions, ethnicities, body sizes, economic levels, professions, sexualities, levels of education, and decisions people make. Notice the areas where you feel strongly about something. How would you feel if you could help your brain go back to neutral? Might it allow you to see the issue differently with a fresh start? There is peace in returning to neutral and then exploring how you really feel about something without the opinion of others or what you've been taught.

SHAKE IT OFF

Ever notice how a dog or cat shakes their whole body at random intervals? There's a simple explanation for that: they do it to release stress. Wild animals do it, too, after successfully fleeing a predator. Shaking works to process the unused "fight or flight" adrenaline that's flooded their system, releasing tension and returning their bodies back to a relaxed state.

Even Michael Phelps famously "shakes it off" with the wild, double-arm swing he executes to release stress before every race (maybe that is why he is the most decorated Olympic athlete of all time!).

Have you ever started shaking before speaking in public, or some other anxiety-inducing event? That's your body trying to release stress. Your "fight or flight" response can cause you to freeze up, and your nervous system needs to let that go.

We humans are also good at dissipating stress when we're young. Those crying fits, tantrums, and flailing-on-the-floor episodes are all ways our body tries to return to normal. Unfortunately, we're quickly conditioned out of those, because they're inconvenient or disturbing to those around us. That's when we learn to repress emotions and suppress our innate abilities to dissipate our stress.

Shaking is such an easy practice, and such an effective way to unfreeze ourselves and restart our nervous system. The "fight or flight" response brought on by stress also speeds up your heart rate and gives you a burst of energy, which can take a toll on your body if not properly processed. Shaking takes care of that, too.

How do we survive times filled with fear? Whether you survive being chased by a lion or you're just feeling the normal stressors that come with the human experience, get that fear out. Burn that energy. From your head down to your toes, shake it all off.

TRY THIS

Do some shaking now, even if you're not stressed, to see how it works. Start small and work your way up the body. Notice where you feel tense. Is it your shoulders, neck, hands, hips, or back? Is it your jaw, forehead, or temples? Are your upper arms and upper legs tight? Do your wrists, hands, ankles, or feet feel stiff? Shake and move that part of your body.

Now, try your whole body. Allow yourself to release all the stress living inside of you. Don't let fear of looking awkward keep you from embracing it: find a private place and let it all out.

EXPLORE "IT MIGHT BE FANTASTIC!"

One of my clients spent over a decade in upper management in an unhealthy corporate culture. Her company has tremendously high turnover and an inner circle of top executives who won't address the systemic problems in the organization.

For a few years, we talked about how to survive in this toxic environment because she financially needed to stay in this organization. But over time, I watched her lose her passion because of her work environment. One day, she came into her appointment ready to make a plan to leave that job and find a new one.

As we talked through the plan, she felt relief and excitement. Her face lit up with hope. This lasted a few minutes and then I watched as fear began to flood her brain. She expressed doubt that she could match her salary. She worried that the next organization might be just as unhealthy. She was afraid of giving up great benefits and flexibility earned by her long tenure. She doubted her interviewing skills. She realized she enjoyed most of the people who worked on her team, except for five or six very difficult people.

After listening to her and noting her worries on the whiteboard in my office, I could hear her talking herself into staying in this job. She said: "what if the next place is worse?"

I answered, "it could be." Then I asked in a soft, low voice..."but what if it is fantastic?"

We both paused for a few seconds to take that in.

What if her salary could be even higher and she didn't have to fight hard for what amounted to a very small raise every year? What if the next organization was thriving and full of emotionally healthy people? What if the benefit plan and time off was better than she had ever been offered before? What if she loved everyone on her team and everyone loved her?

What if she were finally treated with the respect and admiration she deserved? What if her ideas were valued and implemented? What if she found friends and mentors who helped her soar even higher? What if going to work felt fantastic?

Our brains default to keeping us safe and considering everything that could go wrong. We are great at imagining worst-case scenarios. And many times, that instinct helps us avoid danger. However, when we are trying to make a decision, it is important for us to guide our brains to imagine the fantastic scenarios as well. The more we practice this, the more easily our brain defaults to considering what could happen across a spectrum of options, not just the worst scenarios.

When we look for the bad, we find it. When we look for the fantastic, we find it. I think fantastic sounds like a lot more fun, doesn't it?

That thing you are worried about...it might turn out to be fantastic.

TRY THIS

Stretch your brain into imagining all that could go right when you notice that you are imagining all that could go wrong. Consider:

- decisions you are making
- conversations you are afraid to have
- the futures of children you are worried about
- relationships you fear ending
- relocations you are exploring
- upcoming life events

Imagine fantastic outcomes and notice how you feel.

PICTURE YOURSELF IN
A SNOW GLOBE

A few years ago, I was talking to my son, who was worried about an upcoming test. We were talking about ways to manage his racing mind when I saw the snow globe of Cincinnati that sits on his bookshelf—a reminder of where he was born—and it hit me: it was the perfect way to help visualize the flurry of thoughts that can overtake us when we're feeling anxious.

We shook it up and talked about how it feels to have a flurry of thoughts.

When your brain is racing and your thoughts are swirling, here's a visualization exercise to try: start by closing your eyes and taking a deep breath. Imagine those thoughts quietly falling to the ground, one by one, like flakes of snow. If a new thought appears, observe that it is just a thought and allow that thought to drift downward.

With each deep breath, imagine your mind getting clearer as the intrusive thoughts drift away and fall to the ground. Remind yourself that you are equipped to manage your racing mind and establish a sense of calm. Just as the snow in the globe settles down into clarity, so too can you.

Anxious thinking often runs high even in the healthiest of brains. No matter what, we all need tools to help us when we don't know whether our safety, stability, or peace will be shaken. Tools to help us cultivate a sense of inner quiet and calm—much like after a snowfall, when our surroundings are covered in a blanket of peace.

TRY THIS

Do you have something stressful coming up? A task or event that you're dreading, or can't stop thinking about? Take a moment to sit with those thoughts, taking deep breaths as you imagine them falling to the ground, one by one.

If you find this practice useful, consider purchasing a snow globe to keep nearby as a visual reminder of how to manage your thoughts on a daily basis.

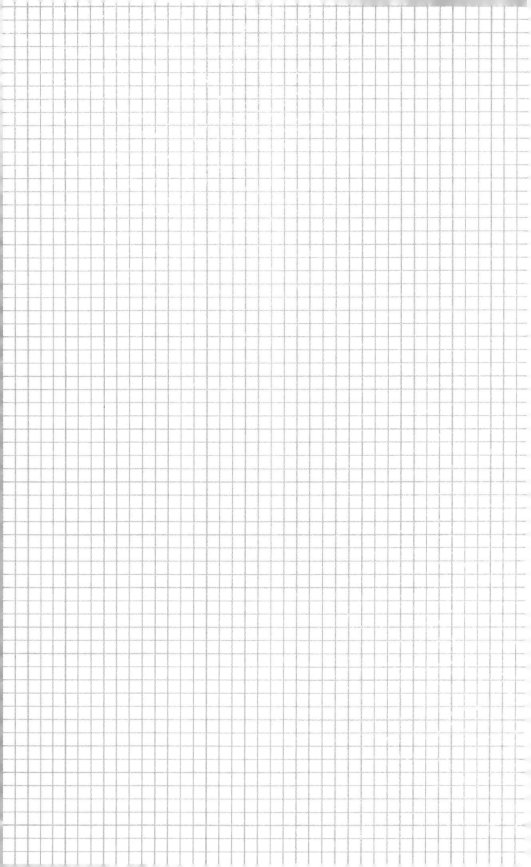

GET UNSTUCK

Feeling stuck is a very common part of being human. We all have circumstances we can't change, but our "stuck" mindsets are something we can change.

Stuck is just a feeling. Most times, we aren't as stuck as we think we are. These tools are here to help us unstick ourselves and start moving forward. I've used all of these tools throughout my life and return to them often.

When I feel really stuck, I reflect on Victor Frankel's words in Man's Search for Meaning: "Everything can be taken from a man but one thing: the last of the human freedoms—to choose one's attitude in any given set of circumstances, to choose one's own way." Frankel spent 1942-1945 in concentration camps Auschwitz and Dachau. Prior to World War II, he was a physician and chief of the University of Vienna Medical School's neurology and psychiatric clinic. Frankel's contribution to helping humans find meaning as a tool for psychological well-being no matter our circumstances is timeless.

Let's all remember that our greatest freedom is to choose our attitude despite our circumstances. I hope these tools help you with the "how" of getting unstuck.

REMEMBER THAT
YOU HAVE OPTIONS

A number of clients I've seen struggle with making big decisions.

"Should I take this new job?"
"Should I stay in this marriage?"
"Should I go back to school?"

One of the most powerful things I do with clients who are frozen by indecision is to go to a whiteboard and ask them: "what are your options?" Then we write down the options and make notes about each one. We discuss each option and it is amazing how seeing them on the board allows the client to gain clarity.

A recent example is a client who was struggling with whether to stay married. Together, we came up with her options:

- I stay in this marriage; status quo.
- I stay, but I speak up for myself.
- I get a divorce.

Seeing her options in front of her, laid out so plain and simple, she then said: "I can't get a divorce." So we crossed that one out. After a few minutes, she said: "but I can't stay in this marriage status quo." And there we had it—she knew she needed to speak up for herself and address some of their issues. She had her clarity. She was no longer stuck. Now we could determine what she needed to say and how she was going to say it.

So often, we feel trapped when we're facing a big decision because we forget that we actually have many options. There are always options. Many times, we only see two options and forget there are nuanced options in between the obvious choices.

Remember, always, that you have agency. Agency means that we get to make choices. We get to design our lives. Forgetting that can trigger a primal feeling of being trapped. That's why reminding yourself that you have multiple options is so important. You get to decide what you will do next.

TRY THESE

1. Consider a decision that you're faced with at the present time, or one that may come up down the road. Write your options down across the top of a piece of paper, with ample space under each one.

2. Consider the outcomes: in the space under each option, do an old-fashioned pros and cons list, but add a little twist of considering the option over the course of time. For example:

    - Pros, short-term:
    - Pros, long-term:
    - Cons, short-term:
    - Cons, long-term:

3. Consider how it will feel. After you consider the outcomes of each option and evaluate both short-term and long-term impacts, let yourself imagine how you will feel.

- Immediately, I might feel...
- Over time, I will likely feel...

4. Listen to your body. Some of us are more experienced at this part than others, but if it feels comfortable to you, physically embodying a decision can be a helpful practice in finding clarity.

   - My gut says...
   - My heart says..
   - My mind says...
   - My soul says...

5. Name your fears. Complete this sentence for each option: "choosing this option feels scary/dangerous/risky because...."

6. Imagine the possibilities. Complete this sentence for each option: "choosing this option feels exciting/hopeful/fun because...."

7. Decide to take action...or not. You don't have to take action every time. This process helps you get the noise in your brain out of your head and onto paper. You can let it bake for a while. Just knowing you have options will make you feel better.

START WITH YOUR EASY

A client of mine, Tess, came to me feeling really discouraged. She had become bored in her current job and couldn't figure out what she wanted to do next. She felt, in her words, "frozen in stuckness." The only thing she could come up with was to go back to school—something at her core she knew she didn't want to do. It felt too difficult, expensive, and time-consuming.

I love working with clients like Tess. Tess, like me, forgets that things can be easy. Many of us think we have to do hard things to get unstuck, but I have found that the path out of stuckness is often actually a very easy path. We just need help seeing it. We can begin to see it by asking ourselves this question: "what comes easy to me?"

We get stuck because we're looking at hard things. Paths that would require more resources than we're willing or able to give up. But when we think about what comes easy to us, we can take into consideration the strengths and gifts that we already have. The ones we so easily overlook.

For Tess, she realized that what came easy to her was journal writing and talking about her writing process. As we explored that further, she started to consider what it would look like for her to teach writing. I watched the light come on in her eyes as she began to consider what it would mean to do something that already came naturally to her—that she already was passionate about.

The important thing to remember, and what we so often forget, is that what comes naturally to you looks like magic to someone else. What could you do with that magic? How could you pass that along to someone else? We're all good at different things, and we all want to learn.

When we celebrate what we are naturally good at doing, we find the path out of stuckness and start walking with more confidence, knowing the unique contribution that we bring to the world.

Spend some time thinking about what comes easily to you. Someone else is amazed by your ability to do that. Someone out there struggles with the very thing that is a cakewalk for you.

Everyone has something to offer, and your magic is what comes most easily to you. Focus on what comes naturally to you and start to think about how you might be able to do more of that. Start with you.

TRY THESE

1. Ask yourself the following questions to start exploring what's easy for you:

    - What flows naturally to you?
    - What could you talk about off the top of your head?
    - What do you not have to prepare for?
    - What could someone interview you about and you wouldn't need notes?
    - When do you lose track of time?
    - What's easy for you to do?
    - What excites you?
    - What lights you up?

2. Brainstorm ways you can do more of what comes easy for you. In what ways could you share your talents to help others? Are there other careers or pursuits where you could put those skills to use? Is there something people need that you can easily do? Even if you can't answer every question, consider how you could do more of what comes easy for you every day. You may soon find the answer just by practicing more of it.

GO FROM ZERO TO ONE

Not long after I started coaching people, I found myself thinking: "I want to write a book." The prospect was more than overwhelming, though. I hadn't written much at that point, but felt a deep desire to. I only knew that there was so much I was interested in teaching others that I wanted to somehow get it on the page.

I was frozen with inaction, and had no idea where or how to start. Then one day, it hit me: why not try writing a weekly email? That felt doable. I started by making a list of clients and friends who I could send that email to. From there, I wrote an email that went out every Tuesday morning with a new piece of research I had discovered or a quick tip. I created a small thing each week, and those small things added up to the book you are reading right now.

That course of action is a practice I call "Zero to One." Whether you want to write a book, run a marathon, or pursue a new career, the prospect of starting something can be terrifying. We expect ourselves to go straight from 0 to 10, and to accomplish that goal as quickly as possible.

But here's where science steps in to make that virtually impossible: our brains actually block us from moving from 0 to 10. The fear center in our brain makes us feel like there is too much danger in making that much change. Our brains resist us. When we expect big leaps but don't make them we begin to feel like a failure—when really, it was just our brains trying to keep us safe.

Big change will always sound the danger alarms. "Zero to One" is a way of working with your brain to feel safe and helps us reach success. With "Zero to One," you start by taking one tiny step. Then, the next day, you take another.

Here's an example: let's say you want to run a marathon. Going from zero to one means you get your running shoes out so you can easily see them. And that's it. Then, maybe one to two is you put them on and take a five-minute walk. And then a 10-minute walk. You don't immediately start running 26.2 miles. You don't even go immediately to running one mile. Those leaps are too big to sustain the progress you need to reach your goal.

Most of us want to do things well and be experts immediately. We have to remember that the experts started at zero and moved to one, then two. Give yourself time to get to 10 and allow for mistakes along the way. Our fear of making mistakes keeps us stuck at zero.

That thing you've been thinking about doing? Forget about doing it perfectly. Just start and move from a zero to a one—that's the hardest part. Once you have momentum, things will fall into place and your fear will lessen. Take a deep breath and just begin. One small step at a time.

TRY THIS

What's something you've been hoping to try? Or a goal you've been wanting to achieve? Write a note that says "zero to one" and put it somewhere you can see. When you're ready to begin, tell yourself, "zero to one." Consider changing that note after every step ("one to two," "two to three," etc.) to remind yourself to go slowly. Repeat those steps to yourself every day as a reminder. With time and consistency, those tiny steps will add up to progress.

Remember that often, going from zero to one helps our

brain get on board with where we want to go. Here are some examples of what that might look like:

- Pursuing a new career: ordering a book on the topic, or looking through your contacts to see if there's someone you could ask to coffee
- Wanting to get healthier: drinking one extra glass of water each day
- Tackling a big home project, like organizing your closet: starting with your shoes, then tops, then pants, or searching online for tips
- Taking up a new hobby, like painting: looking up local classes

TURN JEALOUSY INTO ACTION

Jealousy is often thought of as a negative feeling we have toward someone who has what we desire. Often, we end up criticizing that person or resenting them.

But an uncomfortable emotion like jealousy can be a helpful messenger to us: a practice we can use for insight and action.

A client of mine, Karrie, came to me frustrated. While she loved staying home every day raising her two young children, she missed being around adults and felt like she never had any time for herself. Meanwhile, she felt frustrated every morning, jealous of her husband when he left for his job— which to her meant that not only did he get to be around other adults, he had freedom during the day. The jealousy she carried was starting to take a turn toward resentment, and she knew it was time to address it.

What Karrie and I worked on was the idea that feeling jealousy can sometimes be just what we need to get unstuck.

With some intentional thinking, we can reframe jealousy into action for ourselves instead of ill will for someone else.

For Karrie, that meant thinking about what she could do for herself to start easing those uncomfortable feelings. Was there a moms' group she could sign up for to connect with others in her position? Was there a hobby she could explore during the evenings when her husband was home with the kids? Was a part-time job worth considering? Once she realized there were a number of options she could act on, her resentment began to fade away and her jealousy turned into action.

Here are some other examples of how we might reframe our jealous feelings:

- "Beth is so much more active than me." → "I'll take a brisk walk today."
- "Susan just bought a beautiful new house." → "I'll repaint a room in mine this weekend."
- "Lydia got a book published." → "I'll try writing 500 words every day for a month."
- "Jake found a partner." → "I'll sign up for a dating app."

Instead of shaming yourself for feeling jealous, see it as a message of hope. Harness the energy of jealousy into action. And while you're at it, here are some helpful things to say to yourself when you feel comparison and jealousy creeping their way into your mindset:

- "She's successful, and so am I."
- "They're happy, and we are too."
- "She's active, and I can be too."
- "He's a great parent, and I am too."

With a little work, not only can you shift out of jealousy and into action, you can also shift your mindset from self-pity to self-compassion: the best antidote to self-pity. Where self-pity isolates us, self-compassion reminds us we are experiencing what it means to be human. Compassion reminds us that we are all striving and longing for the same things in this great big human experience.

TRY THIS

1. Divide a piece of paper into three columns.

2. In the first column, list everyone who makes you feel jealous when you think of them.

3. In the second column, write a few words on why you are jealous of them.

4. In the third column, name one step you can take to obtain what they have or create something even better in your life. Shift out of jealousy and into momentum toward your goal.

PREPARE FOR THE BEST CASE

I once had a teen client who wanted to run for student office, but was afraid to submit the application. He was terrified by the prospect of losing and embarrassing himself. He spent so much time imagining losing that he talked himself out of running at all.

So I posed this question to him: what's the best-case scenario? What if you win? He didn't even want to think about it, because he didn't want to set himself up to be disappointed.

But I encouraged him to imagine winning. I watched his body language change just from the hope he began to give himself. He looked lighter even talking about it.

I understand being scared to imagine the best-case scenario. I am often afraid of setting myself up for disappointment too. But if we can force ourselves to imagine the best outcome, then we give ourselves a dose of hope and that might be enough to help us move toward getting what we want. Ultimately, we can't control what happens, but we can learn how to give ourselves hope, which is more likely to help us move forward.

When we worry and imagine the worst outcomes, our body produces the stress hormone cortisol. Which—if we're not actually being chased by a lion—has long-term effects that can harm our bodies. We're creating a harm and a stress that's totally optional. Our imaginations can be both harmful and helpful; they can conjure up the worst things that can happen, or they can give us hope and possibility. When we harness our imagination for good, great things can happen.

Train yourself to say: what's the best that can happen? What great things could come of this? You will feel an energetic shift when you do so: the worst-case scenario often feels heavy and awful, but the best-case feels lighter. You can give yourself hope. You can spend time in possibility. You can grow more optimistic.

Our brains will default to worst-case scenarios until we teach it to also consider the best-case scenario.

TRY THIS

1. Is there something either in the present or the near future that you're dreading, or that is causing you anxiety? Imagine the worst-case scenario, and write it down if it helps to capture your thoughts. What do you notice in your body? Does it feel heavy or dreadful?

2. Now do the same thing, but imagine the best-case scenario instead. What do you notice in your body? Do you feel lighter, more hopeful?

3. Next time you notice worst-case-scenario thinking, remind yourself to consider the best-case-scenario too.

IMAGINE YOUR FUTURE SELF

Many of us feel adrift and forlorn when we aren't happy with the way our lives are going. We know we don't like where we are today, but we aren't sure what we want instead. I've experienced this and I've seen it with many clients. We aren't sure what we want.

I had a client, Debbie, who had been fired and came to me for coaching. Her department was eliminated and she didn't see it coming. She felt lost and very unsure of what she wanted to do next.

We started by building a picture together of her ideal vision for the future. I took her through a series of questions: What type of person do you want to be? What's the feeling you want to have about your job? What accomplishments are you striving for? What kind of life do you want to lead?

Once she found answers, we worked on envisioning her life as if everything had already fallen into place and showing gratitude toward this future version of Debbie: "I'm grateful that Debbie found the perfect job. I'm grateful that Debbie can share her talents and give back. I'm grateful that Debbie is leading a life centered around helping others." She loved the way this exercise felt and began to feel more hopeful about her future.

Imagining your future self can do wonders to pull you out of a pit of stuckness. When you do so, not only are you giving yourself hope, you're making all your desires, drives, and goals feel like they could be real.

By imagining future you, you are solidifying what you want, and actually taking the first step toward creating that reality. Plus, if you find yourself getting excited at what you envision, that is a clue that you are on the right path.

Directing gratitude to your future self is a sneaky little way to trick your brain into figuring out what you want—and helping yourself get started toward that path. Future you can help present you get started today.

TRY THIS

Take a moment today to thank your future self for the life you hope to have. If it feels like a lot or it feels too lofty, then try going more general: "I'm grateful that I have found a job. I'm grateful that I now feel at peace." Here are a few examples that might help:

- I'm grateful that [*a problem*] has been resolved.
- I'm grateful that I feel [*desired feeling*].
- I'm relieved that I now have [*something you desire*].
- I'm grateful that [*a person*] is peaceful.
- I'm grateful to be filled with hope.
- I'm grateful for the help I have received.
- I'm grateful to be free and independent.
- I'm grateful for [*accomplishment*] and I'm glad I stayed dedicated.
- I'm grateful that life has turned out the way I had hoped it would.

GAIN MOMENTUM

Remember the merry-go-round on your elementary school playground? You may need to be over 40 to have experienced a merry-go-round. It was a round metal platform that spun, and we all held onto metal bars while yelling "faster" and screaming a lot.

If you wanted to get onto the spinning merry-go-round but the kids wouldn't stop to pick up new passengers, you had to start jogging alongside it to gain momentum. When you were running as fast as it was spinning, you could jump on. It was impossible to jump on from standing still. The kids that tried that ended up on the ground.

I use this imagery when I need to remember that I have to build momentum to reach my goals. We can't jump right in and get to where everyone else is immediately. We have to start moving forward first and gain some speed to make progress. Then we can get to where they are.

In physics classes we learned that an object at rest will stay at rest. At rest, momentum is zero. And not only is there no momentum, there is inertia. Inertia can be thought of as resistance to change. An object will stay still until we move it, and it takes a little effort to get it started. Once there is momentum, then the laws of physics help keep it moving.

Is there someplace in your life where you are struggling to find motivation?

For many of us, motivation actually follows momentum. Often we wait to feel motivated, but actually moving forward starts the momentum that feeds your motivation.

Consider this image of the merry-go-round next time you feel stuck. Start moving around the outside. It's a little uncomfortable to get started, but soon you will be shrieking with delight in the middle of the figurative merry-go-round.

TRY THIS

Think about projects you've finished—did you have a slow, resistant start but then once you were rolling you found it easier to keep going? Where could you use a little momentum right now?

Ask yourself: what small thing would help me get started? Doing this small thing will get you unstuck and moving forward. Then the motivation is more likely to show up. Momentum first. How can you get moving?

TRY SOMETHING NEW

In 2020, I finally tried something I'd always wanted to do: paddleboarding. Prior to that, I'd watched paddleboarders in the ocean and on lakes and always felt envious. I didn't think I had the balance or strength to do it. For years I wanted to try it, and yet never once made the attempt.

But then, that unforgettable year of 2020 came around, making everything unpredictable, and I thought: "what the hell do I have to lose?" Finally, I tried it at a nearby lake that rented paddleboards. And I loved it! Was I great at it? Not really. But I felt alive. I was lit up by the experience, finally unstuck from the fear that had stopped me before.

So often, we trudge through life, letting fear and uncertainty stop us from moving forward. We freeze in place, feeling stuck. One easy way to get out of that rut? Try something new. The thrill of a first-time experience can help to awaken something in you again. It can help you feel more alive.

I would venture to guess this is why, during the pandemic, we saw people trying to bake sourdough bread for the first time, taking rookie RV trips, and learning to do things like knitting and DIY home projects. Subconsciously, we know that we need to learn new things or do something we've never done before in order to feel alive.

When was the last time you felt the thrill of trying something new?

When you're stuck, dare yourself to take a risk (even a small one!). It can help you feel more alive—and help you believe in yourself more.

Inspiration and creativity come when we step outside of our comfort zone. Scientifically speaking, you're also causing a release of the feel-good hormone dopamine, which feeds your brain. Ideas form. Lightbulbs come on. Stuckness fades.

We all want a sense of adventure in our lives. We wither away if we aren't growing. If you feel like you're in a rut, try something new and watch yourself come back to life.

TRY THESE

Below is a list of activities to help you feel more alive. Choose a few and dive in. Or—begin your own list and challenge yourself to do something new each week.

- Watch a sunrise (or sunset)
- Handwrite a letter of gratitude to a former teacher
- Experiment with a new recipe
- Have a completely tech-free day
- Drop books, movies, or puzzles off at a nursing home
- Compliment a stranger
- Try a new international food
- Watch a YouTube video on an art medium you've always wanted to try
- Build something
- Send a card for no reason to someone you love
- Place an anonymous gift by a neighbor's door
- Fill the house with music and dance
- Post a book review online
- Write a note of appreciation to your favorite musician, author, or actor

WRITE YOUR WAY OUT

Journaling gets a bad rap. Even the word "journaling" can cause my clients to roll their eyes and groan. They've tried it before, they didn't know what to write, they couldn't stick with it. There are so many reasons why it is hard.

Even so, journaling is one of the most effective ways to get unstuck, and one of the recommendations I make most often. You just have to know how to do it in an easy and sustainable way so that it can become a regular practice in your life.

First, a quick rundown of what journaling has been shown to do:

- It boosts your immune system
- It improves your sleep
- It improves your focus and memory
- It helps to process and regulate your emotions
- It lowers your cortisol levels
- It reduces symptoms of anxiety and depression

There's no doubt that journaling is a practice worth pursuing, especially when you're feeling stuck or hopeless. Write what you hear your inner roommates saying. Your inner roommates are, simply put, the commentators who live in your head. They can be critical and obnoxious, and if we don't help them feel heard, they can end up running the show. When that happens, our brain becomes a very noisy place. We feel anxious and uncertain.

Writing down what your inner roommate is saying is a great way to get at what's keeping you stuck. Deep down, we often know what we want. We're just not listening to ourselves. Journaling what we hear that roommate say is the path to getting to the heart of what we want and how we feel.

Not only that, but writing really does quiet your brain—thinking through a challenge moves your brain activity out of the amygdala (fear center) and into the prefrontal cortex (planning center). When we have a plan, we feel safer.

Writing is cathartic and healing for your soul. It quiets your brain. It validates your feelings. It helps you process your thoughts and connect your own dots. You don't have to make this a formal practice; just write down what comes to you and toss it in the trash if you don't like it.

Give yourself the gift of writing down your thoughts and beginning a conversation with your inner roommates. Helping them feel heard can help your brain find peace.

TRY THESE

1. Set yourself up for success by starting small: grab a notebook (the plainer, the better) and commit to just one sentence or paragraph a day, working your way up to one page.

2. If you can't hear what your inner roommate is saying, simply write about your surroundings or anything else that comes up. All writing helps and anything counts, as long as your pen is moving.

3. As you grow more comfortable with the practice of getting a few words down on paper, start to get the thoughts you hear down, too. They can be perfectly mundane ("I need to start the dishwasher").

4. Keep writing down your thoughts until you're relaxed enough that some deeper ones start to bubble up. Pretend that you're dictating for your inner roommate. Ask it: "what do you have to say? What do you need to tell me?" And get it all down. Keep repeating this process on a regular basis and not only will your brain quiet down, you'll be surprised at what longings, emotions, and ideas come up.

BE RIDICULOUS

So often, we play small in life because we are afraid to think big.

We think big when we are children. How many of you said you would be President or an MLB player or a famous actor? How many of us dreamed of a life that seemed totally plausible when we were young? What happened? What happened is multi-faceted:

- We learn what it takes to become those things and assume we don't have the innate skills.
- We listen to the voices that are trying to keep us safe who encourage us to find "a real job."
- We grow in self-doubt as we have setbacks.
- We age and realize time is finite.
- We gain perspective in the cost and benefit of our choices.
- We find out that there are other things more important to us than pursuing that original dream.
- We change over time and our interests change.

Many things alter our course, but we have to be careful not to get in a habit of thinking small.

If you feel stuck, it can help to check in with your big dreams again. Go back and think big again. Consider something that is ridiculous.

What would be something totally ridiculous to do in your life right now?

Can you feel the energy that comes into your body when you think that thought?

It feels like a rush of excitement for a split second, then we usually start diluting it with reasons why that won't ever be possible.

I invite you to stay in the ridiculous a bit longer. Don't cancel it so quickly this time.

What if you could do that ridiculous thing?
What would it be like to live that life?
How would you feel about your life?

Can you stay there for a bit longer? Stay in the dream. Go back to being seven years old and thinking you could be anything. Hold that imaginative energy a bit longer.

We are conditioned to play it safe. The longer we live, the more safety we seek. Financial safety. Success safety. Relationship safety. We try to make "good decisions" our whole lives which serve us well usually, but might quiet our zest for life.

Your brain might not be liking this as you read it. Your amygdala's whole job is to keep you safe from harm. It is likely sending you messages right now saying, "playing it safe is better than having zest." If that feels true to you, then seeking safety is a good path for you. But, if you want more zest or feel stuck and don't like where you are, then try thinking on ridiculous levels and see what you notice.

We tend to use our imaginations for the bad stuff that could happen, but we forget to think big. We forget to imagine the ridiculous. We often limit our thinking and as a result limit our potential. There are great clues to your happiness in dreaming bigger. Explore the ridiculous this week and see how it feels to dream big again.

TRY THESE

1. Reflect on those dreams you had as a child. Why did you dream of the things you did? How did it feel to be limitless?

2. Write down a few things that you're struggling with. What would help you? Then, think bigger. Then, think about what ridiculous solution would help. Can you feel the possibilities return to your spirit?

3. Think of dreaming like stretching a muscle. We can go further each time we stretch a little more. Stretch your imagination. Play with this exercise in mind stretching:

   - Make three columns on a page of paper and title the columns: Idea, Bigger, Ridiculous.
   - In the left-most column write an idea you have.
   - In the middle column stretch that idea into something bigger and write a description of that idea.
   - In the right-most column imagine a ridiculous version of that idea (if money, time, success, qualifications, what people thought, etc. were no issue) and capture it in a description.
   - Now review your three columns. Isn't it amazing how the left column now feels too small? Explore all the areas between small and ridiculous and you will find something with which you can move forward.

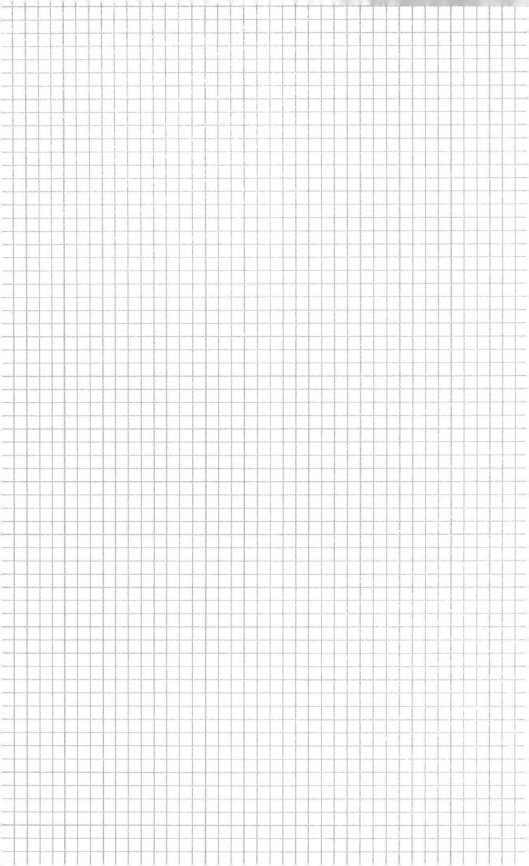

QUIET YOUR BRAIN

Smart, capable, loving, funny, kind, busy human beings have busy brains. I'm guessing that is you if you are reading this book. You have a lot of ideas, worries, talents, dreams, desires, and thoughts. But sometimes, your brain feels like it is spinning and you need some peace. The practices in this section are here to help you find that inner quiet you long for. We love our brilliant brains, but sometimes we need a break.

These practices will help you manage fears, worries, angst, iciness, and stress. Give them a try and practice these tools often. Over time, you will rewire your brain to be less reactive and more receptive to peace. You won't see instructions on how to meditate in this section; although I am a big fan of meditation, these practices are more about helping you stop your mind from racing so that if you want to meditate, you can. I find many people can't just sit down and meditate—so these practices are intended as pre-work for the day you want to try meditation.

Form a relationship with your brain first. Then you can take it where you want it to go, rather than it driving you to places you don't want to be. I have a very busy brain, and these practices have helped me quiet my brain quickly when I feel overwhelmed or am flooded with worry. It takes practice, but you and I are getting closer to peace together.

WORK WITH YOUR BRAIN

Ever wonder how big your brain is? Follow these steps to get a feel for its size:

1. Make a fist with each of your hands and hold them out in front of you with thumbs pointing to the sky.

2. Now, bring your hands together so your knuckles touch.

3. This represents the two hemispheres of your brain and the size of your brain is close to the size of the shape your hands just created.

Most people think their brain is larger than it actually is. But it is the most complex and powerful part of your body. It weighs around three pounds and is responsible for keeping you alive: all of your behaviors, the words you speak, your skills, who you love, the stories you tell, the things you create, how you interpret the world around you—everything you experience in life is processed in this beautiful bundle of cells inside your skull.

The human brain may truly be the most amazing engineering project in all of creation. But why aren't we taught how to use it? I joke that when I got a new car, they taught me more about the climate system in my car than anyone had ever taught me about my own brain.

Working with your brain is one of the secrets to living a happy, peaceful, hopeful, and compassionate life. The more I have learned about neuroscience, the more compassionate I have become toward myself and every human being on this planet. We all have very complex brains and aren't taught how to use them. Understanding how our brains work might help us solve a lot of humanity's challenges.

Here are some very simple descriptions of a few parts of your brain and how to work with them:

- The amygdala: sits in the middle of your brain and is about the size of an almond. This part of your brain is responsible for triggering feelings of fear and the fight-or-flight instinct.

  A quick tip: when you feel afraid, make a plan. In functional MRIs, only the amygdala or the frontal cortex can be lit up (not both at the same time), which means when you feel afraid and then make a plan, you are shifting out of your amygdala and into a different part of your brain, thus reducing your feelings of fear. Afraid to walk into that meeting? Make a plan for where you will sit, what you will say first, how you want to be perceived, and what time you will leave. You just helped your brain feel less afraid.

- The limbic system: where our impulsive behaviors and desires come from.

  A quick tip: when you feel tempted to do something you promised yourself you wouldn't do, talk to your limbic system. Something like: "I see you trying to tempt me to act impulsively, but I don't want to do that right now." Think of this part of your brain like that person who wants to get you into a little trouble because it is fun to watch. Tell it no—you are more in control of this situation than you think you are.

- The frontal lobe: sits directly behind your forehead, and is responsible for decision making, problem solving, reasoning, and planning.

  A quick tip: think of the front of your brain as the wise leader of the other parts. When the amygdala feels anxious, like a lizard darting in and out of the wood pile, imagine the frontal lobe assuring the lizard it is safe to calm down and lay in the sun. When the limbic system is tempting you to do something you know you shouldn't do, imagine the frontal lobe giving you greater perspective on the long-term effects of this decision.

That's just a quick and simplified summary, but I hope it inspires you to become a little more familiar with your brain.

Remember, you control your brain. You tell your brain where you want it to focus, what you want it to process, and how you want it to react to your circumstances. Just like you adjust the climate system in your car to keep you comfortable, work with these parts of your brain to shape your day the way you want to.

Learning how to manage your brain helps you manage life. You have an amazing brain full of potential for helping you get where you want to be.

TRY THIS

Tune into your amygdala, limbic system, and frontal cortex, and get to know how your brain operates.

When you feel afraid, what helps you: is it making a plan, or talking to yourself, or finding out more information?

When you feel impulsive or tempted, what helps you: is it noticing the urge but talking yourself out of it, or asking for help, or personifying it as a tempter who is trying to hurt you?

When you are uncertain of what to do, what helps you: is it making a list of pros and cons, or doing more research, or asking someone for advice?

Learn what works for your brain, and do that. You are the driver of your brain, not a passenger in the back seat.

STOP WHEN YOU'RE OVERWHELMED

A teen client of mine, Lola, had a pattern of letting anger take hold of her emotions, often causing her to say things she later regretted. We talked about how, sometimes, the real reason we feel angry is because we're overwhelmed by all the thoughts racing through our brains.

When that happens, a mindfulness practice is an especially helpful way to pay attention to your thoughts, without judging yourself or letting them overtake you.

One of the best practices to help you do that, and one I use often, is also easy to remember—a practice known as STOP: Stop, Take a breath, Observe, Proceed. When you're feeling overwhelmed, take a time-out to:

- Stop what you're doing and close your eyes.
- Take a deep breath.
- Observe how you're feeling and what's going on inside your body: notice the stress you feel, what's causing it, and why.
- Proceed with care for yourself and those around you. Decide what the most compassionate next step would be—and do that.

Lola was able to use STOP when she got into an argument with her boyfriend at a school dance. She felt herself getting frustrated and realized that if she wasn't careful, she might say something to ruin the relationship, so she excused herself and went into the bathroom to work through each step in her mind. She was able to calm herself down, and the argument dissipated.

A mindfulness practice like STOP allows you to observe without judgment and become aware of your inner dialogue. Once you're aware of your thoughts, you can understand your emotions, identify what's going on beneath the surface, and think more clearly about your next action—instead of shifting from overwhelm into anger.

TRY THESE

1. Think about the last time you were angry. Place yourself in that moment, and think through how using STOP might have helped bring awareness to what you were thinking and feeling.

2. If you know there's a situation in your near future that could cause you to feel overwhelmed, write "STOP" on a sticky note and keep it with you as a reminder. You can also prepare by thinking through what a few compassionate steps might look like, such as waiting a day to react, or engaging in an activity that centers you, like taking a walk, reading, or connecting with others.

MAKE SPACE
BETWEEN YOUR THOUGHTS

Our lives can become very chaotic, but inner peace is always available to us. I have found that it is often my rushing thoughts that contribute to life feeling like chaos. Learning to pause my thoughts has helped me quiet my mind.

Our brains are noisy places: estimates vary, but it's estimated by the Chopra Center that we have more than 80,000 thoughts per day[4]—that's a lot of nonstop chatter. Our thoughts commentate in real-time, noticing every move we make, what everyone around us is doing, and a vast number of other things, all at once. Add on top of that the constant swirl of thoughts from the past and future, and it's no wonder how rare it is for us to feel at peace.

Maintaining inner peace is easier said than done, but it is possible. During times of uncertainty, your thoughts are one of the only things you can control. While none of us can ever truly exist without any thoughts, there are ways to quiet them, to pause them, and find a little space in between.

---

[4] "Why Meditate?," *Chopra*, February 2013. Retrieved from https://chopra.com/articles/why-meditate.

TRY THIS

1. Notice Your Thoughts

   - Set a timer on your phone for two or three minutes. Then, sit comfortably on the floor or in a chair with both feet on the floor. Straighten your back, lower your shoulders, and relax your jawline.
   - Start by noticing your natural breathing. You don't have to take a deep breath. Just notice the air flowing in and out.
   - As thoughts creep in, just notice, "oh there is a thought...and there is another one."
   - Become a watcher of your thoughts. Notice how busy your mind wants to be; observe the thoughts as they fly through your brain.

2. Add Space

   - Return to watching your breath move in and out.
   - Now, see if you can create space between the thoughts, like white space between sentences on a page. Maybe it is just a slight pause right now, but eventually, little by little, you can try to hold more space before a new thought comes in.
   - Notice that in the space between thoughts, there is the quiet of thoughtlessness.
   - Consider how good it feels to practice thoughtlessness.
   - Pause and be silent like this multiple times throughout your day. Allow yourself to be without thought. Allow quiet. Space. Calm. Notice the experience of freedom from thinking.

3. Assess Your Thoughts

- When you notice a thought, assess whether it is helpful or harmful to your peace. If it is harmful, let it pass. If it is helpful, invite it in and hold on to it.
- Begin to identify if a thought came from the past or the future, imagine pushing the thought aside to make space for noticing the present moment. The idea is to make space for right now.
- When you notice a thought about something in the past, think: "past."
- When you notice a thought about something in the future, think: "future."
- As a Kansas cattle ranching girl, I picture sliding barn doors for this exercise. I picture pushing open the doors like I am pushing thoughts of the past and future off to the side, so I can enter the present moment.
- Be patient with yourself; it takes practice to learn how to stay in the moment. When your thoughts creep in and derail your peace, continue to push them to the side and return to the now.

BYPASS THE ALARM

Learning to bypass the alarms in your brain can be a helpful practice to quiet our racing minds. Our brains work like the alarm system on a house, trying to detect threats and warn us that we are in danger. But sometimes the sensors are too sensitive and exaggerate the alarms. We can learn to bypass the alarms by understanding how our brain works. Our brain warns us that devastation is looming, but it forgets that we have been there before and survived. We have built a resilience that we sometimes forget about.

There are moments in our lives that devastate us, like your first major breakup or getting let go from a job. These things feel impossible at the time and we fear them happening again. We worry that it will always be this hard; that any potential future breakup or job loss will be just as devastating.

The good news is, after you've made it through those life-changing moments, you've already survived the hardest part. Those moments help you build resilience, so it will never be that hard for you again.

I've witnessed this phenomenon many times: a client will ask to see me immediately, because life feels so horrible that they feel as though they can't stand it. But by the time they come in, they are already a little stronger.

As a new coach, I would panic when I couldn't work them into my schedule immediately. I've since learned, though, that often they just need time to let things sink in. And not only do they feel a little better by the time I see them, their emotions are less raw, so we can do even deeper work.

Even when we think we're doomed, or that we couldn't possibly make it through something difficult again, we're actually almost always doing better than we think we are. Blame that partially on our brain, and specifically, the amygdala, which sounds the alarm when it thinks that we're in danger.

The amygdala is sounding alarms like it is created to do. Its job is to keep us alive by detecting threats. That reaction was useful back when everything was dangerous—when we were in danger of being chased by a lion, and our brains were telling us to stay in the cave.

In reality, we're not in imminent danger like our brains are telling us. We can handle the lions, so to speak. And when we do, we become more and more resilient, which makes us even more capable of whatever might come our way.

You're not doing as bad as you think you are: that is almost always true. No matter what your brain is telling you, remember that it's not actually the end of the world. There are no lions chasing you. This is just everyday life as a human today. Bypass the alarms. And reassure yourself that you will be okay.

TRY THESE

1. Think back to some of the toughest moments of your life up to this point. How did you feel right after they happened? How did you feel a week after? A month after? A year after? Remember that progression toward feeling better the next time a difficult situation arises.

2. Take time to consider which events in your life have made you more resilient. How does that resilience show up for you today? How might it help you the next time a difficult situation comes up?

3. The next time you feel devastated, or unable to visualize how you'll make it through something, try saying to yourself: "okay, amygdala. I know you're trying to protect me, but I can handle this. I'll get through this and life will get better."

RELEASE ANGST

Angst is that feeling you get inside when someone is irritating you, something frustrates you, or you feel upset over something that occurred.

Here are some common things that cause us angst:

- Someone cuts you off in traffic
- The line you are standing in isn't moving
- The technology you are using glitches
- You can't find what you are looking for
- Your restaurant order is wrong
- You encounter an opinionated person you disagree with

These moments might trigger in us a response of: "[*curse word*], why does this always happen to me?" Then the angst begins. The event happened, the event is now over, yet the angst lingers. Angst stays in our minds and bodies long after the moment that triggered the angst. When we focus on angst, it grows. Angst causes internal suffering and prolonged internal suffering can lead to toxicity in our bodies. We all need to hone our skill of releasing angst so that we aren't storing toxicity in our cells.

Think about that guy who cut you off in traffic—he's going about his day, yes, driving like an idiot, but he's not upset about it. His body is free from angst. It is you who is hanging onto the angst. As he drives away, you are stewing.

You are giving him the power to ruin your day. You replay the moment and fixate on what a jerk-idiot he is. You feel wronged, violated, and attacked. And yet, he drives away carefree.

Who is suffering here? You. Not him. Let's stop torturing ourselves by replaying everything wrong in the world. Why would we choose to bring more suffering onto ourselves? Life is hard enough, let's not pile it on by choosing to add even more angst into our bodies.

The more you can allow things to be as they are, even when you don't like them, the less angst you will feel inside. And when we reduce our levels of inner angst, we are less triggered by being wronged. It creates a positive cycle toward inner peace. And more people walking around with inner peace contributes to a more peaceful world.

This doesn't mean you become a doormat that others walk on. This is an exercise in helping your brain be less overreactive in moments of stress. Our brains throw tantrums when we are inconvenienced and can't control the world around us. But, truly, we have an amazing sense of inner strength that can help us through difficult moments if we train ourselves to override the tantrums.

High levels of angst can indicate that you have unmet needs, so dive into that a little deeper if you need to. If you feel like you are never getting what you want or need, then you might be easily triggered by things not going your way. Love yourself through those moments. You be the one that fulfills your needs, don't wait for someone else to take care of you. You care for you. The more you care for yourself the way you care for everyone else, the less angst you will feel inside. Less angst, more peace.

TRY THESE

1. Think through or make a written list of the things that cause you the most angst. What really pushes your buttons and makes you mad? Why is this so triggering to your brain? What might this be signaling? An unmet need? Explore this with yourself. Investigate what is under your angst. Help yourself uncover what is going on beneath the reaction. There is peace on the other side of this introspective work.

2. Once you become aware of what brings you angst, explore why. After you identify some reasons, see if you can gently talk yourself through your triggering moments. For example, maybe next time you are cut off in traffic, you say to yourself: "that person is clearly in a hurry, so I'm going to let them do what they need to do. I don't have to get angry about this, and I'm not going to let their choice ruin my day."

GUIDE YOUR 3 A.M. BRAIN

Do you ever wake up in the middle of the night and your brain starts a failure debrief meeting? Past regrets...future worries...things I'm afraid I will forget to do...things I did that I shouldn't have...things I didn't do that I should have. This used to happen to me a lot, usually around 3 a.m. I would be lying in bed, asleep, and then wake up just enough for an alarm to sound inside my head. My brain was up and at 'em: "time to list everything we're worried about!"

When you wake up in the middle of the night, often it triggers anxious thinking. We've all been there—our bodies exhausted and our brains in overdrive. There is actually a biological reason for this. Here's the neuroscience behind waking up in the middle of the night: when you awake, your amygdala—your brain's "fear center"—gets triggered and goes into "fight or flight" mode. Which was useful millions of years ago, when a bear may have wandered into our cave. Not so much now, though.[5]

When triggered, our brains turn to the nearest fear risk: often, the anxieties and worst-case scenarios stored elsewhere in the brain. It runs through that list in an attempt to keep us safe. And there we lie, thoughts racing, wide awake.

---

[5] Greg Murray, "Why Do We Wake Around 3am and Dwell On Our Fears and Shortcomings?," *The Conversation,* October 2021. Retrieved from https://neurosciencenews.com/night-waking-fear-19488/.

Understanding why your brain is racing is the first step toward helping to quiet down.

Remind yourself: "nothing good happens in my brain at 3 a.m." You are not going to experience positive thinking. That's not how we are programmed.

What you can do, though, is have a plan in place. Have something ready to help manage that busy brain. Give it something more productive to work on. Here are some examples:

- I'm going to do some deep breathing.
- I'm going to make a list of my favorite songs (or movies, shows, etc.).
- I'm going to relive a favorite vacation.
- I'm going to start planning a fun project.
- I'm going to think about what I can do tomorrow to have a good day.
- I'm going to talk to my higher power.

Ideally, your plan should be something you can do while lying in bed so that you can drift off back to sleep. Be gentle with yourself: it may take some time to quiet that impulse in your brain.

TRY THIS

Write yourself a note and put it by your bedside as a reminder before you go to sleep: "nothing good happens in my brain at 3 a.m." Then, if you wake up, you might read it and stop the negative thoughts before they begin. With a plan in place, we can quiet our beautiful brains that are trying so hard to protect us.

You deserve inner peace. To achieve it, we each have to learn to work with our complex brains. You are the driver of where your brain goes. Take it to peaceful places, not scary ones.

SEE WORRY AS AN INVITATION

I worry a lot. I bet you do too. Worrying is not usually an enjoyable activity, but it often invites us deeper into a conversation with ourselves. Our worries help us know more about ourselves if we take the opportunity to look.

Worry invites you to notice:

- Who you love
- What you care about
- Where you want to grow
- How you want to do things

You worry about the people you love. You worry about what is most important to you. You worry about areas that require you to step up and grow. You worry about doing things well.

Next time you sense a worried thought pass through that beautiful brain of yours, see if you can pause and go a little deeper. What does this worry have to teach me about myself? Is this worry a messenger of something bigger happening within me?

Maybe your worry is an invitation to surrender or release the need for control. Maybe your worry is inviting you to level up your life. Maybe it is a reminder to limit unhelpful beliefs about yourself.

Here are some examples from my client conversations:

- I'm worried about my children = I love them so much and want them to thrive.
- I'm worried about this first date = I really like her and I want her to like me.
- I'm worried about an evaluation = Doing my work well is important to me and I hope that is how I'm perceived.
- I'm worried about how this speaking gig will go = I want to make a positive impact on people's lives.
- I'm worried she's mad at me = I value our friendship and don't want there to be a conflict between us.
- I'm worried I can't get pregnant = I deeply long to be a mother and share my love with a child.
- I'm worried I said the wrong thing = Doing no harm and choosing words carefully really matters to me.
- I'm worried I don't have what it takes for this = I really want to grow and learn something new.

Your worries are an invitation inward. Your worries are trying to tell you something. Listen. When you can identify the deeper message, your brain quiets down a notch. Worry invites you to see what you value, and then you can approach it from a place of love instead of fear.

TRY THIS

Write down a list of your current worries. Big ones, small ones, things that feel ridiculous to worry about—write down anything that comes to mind. Now, look at that worry a little deeper and see what is underneath it. What is it showing you about what you really care about? Why are you worried about this? What is at stake? After you can see the deeper meaning, then speak to yourself gently about it: "you are worried about this because you care so much, it makes sense that you are worried, what would help you feel a little more peaceful or bring some comfort to you right now?"

TELL YOURSELF: "NO BIG DEAL"

One of my favorite meditation teachers, author Pema Chödrön, tells a story about a life-changing learning from her own meditation teacher. She watched as students shared their experiences and struggles, to which he simply responded: "no big deal." This wasn't due to a lack of compassion; the guru was actually teaching them a valuable practice to help find inner peace.[6]

When you say "no big deal," you train your brain that nothing's really a big deal. And when you think about it, many of the things that upset us really aren't big deals.

I once had a client who was feeling worthless and filled with the feeling: "I can't do anything right." I had her talk me through examples of when that popped up in her mind, and some were as small as when she burned dinner. She, like many of us, ended up crucifying herself for something tiny and insignificant—something that was truly no big deal.

Our self-critic can be ruthless. You burn the cookies, and you think things like: "I mess up everything." When really, what you should be thinking is: "no big deal."

---

[6] Pema Chödrön, *How to Meditate: A Practical Guide to Making Friends with Your Mind*, (Boulder: Sounds True, Inc., 2013), 13-14.

And not only is "no big deal" a great practice to silence your inner critics, it's also a great anti-panic practice. When we train our minds to react to small problems calmly, we are better able to weather larger challenges without all the stress.

People ask: but what if something is a big deal? This practice will still help you, no matter what. If you're working on a change in the neural pathways of your brain—which you are, if you're training yourself to say "no big deal"—you'll end up approaching bigger deals much calmer. You'll find yourself saying: "okay, this is a big deal, but I can figure it out." Your default mode will no longer be panic.

This is also a practice that helps you get in the habit of asking yourself: am I making this bigger than I need to? Am I adding to my stress level? Could I be more compassionate with myself at this moment? You'll find that learning to say "no big deal" can end up helping you in a very big way.

TRY THESE

1. Think about what little things always stress you. Commit to saying "no big deal" on things big and small and see if you notice a less reactive way of living, a lower level of stress, and clearer thinking in moments of struggle. Here are some examples:

   - You don't wake up to your alarm: no big deal.
   - You don't receive a quick response to an email: no big deal.
   - You have to wait in a long line: no big deal.
   - You eat an extra piece of cake: no big deal.
   - You spill a beverage: no big deal.
   - Another driver cuts in front of you: no big deal.
   - You show up for an appointment late: no big deal.

2. Write "no big deal" or "NBD" on a notecard and carry it with you or put it somewhere you can see it. Continue to say it in the days and weeks to come; remind yourself that you're rewiring your brain, and that this takes time.

CARE LESS, LOVE MORE

We care what people think of us. That's because we are naturally wired to take things personally. When people are unhappy with us, it triggers fear in our primal brain. Our ancestors, dating back to prehistory, were afraid of being exiled because they could not survive alone. Centuries later, well after that response stopped serving us in the same way, our brains still carry that wired-in fear.[7]

From an early age, our brain is wired to tell us: "if I make a mistake, I might get kicked out of my group and have to survive on my own." Caring what people think—whether they're happy with us or not, or whether they like us or don't—isn't a weakness. It's science.

Even knowing the scientific reason behind it, caring what people think has a down side. It can become unhealthy if we:

- Don't allow ourselves to make mistakes. And if we do make a mistake, we don't let ourselves off the hook. We punish ourselves, and we feed our inner critics
- Let others criticize us, and diminish our self-trust

---

[7] Miguel Ruiz, *The Four Agreements* (San Rafael, California: Amber-Allen Publishing, 1997), 58.

- Fear disapproval and rejection so much we freeze with inaction
- Believe we are never good enough, which leads to us to move the finish line further and further away
- Try to control how we are perceived and end up getting defensive and argumentative, often alienating people in the process
- Long for people to approve of and love us and end up denying our own needs, often lying to ourselves and allowing unhealthy relationships to continue

It's part of our survival instinct to care what people think of us, yet over-caring what people think blocks us from our own growth. We sometimes attempt to overcome that by telling ourselves not to care what anyone thinks, but what is more effective is to help ourselves through those moments when we find ourselves overwhelmed by seeking the approval of others.

There are several ways you can help yourself overcome that primitive wiring in your brain:

- Remember that a person's words and actions say more about them than they do about you. As the well-known adage goes, hurt people hurt people. Often, that person is projecting their own insecurities and shame onto you.
- Spend time with people you trust and who make you feel good.
- Consider the wisdom of Don Miguel Ruiz, author of the influential book, *The Four Agreements*: "If someone is not treating you with love and respect, it is a gift if they walk away. If that person doesn't walk away, you will surely endure many years of suffering with him or her. Walking away may hurt for a while, but your heart will eventually heal. Then you can choose what you really want. You will find that you don't need to trust others as much as you need to trust yourself to make the right choices."

Above all else, trust yourself. It's okay to seek feedback, criticisms, or opinions, as long as they're delivered with respect, mutual benefit, and compassion.

Work at overriding that pesky brain wiring by listening to your inner advocate as much as you listen to your inner critic. Then, you're far less likely to hinge your level of happiness on the approval of others. Life is so much more peaceful that way.

TRY THIS

Take note of when you find yourself caring what others think. In each instance, try one or all of the following:

- Remember what you know to be true about yourself, and repeat those things to help build new neural pathways into your brain. For example: "I am kind, compassionate, trying to help, and doing the best I can."
- Separate what is fact from what is story. Consider these examples: "this person is angry with me" is a fact; "our friendship is over" is a story—unless you decide that it's best to move on, which is also allowable.
- Practice being assertive. Ask for what you want and say no to what you don't want in a respectful, honest, clear, and direct manner.
- Think about loving more and caring less. Tell yourself: "I will send them love and release my worry about what they are thinking of me."

MELT THE ICE

In graduate school, I had a professor I was icy toward. I couldn't help it. I found her abrasive and confrontational—she would argue so much with students that I could feel myself starting to shut down in her class.

At some point, though, I realized that the dread of going to her class was getting heavy. I was the one making myself suffer. Finally, I asked myself: How can I make this better? How can I not be so angry? How can I open back up, instead of shutting down?

I worked hard, focusing instead on respecting her knowledge, regardless of how I felt about her delivery system. It helped immensely, and I was better able to move forward, without all that dread to slow me down.

I once heard the metaphor of ice used to illustrate the opposite of compassion. It's easy to become frozen, hard, and rigid in our opinions, so much so that we can become solid and immovable. If we aren't careful, we lose the ability to listen, understand, and open our hearts to those who aggravate us or those we disagree with.

Visualize what happens when a tree is covered in ice: the limbs start to get heavy. Some branches can't handle the weight of the ice and fall to the ground.

Ice is heavy. And sometimes, it causes us to detach.

Anger, bitterness, judgment, isolation, disappointment, fear, and sadness can feel like ice forming around our hearts. It becomes a heaviness we carry inside that hurts our relationships, energy, and ability to live to our fullest potential.

We can choose to melt our inner ice, though. It is a choice we get to make. When we melt that ice, we choose to replace those cold feelings with ones of warmth, openness, and compassion. We experience fluidity again.

We allow our minds and hearts to soften and find our way to a more peaceful place.

TRY THESE

1. Think of someone who really annoys you. Recognize that the coldness you feel is heavy and toxic to you. Ask yourself if you could warm up to a part of this person. Is there something you can find to admire or respect about them? How could you soften your heart and lift that heaviness? How could you melt that ice, even just a little?

2. Now bring to mind someone you love dearly. Connect with the warmth you feel when you think of this person. You care about them, you wish to alleviate their pain, and you want what is best for them. This comes naturally to you. Treasure this feeling of warmth for a few moments.

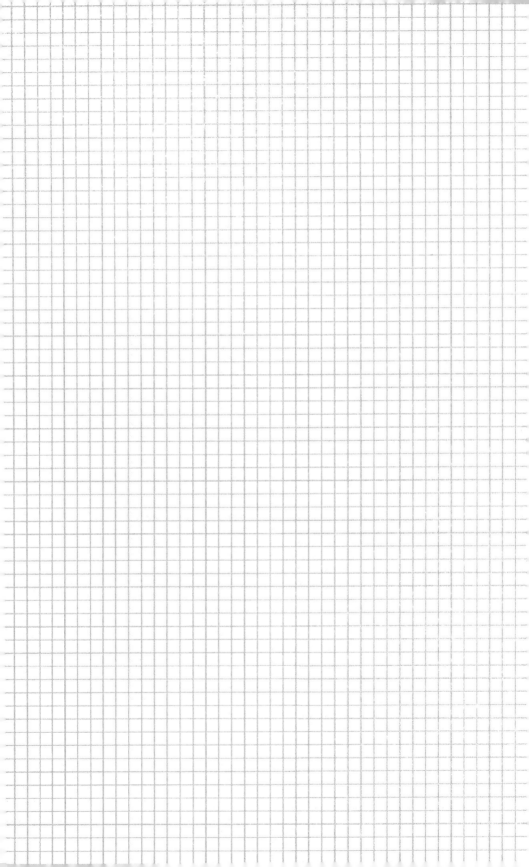

BEFRIEND YOURSELF

Befriending ourselves can be some of the hardest work in our lives. It sounds so simple, but if you struggle with feelings of low self-worth, were overly criticized as a child, or find insecurities hard to overcome, then you know how hard it is to befriend yourself. I have had clients say: "I don't think I will ever be able to love myself." If that seems hard to you too, then this section is the place to start. Let's just start with befriending ourselves.

Step one in befriending yourself is noticing how you talk to yourself, especially your inner criticisms, then asking yourself: "would I say that to a friend?" If you wouldn't say that same criticism to a friend, then don't say it to yourself. If I'm about to go onstage to speak, my critic may say: "you aren't good enough, you aren't prepared or ready yet, they aren't going to like you, this is going to flop and be horrible." I would never say those things to a friend before she went onstage. To her, I would say: "you've got this, you know your stuff, they are going to love you." Treat yourself as you would treat a friend.

This section is full of practices to help you create a friend-ship with yourself. Then you can build on that with the practices in the sections on trusting yourself and practic-ing self-compassion. This work is truly life-changing—I've watched it have a profound impact on my own life and the lives of my clients.

SAY YOUR OWN NAME

Ethan Kross, a professor and director of the Emotion and Self-Control Laboratory at the University of Michigan, has done extensive studies on the power of using our own names when we talk to ourselves. He's found that speaking to ourselves in the third person can alleviate anxious thinking; our brains feel less worried when they hear from an inner coach helping us through life.[8]

I used to feel silly talking to myself when I was home alone, but once I found Kross's research, I started doing it more intentionally. I use this as a tool to reassure myself, give myself permission to do (or not do) something, get myself back on track, help me make decisions, and encourage myself.

Our brains pay attention when we hear our names.[9] Think about in social settings when we hear our name, we tune into what is being said about us. So, make sure when you talk to yourself, you are using your first name to get your brain's attention.

Another researcher, Jason Moser, found that emotional distress decreased im-

---

[8] Lenny Picker, "Talking Head: PW Talks with Ethan Kross," *Publishers Weekly*, October 2020. Retrieved from https://www.publishersweekly.com/pw/by-topic/authors/interviews/article/84753-talking-head-pw-talks-with-ethan-kross.html.

[9] Dennis Carmody and Michael Lewis, "Brain Activation When Hearing One's Name and Others Names," *Brain Research* 1116, no. 1 (2006): 153-158. doi: 10.1016/j.brainres.2006.07.121.

mediately—within one second—of the participant using their own name in an encouraging sentence. He summed it up like this: "essentially, we think referring to yourself in the third person leads people to think about themselves more similar to how they think about others, and you can see evidence for this in the brain. That helps people gain a tiny bit of psychological distance from their experiences, which can often be useful for regulating emotions." [10]

The next time you feel anxious about something or afraid to try something new, start with a piece of third-person encouragement as simple as: "[*your name*], you can do this."

Experiment with saying your own name and coaching yourself out loud, no matter where you are or who will hear you. If you feel like you will be judged for talking to yourself in public, share this research with them and encourage them to try it out too.

The more we say our name and then something encouraging to ourselves, the more likely we are to trust ourselves. The other bonus to this practice is it helps you feel less alone in the world. If you feel unheard or unseen, this practice helps your brain feel heard and seen. It doesn't care where it is coming from, our brains light up when love is felt.

TRY THIS

Practice talking to yourself in the third person today— whispering to yourself counts, too! Try saying your name and offering encouragement like you would to a friend. Example: [*your name*], I see that you are [*frustrated*]. Remember that you are [*positive quality*] and you can figure this out.

---

[10] J.T. O'Donnell, "New Research Says This 1 Odd Skill Makes You Better at Controlling Stress," *Inc*, July 2017. Retrieved from https://www.inc.com/jt-odonnell/new-research-shows-this-odd-skill-makes-you-better.html.

Here are some scenarios in which you can give it a try:

- When you feel like you're not getting recognition: [*your name*], I see how hard you worked.
- When you have a misunderstanding with someone: [*your name*], you were trying to help and it was misunderstood.
- When you make a mistake: [*your name*], that wasn't the big mess-up you thought it was. Just clean it up and you will be fine.
- When you need hope: [*your name*], this pain is temporary, brighter days will return, it might not feel like it right now, but it will get better.

LOOK AT YOUR HANDS

When I speak to groups of nurses, they share that they spend so much time and energy taking care of others that it's easy for them to forget about taking care of themselves. This can, over time, threaten their own health and well-being.

There's an easy technique I like to teach those groups that offers them a quick, physical way to remind themselves to practice self-compassion. They start by putting their hands in front of themselves, and I ask them to think of all the ways they use those hands to care for others: administering IVs, providing comfort to patients, or holding the hands of grieving family members.

Finally, I have them place their hands on their hearts—which can help release oxytocin, a hormone that helps to lower stress. I then ask them to close their eyes and consider what it might be like to give themselves the same care they show others. I encourage them to say something loving to themselves. After a few minutes of silence, I have them open their eyes; often, there are tears on almost every face in the room. They've realized how much they pour into others, and how important it is not to forget themselves.[11]

---

[11] Kerstin Uvnäs-Moberg, et al, "Self-soothing behaviors with particular reference to oxytocin release induced by non-noxious sensory stimulation," *Frontiers in Psychology* 5 (2015). doi: Self-soothing behaviors with particular reference to oxytocin release induced by non-noxious sensory stimulation.

Like nurses, we all spend so much of our lives doing kind things for others, but it can be so easy to forget to show ourselves that same kindness.

Our hands do so much to show compassion and love. They prepare food, drive, send texts, tuck in children, pray for people, fold laundry, clean bathrooms, pet dogs, feed cats, take out the trash, pick up the phone to check on someone, write letters, open doors, give hugs, and hold the hands of others. Taking notice of those hands is a powerful way to remind yourself: you deserve all that compassion, too.

TRY THIS

1. Place your hands in front of you.

2. Consider all that your hands have done so far this week to show compassion and love. Maybe even make a list—you may be amazed at how many you can come up with.

3. Look at your hands with adoration as loving instruments that show compassion and kindness to others every day.

4. Now place those loving hands on your heart and take a deep breath.

5. Say something kind to yourself. Give yourself encouragement. Make a loving statement to yourself. If this seems hard to do, imagine what you would say to a dear friend. Be the friend you are to others to yourself this time. When I do this, I place my hands on my heart and say something like this: "Ginger, in this moment, you are okay. You are enough." Find the phrases that feel true and restorative to you.

F.I.X. YOUR INNER DIALOGUE

Imagine you're walking along a sidewalk and someone in front of you falls to the ground. You become aware that this person may have an injury or need your assistance. You feel a human connection to this person; you know what it feels like to fall and be in pain, or be embarrassed, or need help to get up. You give them words of encouragement, or if they're badly injured, you call 911 and assure them that you'll stay with them until help arrives.

We all have the universal capacity to show compassion, a word that comes from the Latin word "compati," which means "to suffer with." It's something we do instinctively.

Yet when it comes to self-compassion, it's so often a different story. We don't give ourselves nearly as much compassion as we give to others.

Usually, when we're the ones falling on the sidewalk, our inner chatter sounds like this: "why wasn't I paying attention? How could I be so stupid? I knew I shouldn't have worn these shoes. You are always running late!" You tell the person trying to help you: "I'm fine." And on and on and on.

Becoming aware of our self-talk and showing ourselves the same compassion we so freely give to others is truly a game-changer. And, as you become more compassionate toward yourself, you naturally become even more compassionate toward others. It moves the needle toward love for everyone.

Self-compassion research done by Kristin Neff at the University of Texas, Austin, found three elements present in the practice of self-compassion: self-kindness, common humanity, and mindfulness. [12]

To help remember those three elements and put self-compassion into practice, I came up with the acronym FIX: a strategy to help stop my clients from beating themselves up, and point them instead toward a more hopeful, kinder, self-compassionate place.

FIX stands for:

- F: "What am I **F**eeling about it?"
  Get curious about what you're thinking, feeling, and experiencing at this moment. Notice if you're in pain, sad, alone, helpless, or upset. Tell yourself: "this is a hard thing to do and it makes sense that I am anxious."
- I: "**I** am not alone."
  Remind yourself that you're not alone; others feel this same way. Part of the human experience involves suffering. Millions of people have had similar circumstances or experiences. Tell yourself: "what I am feeling right now is part of the human experience, and other people feel this way too."
- X: "I will be **X**tra gentle to myself."
  Offer yourself kind words of encouragement and remind yourself that this feeling is temporary. Give yourself hope that the situation can improve, allow yourself to see that you will be okay soon, and ask yourself what you need to feel a sense of comfort.

As human beings, we are going to encounter struggles, but there is always hope if we FIX our inner dialogue: investigate what we're Feeling, remember "I am not alone," and practice being Xtra gentle with ourselves.

And when we fall, we can be the ones to help ourselves back up.

---

[12] Kristin Neff, *Self-Compassion: The Proven Power of Being Kind to Yourself* (New York: Harper Collins, 2011), 41.

TRY THESE

Reflect on a time when your feelings got hurt—maybe when a family member said something that stung, or when you felt left out of something.

- F: How did that make you feel? Get specific; name all the emotions that arise when you think back.
- I: Consider others who have felt the same way. Think of loved ones who have been through something similar; take a moment to feel the shared experience of what it was like for them, knowing you're not alone.
- X: How might you be extra nice to yourself if a similar situation arises in the future? Is there someone you could check in with who always makes you feel good? Or something you like to do that makes you feel happy and calm? Keep those things in mind so that you're always well-prepared to show yourself the self-compassion you so fully deserve.

THINK OF YOURSELF AS A STUDENT

A client once shared a story about her young granddaughter staying at her house for the weekend. As my client was having her morning coffee, the little girl came into the kitchen in her jammies, blankie under her arm, face lit up with excitement. "Grandma!" she exclaimed. "It hasn't ever been this day before!"

Her grandmother loved her joy and so did I. I love how she approached the new day with awe and bewilderment, like a student seeing everything for the first time. It's important for all of us to remember that no matter our age, our experiences are always new to us. We'll always be students, and we'll always be learning new things.

Author Elizabeth Gilbert once mentioned in a social media post that she wrote "student" on her hand as the "best defense against self-abuse, shame, perfectionism, failure, and regret." When I saw this, I was in the midst of feeling some severe stage fright as I was preparing for a few major speaking engagements. I realized that with a student mindset, I could drop the expectation of being perfect from the start, and notice instead that I improved every time I was on stage.

I would tell myself: "it doesn't have to be perfect today because you are still a student." It did wonders to help my stage fright go away and is a practice I continue to this day whenever self-doubt appears. When I experience times of deep self-doubt, I write "student" on my hand to remind myself that I am always learning and growing.

Reminding yourself that you're just a student is also helpful during uncertain times, much like what we've all been through over the past few years. When our shared experiences are particularly challenging, it's important to remember that no one has lived through such a time before. We are all just students of life, no matter what it brings.

We're all works in progress, as individuals and as a society. Humanity has never been here before. Be gentle with your expectations of yourself and others. We are in a constant state of learning. We are all just students.

TRY THESE

1. When you feel fear, self-doubt, confusion, anger or any other uncomfortable emotion, ask yourself the following questions through the lens of being a student:

    -   What can I learn from this experience?
    -   What can I learn from this person?
    -   How would I feel if I admit I do not know the answer?
    -   How would it feel to tell someone that I have never done what I am doing before?
    -   How does it feel to remind myself that I am still learning?
    -   Can I release the need to do this perfectly?

2. Try writing "student" on your hand for a day. Do you notice a shift in your thinking? Does it remind you to be gentler to yourself or to others?

MAKE A "GOOD LIST"

Whether it is our spouse, children, parents, coworkers, or friends, it's easy to get frustrated with others. We're only human. Often, that frustration bubbles over into criticism, and if we're not careful, we risk alienating those we care about the most.

What is important, though, is making certain that we balance those criticisms with seeing the good those same people do in our lives. If not, our relationships might tip too much toward the negative and become difficult to recover.

I often work with teens who get so frustrated with a parent or sibling over something small that they let the frustration fester to the point of near-explosion. I listen as they describe the list of things that are going wrong, and if they want to lessen their anger and work on healing the relationship, I ask: "what do they do well?" Inevitably, after some thinking, their face softens as they begin to share with me a "good list" of wonderful things about this person.

Sometimes we forget the good stuff.

We can so easily and unconsciously enter into a criticism loop where we only see the negative. Think about the people you live with—often, we default to seeing what they do wrong: the dishes not put away, the towel on the floor, the unfinished projects, all their annoying idiosyncrasies.

We do this to ourselves too. You might be self-critical that you didn't get enough accomplished today. Maybe you replay the mistakes you made in your life. Perhaps when you talk with friends, you discuss all of the things that are horrible in your life to bond with them in misery. The to-do lists, regrets, and scorecards can loop through our brains for eternity if we don't learn to change our thought patterns and start keeping track of the good.

Scientifically, learning to make "a good list" works in our favor: self-compassion research shows that celebrating your accomplishments results in higher levels of motivation than punishing yourself for a lack of accomplishment.[13] And making a "good list" for others also trains our brains to more easily remember those qualities the next time we feel frustrated.

Take time to make your "good lists," and chances are, you'll soon find even more good coming your way.

TRY THESE

1. At the end of the day, make a written or mental list of the things you accomplished, rather than focusing on what didn't get accomplished.

2. When you think about all that's wrong with a situation or relationship in your life, pause and bring to mind the things that are actually going well right now, or have gone well in the past. Here are some examples:

    •   When a partner or spouse gets on your nerves, think back to your first months of dating and what you most liked about them.

---

[13] Breines, J. G., & Chen, S. (2012). Self-compassion increases self-improvement motivation. *Personality and Social Psychology Bulletin, 38*(9), 1133-1143.

- When you look in the mirror and don't like what you see, remind yourself there are a lot of really great things about you too.
- As a student, when you beat yourself up for procrastinating, make a list of all the things you turned in on time this month.
- When you're annoyed with a friend, look back over your entire friendship and consider the joy that they've brought into your life.
- When work seems mundane, make a list of the things you've accomplished in this role.

For a life-transforming reflection, keep a journal by your bedside to record your daily "good list." You'll fall asleep thinking about all that is right, instead of all that is wrong. Try it and see if you notice higher levels of motivation.

TRAIN YOUR BRAIN TO SAY "...YET"

Years ago, I found myself wanting to try a yoga class. But I kept telling myself: "you're not flexible enough." I said it so much, my brain logged it as fact. And so—surprise, surprise—for a long time, I never once gave yoga a try.

What I didn't know was that I was training my brain with the kind of black-and-white thinking that our minds love: either we can or can't do something. Either we're good or bad at something. Either we like something or we don't. That's because we're hardwired for survival from way, way back—back to the times when our ancestors had to learn things like red berries are poisonous, but blueberries are okay. That kind of thinking kept us safe—it kept us alive.

Millions of years later, we've evolved past the necessity of black-and-white thinking. Thankfully, there's a way to hack our way out of it. It's a practice known as "the power of '...yet.'"

If I say to myself: "I'm not flexible...yet," I'm giving myself a dose of hope. Growth becomes a real and tangible possibility. Wiring-wise, my brain can now see those shades of gray: I can't do it yet, but I can work toward it. That potential for growth can become our default thinking—we can rewire our brains to help us grow. To remember that there's potential. And to keep working toward what we ultimately want.

The study of neuroplasticity tells us that our brains can be rewired by changing our thought patterns; neuroscientists continue to validate the power of positive thinking.[14] We know now that our brains are more malleable than we once thought. We can overcome that black-and-white thinking that's hardwired into us and can sometimes stop us from moving forward.

Practicing tools such as the power of "...yet" allows our brains to make new neural connections and improve our compassion toward both ourselves and others.

The power of adding the word "...yet" to your limiting thoughts is fostering a growth mindset, which means you're teaching your brain that anything is possible. You believe that skills can be learned and that you have potential. Best of all, in a growth mindset, you stop hearing your inner critic and let your inner encourager run the show instead.

TRY THIS

When you hear yourself thinking a negative or hopeless thought, add the word "yet" to the thought. Continue this on a regular basis to give your brain the chance to rewire its black-and-white thinking. Soon, you'll feel hope start to enter in. Here are some examples:

- I'm not good at this...yet.
- I don't know the answer...yet.
- I'm not confident...yet.
- I'm not able to run a 5K...yet.
- I'm not healthy...yet.
- I didn't get the promotion...yet.
- I'm not organized...yet.

---

[14] Carol Dweck, *Mindset: The New Psychology of Success* (New York: Random House, 2007).

- I don't know how to _____...yet.
- I can't _____...yet.
- I don't have _____...yet.

REVISE YOUR "EVERYBODY ELSE" STATEMENTS

Social media has gifted humanity with a new way of connecting, but it's also prompted intense, unprecedented levels of comparison. As we scroll, we see what everybody else is doing, which inevitably makes us all a little bit envious at times.

I've had teen clients who struggle with insecurity, all thanks to the heavily filtered and edited pictures that pop up on their social media feeds.

I've had adult clients who look at their feeds and think everyone else is sailing happily through life, while they struggle with their jobs, their families, with any number of normal human challenges.

We look at social media, and without even realizing it, the "everybody else" statements start flooding our brains:

- "Everybody else has money."
- "Everybody else has plans this weekend."
- "Everybody else has a job they like."
- "Everybody else has a best friend."
- "Everybody else has fun."
- "Everybody else has a child/grandchild."
- "Everybody else has a purpose."
- "Everybody else looks perfect."

Within statements like these lies an unspoken hint of self-pity: "I'm the only one who's missing out." Self-pity isolates us and makes us feel more alone.

But there's a way out of self-pity and isolation: turning to self-compassion instead. Self-compassion connects us and reminds us that we're not alone. Because here's the reality—everybody else longs for something they don't have. What we're all feeling is simply part of the human experience.

We're all in this life together; we all have challenges and struggles. Those don't separate us. They make us all more alike. With that in mind, here's what those "everybody else" statements should start sounding like:

- "Everybody else gets lonely sometimes."
- "Everybody else doubts themselves."
- "Everybody else is afraid."
- "Everybody else is tired."
- "Everybody else wants connection."
- "Everybody else longs for meaning and purpose."
- "Everybody else knows what it feels like to be left out."
- "Everybody else wonders who they can trust."
- "Everybody else thinks something is wrong with them."
- "Everybody else wants to be seen and heard."
- "Everybody else is doing the best they can."
- "Everybody else wishes for more."
- "Everybody else wants to be loved."

When you find yourself comparing your life to others, be mindful of where your "everybody else" statements start to go. See if you can't direct them to a more productive place—one where you can start building compassion instead.

Above all, whenever you find yourself in the trenches of comparing and despairing, remember this: you are never alone.

TRY THIS

The next time you scroll through social media, stop to see if you can't catch yourself comparing yourself to the people in the pictures you see. Stop and flip those thoughts into something more productive and compassionate. Try to imagine what else that person might be going through. In what ways do you both experience the same ups and downs life throws at us? How might they be like you?

ADOPT YOUR INNER CHILD

In a class I teach about connecting with your teen, I share a slide with suggestions my teen clients have for parents. In my poll, I asked teens what they
wish their parents would do more of. Here are some of the things teens said:

- Be less serious
- Laugh more
- Don't freak out
- Say "I love you" more
- Spend time alone with just me
- Like and appreciate my friends
- Have more cozy family nights at home
- Give me small surprises
- Accept who I am
- Respect my room as my space
- Don't keep reminding me of past mistakes
- Give me a little more freedom
- Be silly with me

Being a parent can be so difficult, and yet these things are pretty easy for us
to do. It helps when we remember that there is a child in that teenage body
who still needs assurance, affection, and attention, even though they might
act like they don't want those things.

No matter our age, we all have a child inside us that wants to feel loved and know we matter to someone.

There is an inner child in every human being. That inner child wants to feel safe, adored, and cherished, and often longs for what we did not receive in our childhood. You can give your inner child now what you did not receive as a child. It is known as "re-parenting yourself." Say the things to yourself now that you didn't hear as you were growing up. Be the adult that child needed. If re-parenting isn't a term that resonates with you, try thinking of it as adopting or befriending your inner child.

You can do this by imagining yourself at a certain age. See your home setting, school setting, or activities you were involved in. Notice what you are wearing, what your hair looks like, what personality you have, and how darling that little person is. What does that child need to know? What do they need to hear from a loving adult? What encouragement could you give to them? Imagine that as an adult you are telling that child very loving, encouraging, validating things. Give them hope that it is all going to be okay.

Also, take that inner child of yours outside to play. What did you love to do as a kid? Do some of that now. Swing on the swings. Color with new crayons. Skip. Dance. Create something. Laugh at silly videos. Make lemonade. See the dandelions as wishes instead of weeds. Buy something that doesn't make sense. Use your imagination.

Connect with the child inside yourself. We all have a child who wants to be seen, heard, loved, and understood. Love on your inner child this week. Then you will naturally love everyone else a little more too.

TRY THIS

Find a photo of yourself as a child. Ideally around age 6, as this is the age that research shows we become aware of what others think of us and begin our people-pleasing tendencies.[15] Look at that child with love and admiration. Remember what games she liked to play at this age. Remember what he worried about at this age. Imagine scooping this child up in your arms and taking them out into the yard, away from the stress of the adults. What does this child want to do? Run, find butterflies, do cartwheels, pretend, swing, find shapes in the clouds? Take this child under your wing and protect, guide, and encourage them. They now have a loving adult they can count on...and it is you.

---

[15] Phillipe Rochat, "Five levels of self-awareness as they unfold early in life," *Consciousness and Cognition* 12 (2003): 717-731. doi:10.1016/S1053-8100(03)00081-3.

ADD "...AND THAT IS OKAY"

One of the readers of my Tuesday emails shared that through these weekly messages, she had become aware of how hard she is on herself and how impossibly high her expectations of herself are. She shared that now, in her 60's, she is learning a "more gentle way to live," and I loved hearing that. I've had to work hard to change my own brain from being uber-critical of myself to being more compassionate and gentle. That's why I love sharing these practices with you, so that together we are all finding a gentler way to live.

The "...and that's okay" practice is one of my favorites. A perfectionist friend shared this one with me. She is a Type 1 on the Enneagram and loves her gift of attention to detail. Yet, she can be overly critical of herself if she makes a mistake. She shared with me that she has learned to add "...and that's okay" to the end of her inner criticisms. I loved it and began using it immediately myself and offering it as a practice to my clients.

This is permission-giving in the best way. When you feel unsure of yourself, see if you can add the phrase "and that's okay" to your thoughts.

Here are some things I've heard from clients recently that work well with this practice:

- I binged a series on Netflix this weekend and didn't open my laptop to respond to emails...and that's okay.

- I don't want to volunteer at my child's school any longer...and that's okay.
- I stopped giving money to my religious organization and started giving to a charity that I believe in...and that's okay.
- I want to take the job that has more meaning instead of the job with more money...and that's okay.
- My house is a disorganized mess right now...and that's okay.
- My neighbor came to my back door and saw me dancing in the kitchen... and that's okay.

Being human is a hard job, so let yourself off the hook once in a while. The clinical research on compassion shows that when we let ourselves off the hook, we are more likely to go easier on others too[16]—and that's how we create a more loving world.

TRY THIS

If you notice a shaming inner roommate in your head, see if you can override it with the phrase "and that's okay." This can lead to a powerful shift that reduces stress and helps you feel a dose of self-compassion. It may take some practice to catch those inner criticisms, but when you do, notice the shift in your brain. You might even feel like a burden has lifted off your shoulders. After you get good at this one, offer it to friends when you hear them being critical of themselves.

---

[16] Bruk, A., Scholl, S. G., & Bless, H. (2021). You and I both: Self-compassion reduces self–other differences in evaluation of showing vulnerability. *Personality and Social Psychology Bulletin*, 01461672211031080.

ENCOURAGE YOURSELF

Have you ever written yourself a letter? It might seem weird, but it can be a powerful practice in befriending and encouraging yourself.

Many of us are good at encouraging others, but we aren't intentional about doing it for ourselves. You are a cool human being and you deserve to honor that fact.

We might encourage ourselves through a mantra or positive thought, but writing a letter is more than that. It feels slower and more thoughtful to put your thoughts into a letter. With paper as a medium, our brain senses that the words are more authoritative, as if this encouragement is coming from an outside source beyond the thoughts in your head.

Try it this week. If it feels too strange to write it on paper, type a letter in a word document or use the notes app on your phone. There is something more intimate about handwriting, but if that stops you from this practice, then type a letter to yourself.

Spend some time looking inward. What do you need to hear? Gift that to yourself.

Here are some lines that might help you get started:

- I recognize your ability to...
- I see your joy when...
- You sound excited about...
- I know it has been hard to...
- I understand why you...
- I see you trying to...
- I saw your disappointment when...
- I love it when you...
- I hope you get...
- I think your greatest quality is...
- One thing you're great at is...
- I am proud of you for...
- I know you can...
- I believe in your...

Pick one or a few of these and notice what flows when you start writing. See if you can get out of your own way and let this be a letter from your soul to your heart. Love on you the way you love on others. Write to yourself with encouragement like you would to your grandchild or child. I know you tell them how wonderful they are, so see if you can use that same voice and write to yourself.

Make this practice your own. You can write letters to future you and past you. You can make this a journal practice by writing daily letters to yourself. You can draw or paint something if words aren't your jam. Just find a way to communicate with your own soul and heart.

TRY THIS

Write a short note to yourself like, "[*your name*], you're doing a really good job." Maybe put the sticky note somewhere you will see it throughout the day. Or, make it your wallpaper on your phone or a note in your notes app. Seeing this can be a game changer in your day. Learn to be the voice of encouragement you long to hear. It may feel awkward at first, but push through the discomfort because you deserve a letter of encouragement. You are a great human being; remind yourself of that.

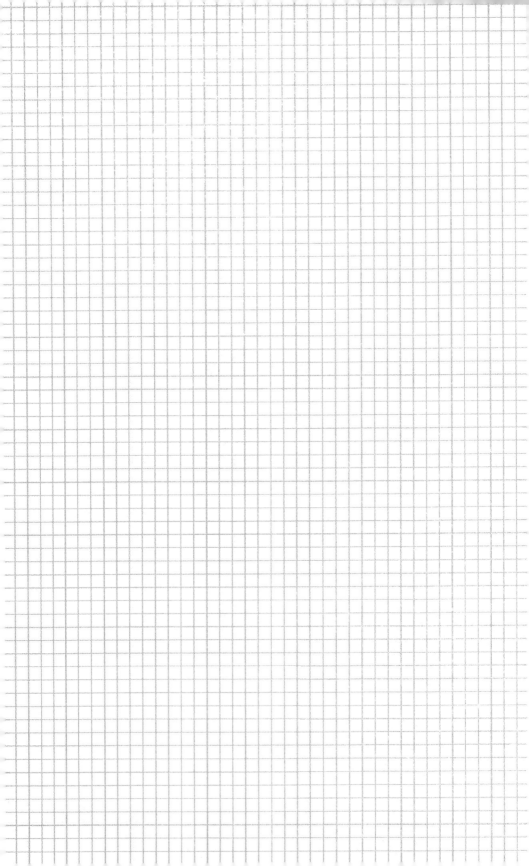

TAP INTO COURAGE

For some of us, finding courage is one of the hardest things about being human. It takes courage to say the things we want to say, to do the things we want to do, and to pursue the dreams we want to pursue.

I see a lack of courage holding a lot of us back. We are afraid of failure, judgment, sacrifice, inconvenience, pain, mistakes, rejection, and regret. But in life, we get to decide if our decisions were good or bad. We tell the story in hindsight, and we can tell it however we want to.

Courage is in you, it just needs to be brought to the surface and strengthened a little. I love the practices in this section and return to them often. Every circumstance allows me to refine how I use these practices, and they never let me down. Courage is a muscle we have to build. We can do it together!

DO BRAVE-ISH THINGS

When you hear the word "brave," do you think of something like skydiving or taking a big risk? Many people associate "brave" with a big scary adventure or something on a grand scale.

Brave-ish isn't a grand event, it is a baby step toward building courage. Brave-ish is doing things like asking for help, trying something new, or saying "I don't want to."

I have talked with so many smart, loving, gifted people who feel stuck because they lack the courage to share their gifts, speak up, share their ideas, or step into their potential. I talk with women who feel resentful because they are afraid to enforce boundaries. I talk with men who feel stuck because they are afraid to share their feelings and emotions. Let's build our brave-ish muscles together.

The way we build our courage muscles is by taking baby steps of bravery. Bravery researcher Dr. Kristen Lee calls this "micro-dosing bravery." Her research has found that a little small act of bravery every day can build resilience, reduce anxiety, spark creativity, and increase your energy levels.[17]

---

[17] Kristen Lee, *Worth the Risk: How to Microdose Bravery to Grow Resilience, Connect More, and Offer Yourself to the World* (Colorado: Sounds True Publishing, 2022).

Here are a few ideas for micro-dosing bravery:

- Speak up in a group setting
- Create something
- Invite someone to something
- Tell your story
- Reach out to an old friend
- Take a class
- Hire help
- Throw things away
- Take a day off
- Dance like no one is watching
- Ask for a raise
- Skip the party
- Say "no"
- Say "yes"

A woman in a class I was leading said she wanted to be more "brave-ish." She wanted to grow more comfortable with being uncomfortable. She was going to try new things and stretch herself beyond her comfort zone. Being brave-ish was how she would start. Small steps toward greater courage.

If we are all a little more brave-ish, we might engage more in social justice, volunteer, contribute, and give. We might speak, vote, and act more bravely. We might see love begin to win.

TRY THIS

Practice small doses of courage this week and see what you notice. Maybe pick one brave-ish thing to do every day this week. Being brave is like going to the gym and starting weight training—we don't just go right for the 150lb barbell, we start with the 5lb weights and move up from there. Quickly, we notice we are able to lift more weight, then more, and then we are surprising ourselves with how strong we are. Bravery works the same way. Start with brave-ish small things and soon you will notice your confidence, resilience, and courage rising.

GIVE YOURSELF TWO OPTIONS: "HELL YES" OR "NO"

A client came to me once who was overwhelmed to the point of exhaustion. She had taken on too much and was at the breaking point. To top it all off, she'd been asked to cohost a party—at her house—with two other women whose personalities tended to be what she described as "bossy." She felt pressured and obligated to say yes.

That's when I interrupted her to say: "This is a no." She looked at me, taken aback by my directness. I told her about a really quick and effective trick you can use to help with decision making: "If it's not a hell yes, then it's a no." It's as simple as that.

When you're already stretched thin and you get asked to do one more thing, remind yourself of your two options: hell yes, or no. What's your gut telling you? Is it a "hell yes I want to do that"? Great! Go for it. Is it anything less than that? Then stop right there: it's a no. For your own health and well-being.

I've met with a lot of clients who have been stuck trying to make a decision. "Should I be the school board president?" "Should I take a new job?" "Should I stay with my partner?" And to all of them, I ask: "Is it a hell yes?" That one question has a really sneaky way of bringing a whole lot of clarity.

Here's why: when we say a "yes" that's not a whole "yes," we're likely to build resentment. This leads us to create unnecessary stress for ourselves, damage our relationships, lose sleep, harm our health—the list goes on and on. Which is why when we say "yes," it needs to be a full-body "hell yes."

There are often clues to help you determine if it's a "hell yes." You feel lit up at the prospect. You feel excited energy instead of dread energy. It feels aligned—it just *feels right*. You can feel it in your body; it's the choice that brings with it no added sense of exhaustion.

A lot of things in life are optional, and especially the things you volunteer to take on. What do we feel like we have to do? Often, those things truly aren't have-to's. This is why we often feel stuck, obligated or expected to do things. We forget that we have a choice. We get to decide. We get to say "hell yes." We get to say "no."

And sure—saying no might upset some people. If you're worried about someone's response, play it through in your head: "If I say yes to this, I'm going to live an angrier existence, which could affect those around me. But if I say no, they're only going to be angry for a few seconds."

We have to learn to be okay with someone not liking our answer. Remember, just because someone doesn't like our response doesn't mean it's wrong. Ultimately, you're trying to take care of yourself. Being mindful of your health and well-being? "Hell yes." Exhaustion and burnout? That's a "no."

TRY THIS

Looking ahead, what are some decisions you might face that could cause you to feel stressed or overwhelmed? Prepare ahead of time by considering whether they feel like a "hell yes" or a "no." Here are a few examples:

- Whether to attend a social gathering
- Whether to assume a volunteer position
- Whether to host an event

- Whether to go on a trip
- Whether to take on an extra work project

A "hell yes" feels like 'without a doubt, I want to do this and I can't wait to do it!" If you don't feel that, explore why. Without that feeling, consider that this is likely a "no."

EXERCISE AGENCY

The word "agency" in psychology refers to our ability to make individual choices. A sense of agency means that we remember: "I can make my own decisions and take action to influence my own life." We each have personal power to design our lives and make our own choices. But it is amazing how easily we forget this when we feel a loss of control.

The opposite of a sense of agency is feeling like a victim.

The more we remember that we have options and can make our own choices, the more freedom we feel. When we believe we don't have options, we feel trapped and stuck. The truth is, you always have options. You have agency. You can always choose your actions, thoughts, words, behaviors, next moves, etc.

Here are some examples that might help to illustrate this concept:

Someone who feels helpless or stuck might say in a victimized tone, "I can't..." but since we have agency, "I can't..." means:

- I won't...
- I've decided not to...
- I choose not to...

Someone who feels trapped in an obligation might say, "I have to..." but since we get to make our own choices, we are saying:

- I choose to....
- I will...
- I've decided to....
- I want to...

Someone who feels they don't have enough time might say, "I don't have time to..." but what we know is really true is:

- I choose not to give my time to...
- This is not a priority for me...
- I'm choosing to spend time on...

The point of agency is to remember that you have it. Most of us reading this are free to make our own choices. We can decide what we spend our time on, what we say yes/no to, and how we live our lives.

When we forget we have agency, we experience higher levels of anxious thinking, depressed feelings, and hopelessness.

You have at least three options in any given situation: move forward, move backward, or don't move at all. You get to decide. You are in the driver's seat of your life.

TRY THIS

When you feel stuck, helpless, hopeless, or overwhelmed, see if you can make a list of your options. List every option you can think of, even if it seems impossible. We don't have to determine the "how" right now, we are just exploring all of your options. Simply seeing that you have options brings a sense of relief, peace, and renewed energy. You are not trapped. You have agency. Don't forget to use it.

TURN MONSTERS
INTO MOSQUITOES

A client, Miranda, came to me not long ago. Her relationship had just ended and not only was she heartbroken, she was paralyzed by fear: both she and her ex had been invited to the same party, and it would be her first time seeing him since they had broken up. She didn't know what she was going to say or if she'd even be able to speak—she was afraid she might have a panic attack.

She was doing what we all do when we're dreading something: we make a monster out of a mosquito.

Whether it's a work project we've been putting off, a tough conversation we're avoiding, or the thought of running into an ex, it's easy to imagine that thing you dread as a huge monster overtaking your life. It keeps you awake at night. It makes you put all joy on hold. It is huge and awful and ugly and you cower in its presence.

Now imagine that same thing as a mosquito: yes, it's annoying, but you are so much bigger than that mosquito and you could smash it at any moment. You don't like it, but you can handle it. You have the power to do something about it. You can control the mosquito.

No question, the things we dread are hard. But our brains like to imagine that they're going to be so much more miserable than they actually are. Our amygdala at the base of our brains are always trying to keep us safe and get us ready for the worst-case scenario.

In Miranda's case, we talked through what that moment she dreaded might be like: yes, it will be awkward. But it's just annoying, like a mosquito. It will only be a couple of minutes that you'll see each other, and then you'll walk back to your friends, and it'll be over.

Instead of preparing for a monster—a panic-inducing moment that could ruin her whole night—could she take her power back? And prepare instead for a hard two minutes—just a mosquito? We rehearsed what she would say when she saw him, ending with: "I'm headed to get a drink." She would then have the power to leave that conversation. It's not that it wouldn't be hard; but it could be brief. And she could be in control. Moment over. Mosquito gone.

Reminding ourselves: "this is a mosquito, not a monster" is an easy and effective way to manage our exaggerating brains and remind ourselves that we have the power. We can deal with this.

TRY THESE

Take something you've been dreading and see if you can transform it from a scary, all-consuming monster into an annoying, squashable mosquito. Here are some examples:

1. Is there a project you've been dreading? How can you make it easier? Can you reduce it down into several small tasks? Can you finish those tasks, one by one? Can you delegate anything?

2. Is there a person that you've been avoiding or afraid to run into? Can you picture it as a quick interaction? Can you rehearse what you might say? Or come up with an exit plan?

3. Is there a doctor's appointment you've been delaying? Can you take control and remember that you're in charge of your health? So that you can be active and have fun with the people you love?

4. Is there a conversation you've been putting off? Can you rehearse how you might find common ground with this person? How might you tell them how you feel? And receive how they feel?

WEIGH THE DIFFICULT

I was on a walk in my neighborhood and stopped to talk with a young mom who had just dropped off her son for his first day of kindergarten. She was describing to me how sad she was, and that it had been a hard morning. She knew he was ready to go to school and that this would just be a tough transition for her mama heart. Then she said: "I guess I could homeschool him, but that would be hard too—a whole different kind of hard."

After we talked, I kept thinking about what she'd said. She reminded me of something I talk about in conversations with clients: that often, when faced with a challenging decision, we forget that we actually get to "choose our difficult." Sending her little one to school was difficult, but so was the idea of homeschooling.

When all of your options seem difficult, ask yourself: "which option is the least difficult?" Or: "which option am I willing to endure right now?"

A few of my clients are midway through college, and they're thinking about changing their major. We talk about how it would be difficult for them to start over, or have to stay in school for an extra year. On the other hand, though, it is also really difficult to be stuck in a profession that is meaningless to you. It is up to them to pick which choice is the right difficult for their long-term happiness.

I have a health and fitness goal I'm working on right now, and it's difficult to stay committed. But it's also difficult to be sick or have low energy. So I have to choose my difficult when I make nutrition and exercise choices. Then, everything becomes clearer and less of a struggle when I know I'm weighing the difficult and making a choice to promote my long-term goal.

This practice helps me whenever my brain throws a tantrum about how challenging something is going to be. I remember that I can evaluate my options and that with every change comes difficulties. I get to choose which path is worth the challenge.

Remembering that you can choose your difficult is a liberating practice to help move out of fear and into empowerment and optimism.

TRY THIS

When you notice your brain protesting something, weigh the difficult. What are your options? They are all difficult in some way—maybe they cause discomfort, pain, or challenge—but likely your brain is imagining that they will be worse than they actually are. A moment of discomfort is tolerable if it helps you reach your goals. Is it more difficult to push forward or to regret not pushing forward? We all have to face decisions like this. Many times, our brains want to take the path of least resistance, but it is up to you to choose your path and help your brain understand why. Remember, you are stronger than you think you are!

DISAPPOINT SOMEONE

When I ask people about their greatest fears, I often hear phrases like:

- Disappointing someone I love
- Being a disappointment
- My parents being disappointed in me
- Feeling disappointed if things don't go the way I want them to
- Disappointing myself

We all face disappointment in life, so why are we so afraid of it?

If you really examine disappointment, it is a feeling of sadness that our expectations were not met. So, let's break that down even more: We are afraid of a feeling. A yucky, uncomfortable feeling. A feeling that comes because we imagined one thing and experienced something different than that.

The COVID-19 quarantine days taught us all a lot about disappointment. Events were canceled. We were disappointed. It was a yucky feeling. But did we survive it? Yes. We know we can survive disappointment. In fact, in the case of quarantine, we got used to it. We started to expect to be disappointed. We are getting better at this all the time.

Disappointment is just a feeling, and we can manage our feelings.

Glennon Doyle, in her book *Untamed*, talks about a conversation with her daughter, who feels obligated to join a club her brother belonged to in school. She doesn't want to join the club and says to her mother: "But I don't want to disappoint him." Glennon responds: "Listen. Every time you are given a choice of disappointing someone else or disappointing yourself, your duty is to disappoint that someone else. Your job, throughout your entire life, is to disappoint as many people as it takes to avoid disappointing yourself." Her daughter asks: "Even you?" Glennon responds: "Especially me."[18]

This took my breath away when I read it and it did again as I typed it for you. When I first read this story, I had to go back over it a few times to make sure I read it correctly. Wait—it is okay to disappoint someone? Even a parent? This was such a foreign concept to my brain. I have lived my whole life thinking my job was to never disappoint anyone. My job was to please all of the people and do all of the things, and never ever let anyone down. For the first four decades of my life, I thought it was better to disappoint myself to make someone else happy. I now see that I had it completely backward.

If we live our lives in fear of disappointing someone, do we ultimately live a life of disappointing ourselves? I think so. Here are some examples people have shared with me:

- I want to change my major in college, but my dad will be disappointed.
- I want to call off the wedding, but guests will be disappointed.
- I want to ask for a raise, but what if it leads to finding out that my boss is disappointed in my work?
- I want come out about my sexuality, but I'm afraid of the look of disappointment in my parents' eyes.
- I want to tell the truth, but the person listening will be disappointed.
- I want to start a creative or entrepreneurial project, but I'm worried I'll be disappointed in the result.

---

[18] Glennon Doyle, *Untamed* (New York: The Dial Press, 2020).

As you read those, you might be thinking: "just do it, live your life!" But, when it comes to your own fear of disappointment, is it that easy?

Glennon gifted her readers with this story. A life of pleasing everyone else leads to resentment. Resentment comes when our giving and receiving get off balance. Often, we deny ourselves and then feel mad at the other person after we give them what they want. I have experienced this flavor of resentment many times. Let's do it together—who can we disappoint in order to save ourselves?

TRY THIS

Getting more comfortable with disappointing someone comes through actually disappointing someone. So, answer these questions:

- Who can you disappoint this week?
- What can you say "no" to?
- How can you let someone down, but save yourself?
- How can you stop disappointing yourself?

HANG ON FOR EIGHT SECONDS

Growing up, I spent my childhood weekends at the rodeo. My father had been a rodeo clown and bullfighter in his 20s, and went on to become a rodeo announcer for several decades. He was a corporate executive during the week, but on Friday afternoons, it was rodeo time. It was there that I learned the importance of eight seconds.

In a rodeo, eight seconds is critical: it's the length of time required to qualify in bronc and bull riding. The cowboys or cowgirls must hang on for a full eight seconds while riding a bucking, spinning animal. Not only are they trying to stay alive during that time, they're being judged on their form, too.

To the rider, eight seconds can feel like an eternity. For the rest of us, it's just a blip. It's also a helpful practice we can use for ourselves.

Watching a cowboy hang on can remind us that we, too, can survive for eight seconds. Life can throw us one direction and then another; it can be chaotic and unpredictable. But remember: you're stronger than you think you are—and you can hold on for eight seconds.

When I need a reminder that I can get through something, I count to eight and picture rodeo athletes.

The concept of eight seconds can work in a number of scenarios:

- When you feel like you're ready to give up, keep going for eight more seconds.
- When you're about to say words you will regret, count to eight before you speak.
- When you're overwhelmed and don't know where to start, take a deep breath, count to eight, and see if you find clarity.
- When you feel the urge to do something that you know isn't healthy, think about it for eight seconds, then ask yourself if this is really what's best for you.
- When you have to do a task you're dreading, think of one of those cowboys and consider that if he can do eight seconds on a bull, you can do this task.

To challenge yourself even more, try doing two rounds of eight seconds. Or even more. If you can keep going, you may soon realize that you've gotten through an hour. Before you know it, you will have taught yourself that you can and will make it through anything.

Eight seconds can be a great practice to help you pause, re-group, and remember that you can hang on a little longer.

TRY THESE

Here are a number of ways to incorporate the concept of eight seconds. Experiment with a few and see whether eight seconds helps to ground you, calm you, or center you:

- When you feel overwhelmed: close your eyes and take deep breaths by inhaling for eight seconds, then exhaling for eight seconds
- When you need comfort: pet an animal or hug a loved one for eight seconds
- When you're in a negative state of mind: think a positive thought for eight seconds

- When life feels heavy: think of something you love for eight seconds
- When you have an unhealthy coping urge: suppress that urge for eight seconds
- When you need a boost: smile for eight seconds

SEE THINGS DIFFERENTLY

In these charged times, it's not uncommon to come into conflict with a close friend or family member over politics or any of the other controversial topics that seem to dominate the news. I've been at family dinners with relatives who disagreed with me about an issue; initially, I was frustrated. How could their views be so different from mine?

I knew deep down that I wanted to continue to have a good relationship with these people—they were my family, after all. I had to practice seeing things differently to find compassion for them, and try to understand their experiences and where they were coming from.

By seeing things differently, although I still didn't necessarily agree with them, I was more open to their perspective. I could move past our differences and continue to forge these relationships that were an important and valuable part of my life.

It's human to disagree with others. The reality is, there are many relationships that are too important to lose just because the two of you don't see eye to eye. There are also people you need to peacefully coexist with, like coworkers and the people with whom you live.

You don't have to agree with someone, but can you try to understand their viewpoint through the lens of compassion? Which means pausing in the heat of the moment to put your thoughts down and pick up those of the other side. Examine them. Can you see them differently?

This works for internal struggles as well. When I was first diagnosed with Multiple Sclerosis, all I could think was: my poor kids have to grow up with a mother who's sick. Then, I challenged myself to see things differently: wouldn't they also become more compassionate people because of this?

Examining the other side of my thoughts helped me have more compassion for myself. It pulled me out of that internal struggle and brought me to a place of peace.

To release resentment, judgment, and bitterness, we must change our thinking. Seeing something differently can be the shift it takes to transform your relationships and your peace.

TRY THIS

As you go through your week, stop to notice when you feel frustrated, irritated, or critical—whether it's directed toward yourself or others. Ask yourself: "can I see this differently?" Take time to consider how you might view the situation instead through the lens of compassion. Some examples:

- When you're stuck in traffic
- When someone frustrates you at work
- When someone says something you take personally
- When you feel like you didn't get the credit you deserved
- When you feel jealous of someone
- When you feel hopeless or stuck
- When you doubt your abilities

ADD A MANTRA

Traci, a client of mine, came to me struggling with self-doubt. She'd just gone into business for herself and was crippled by the prospect of sales and self-promotion for fear that she'd be rejected. She was frozen into inaction. She needed something to remind herself of her capabilities. That's when I introduced to her the idea of using a mantra.

In Sanskrit, the word "mantra" means "tool for the mind." A mantra is a word or phrase that helps our minds focus on a positive thought.

When we are overwhelmed or unsure of ourselves, mantras can help us return to helpful thoughts. I often find mantras to be a lifeline, like when I have a speaking engagement and a burst of nerves hits me before I begin. I just say to myself: "be the love in the room." And it works wonders to help me refocus on what I'm there to do. For Traci, we landed on "I trust myself," to remind her that she knew what she was doing, and to keep moving forward.

The use of mantras has been shown to have a physiological effect on our bodies; it creates a feeling of calm, reassures us, lowers stress, and positively impacts outcomes.[19]

---

[19] Ampere A Tseng, "Scientific Evidence of Health Benefits by Practicing Mantra Meditation: Narrative Review," *International Journal of Yoga* 15, no. 2 (2022): 89-95. doi:10.4103/ijoy.ijoy_53_22.

By repeating a mantra to yourself, you're creating a new neural pathway in your brain that not only builds a habit of positive thinking, but becomes your default mindset. The use of a mantra can help you rewire your brain, leading you to feel safer and more optimistic.

Try a mantra for those times when you need an extra boost: like public speaking, walking into a room where you don't know anyone, going into a dentist or doctor appointment, before starting a meeting, before getting out of your car, or before any other situation that triggers social anxiety or self-doubt. Here are some example mantras:

- "I can do this."
- "I choose to be happy."
- "This is good enough."
- "You've come so far."
- "I am okay right now."
- "Go slowly."
- "I am loved."
- "Don't force it."
- "Be you."
- "Let it go."
- "I am doing my best."
- "This too shall pass."
- "I am enough."
- "Breathe."

Mantras are a great way to start a coaching relationship with yourself: tell yourself what you need to hear or what you wish someone would say to you. Encourage yourself through the fearful moments. Talk to yourself kindly and gently. All of this will lead to greater self-trust, fewer feelings of isolation, and an increased sense of worthiness.

TRY THIS

1. Imagine yourself older and wiser: what advice would you give to yourself to make life easier and more peaceful? Write down what comes to mind.

2. Now consider recent times and circumstances during which you needed some encouragement. Write down what you wish someone would have said to you in those moments.

3. Read over what you've written and see if you can create 3-5 short, clear phrases that could serve as mantras for you. Choose the mantras that feel best to you. You might have one for overcoming fear, another for self-doubt, and one for when you find yourself in a conflict with someone.

4. Review your mantras. Are they true, positive, encouraging, and helpful? If not, adjust the words until they are statements that are easy for you to believe when you need encouragement.

5. Practice using these mantras every day. The more often you repeat them, the better your brain will remember the thought when you need it most.

STOP AT BASE CAMPS

Climbing a mountain is often used as a metaphor for reaching a goal, but I don't think we talk enough about base camps along the climb. If we were going to climb a literal mountain, we would have to stop at base camps along the way to rest, acclimate, get used to the new altitude, and review our plans for reaching the summit.

If change is occurring in your life and it feels like you are climbing a difficult mountain, base camps are a critically important part of your journey.

I had a client who said: "I thought I was learning to love myself, but I just fell back down into my self-sabotaging behavior again." I drew a mountain on the whiteboard in my office and said: "you aren't at the bottom of the mountain because you realize you are repeating a pattern of self-sabotage. You just need to spend some time at the halfway base camp getting used to this new way of being. This is like learning a new language; learning to be kind to yourself takes time and practice. Let yourself pause here and remember the basics, then you will be able to climb even higher."

Usually when we think we are failing, we just need to stop along the climb at a base camp and get used to the new air we are breathing.

Too much change at once makes our brains feel unsafe. To help our brains feel safe enough to make a change: do a little, rest, then do a little more. Our brain feels safer when change occurs in small increments. When our brain feels safe, it lessens the resistance to change.

If you get unexpected news, give yourself time to soak it in before taking action. If you are grieving, give yourself time to rest and reflect on the loss rather than running away from it. If you long for change in your life, take a baby step and let that settle in before taking the next step. Give yourself time to adjust to something new before you add in another new thing.

The climb will be successful if you take care of yourself along the way. Pausing at base camp is not weakness, it is necessary.

TRY THIS

What mountains are you climbing right now? Can you notice when you might be in need of a pause?

Give yourself permission to stay there a while. You will know when you are ready to climb again.

MAKE THOUGHTFUL DECISIONS

We make decisions every day about what to eat, wear, buy, believe, do, say, and think. Extrapolate those daily decisions across our lifetime and it is no wonder that we are exhausted from making decisions. Some are small, some are life-changing.

In my coaching practice, I work with a lot of anxious thinkers. Making decisions for them can be overwhelming. In this section, I offer practices to help take the overwhelm out of decision making. I can't make the decision for you, but I can give you practices to help you find your own answers.

Exploring your philosophies around making mistakes is important. If you fear making a mistake, then you are likely to be stymied when it comes to making a decision. If you make decisions from a place of fear versus a place of love, your outcomes change. If you live in scarcity mentality, then you will never make a decision from a spirit of abundance. These are all things you will learn from the practices in this section. Plus, you'll find practices to help you know when to delegate or quit.

This is a section to come back to when a new decision presents itself in your life. Different practices fit different decisions. Become familiar with these practices, and then you will know where to look for them when you need them. They will all be right here waiting for you. Decisions don't have to be overwhelming when we have the right tools in our toolbox.

CONSIDER THE PATH OF LEAST REGRET

Considering the Path of Least Regret is a practice that can help when we are facing a dilemma.

What is regret? It is a negative emotion where we blame ourselves for a bad outcome or wish we had made an alternative choice. Regret is helpful in our youth to gain insights, improve our decision making, and maintain healthy relationships. For many of us, as we age, we tend to regret things we didn't do rather than things we did. Regret can be helpful, but it can also interrupt our well-being when we get stuck in thought patterns that lack self-compassion.

As you think about your options, considering potential regret can be a helpful practice in your decision-making toolbox. Is one option more likely to lead to future regret than another option? Think about what is at stake, what you might beat yourself up for later, and/or what potential consequences might arise from each option. Then think through how you are wired and what types of things you typically regret. This process can help us mitigate risk and regret.

Like many of our thoughts and feelings, regret is something we choose to bring into our minds. However, this practice of considering which path has the least potential for regret can be helpful when we are seeking additional clarity in our decision making.

My husband and I use this practice in our conversations about parenting decisions. Parenting is a constant game of trial and error—considering the path of least regret has helped us find some clarity along the way. We use potential regret as a tool to help us make decisions when it isn't clear which option we should choose.

Regret is a word that most of us dislike because it brings up a gross feeling. But regret can be a helpful teacher and guide in our decision making. We get to decide if we regret a decision or not. So, using it as a predictive tool can help us minimize the gross feelings of regret. We get in front of it, instead of it being a result of our decision.

TRY THESE

1. Make a list of what you are afraid you might regret in life. Most people say things they didn't do more than things they did. For example: I didn't speak up, I didn't push myself, I quit too soon, I wasn't brave, I didn't try, I wasn't kind, I didn't help, I didn't fight for them, I didn't apologize, I wasn't thoughtful, I wasn't strong. This can be a cathartic process of getting it all out on paper. Now, next to each one, note what learning or growth came from that regret. Then see if you can release it as a memory of regret and instead file it in your brain as a valuable lesson learned.

2. Make a list of things you don't want to regret doing or not doing in the future. Think about today until you turn 100, what do you want to make sure you do or don't do? Does thinking about these potential regrets give you more clarity for how you make decisions today?

3. Remember, every decision you have made in the past can be influenced by how you decide to view it. You

can make the case for regret or you can make the case for it having a positive outcome - it is all in how you view and interpret that moment in time. See if you can view regrets through a new lens now.

CHALLENGE YOUR SCARCITY MENTALITY

Finn had been our dog for four years when we decided to add another dog, Chloe, to our family. Chloe, a birthday surprise for our 12-year-old daughter, was tiny, cute, and got a lot of attention. Finn wasn't having it.

If he could talk, he would have definitely said the following:

- "When is she leaving?"
- "Quit touching my stuff!"
- "Is there enough food to go around?"
- "These are MY people. Go find your own!

I think what he was really wondering was:

- "Is there enough love (and food) to go around?"

We know as pet owners that there is more than enough love to go around. But watching Finn's behaviors made me reflect on my own struggle with a scarcity mentality, especially in my former career as a business consultant. Worries would swirl through my head, like:

- "Will I get a large bonus if everyone else gets a bonus too?"
- "Are there enough promotions to go around?"
- "If he's getting recognition, does that mean I won't get any?"

Not only did I find my calling and change careers, I realized there was more than enough recognition, credit, love, kindness—you name it—to go around.

We naturally wonder whether there will be enough for everyone. This wondering is hardwired in our minds for survival. We are worried about not getting what we think we want. But when we realize we already have everything we need, our perspective changes.

When you find yourself wondering whether there will be enough for you, be aware that this is just fear in the form of scarcity mentality. And the best way to cure a scarcity mentality is with what's called an abundance mentality: the idea that there's more than enough to go around.

How do you get there? The quickest way to shift your thinking when you catch yourself in a scarcity mentality mindset is by expressing gratitude for what you already have. This allows you to move away from focusing on what you don't have and retrain your brain to focus on the abundance of good things in your life.

When Finn learned to trust that there was plenty of love—and food!—to go around and that he might even be gaining a fun new friend, the scarcity mentality disappeared. As I watched him process this, I wondered whether a higher power is watching us, too, and hoping that we will trust there is more than enough for all of us.

TRY THESE

1. Think about a resource in your life you may consider to be scarce: is it love, money, time, friendships, recognition, followers, likes? How can you use gratitude to flip into a mindset of abundance? *Ex:* "I don't have as many friends as I used to. But the ones I do have, I feel especially close to. I'm lucky to have them in my life."

2. Quiet your scarcity mentality through inner dialogue. Consider what you have an abundance of, using the following statements:

    I have plenty of _____.

    I feel so grateful for all the _____ in my life.

    There's more than enough_____ in my life to go around.

    More _____ is coming to me soon.

3. Try a visualization exercise of what you want coming to you: imagine your future self receiving what you are seeking now. And, as a compassion practice, imagine everyone else who wants the same thing you do: imagine all of you receiving what you seek. You might also add a wish: "May all who desire _____ receive it in abundance." *Ex:* If you're afraid there aren't many job openings, and someone else is going to get them, try imagining your future self receiving a new position. Now, imagine everyone who wants a new position receiving one. Then, add a wish: "may everyone who wants a new position receive a new position."

ALLOW MISTAKES

How comfortable are you with making mistakes?

How about when other people make mistakes?

Most of us are not comfortable at all with making mistakes. And we don't like it when others make mistakes either.

In working with clients, I have found that most of us need to become kinder to ourselves and others about mistakes. Here are some questions to consider:

- Are mistakes allowed in my life?
- How do I feel in the moment when I realize I made a mistake?
- What are my behaviors after making a mistake? Do I lie, blame, take responsibility, quickly correct, reflect?
- Do I feel differently about small mistakes versus large mistakes? What about private versus public mistakes?
- What does it mean when I make a mistake—does it say something about me as a person?
- When someone else makes a mistake, is it no big deal or a very big deal to me? How do I behave in that moment?
- Do I expect perfection from myself and others?

Of course, we all try to avoid making mistakes. But, I have found most people I talk to have an inner secret policy of "no mistakes allowed...ever." That means when they do make a mistake, as we all inevitably do, their inner critic destroys them with abuse.

You might have grown up in an environment where there was a lot of blame and punishment for mistakes, so of course you are afraid to risk that horrible feeling again. But now as an adult, you get to choose how you handle mistakes.

It is hard to show other people grace when we can't do it for ourselves.

Maybe it is time to give ourselves permission to make mistakes. What would it feel like if mistakes were allowed in your life? Could you breathe a little easier? Maybe your jaw would be less clenched, or your shoulders might relax a notch? Would you do things that you were previously afraid to do? Like start a business, or create art, or attend more social events?

What have you learned from the mistakes you've made? Are you grateful for some of them now? How did past mistakes uniquely prepare you for where you are today?

Maybe it isn't so bad to mess up once in a while. Allow yourself to be a student in human school who is learning by getting it wrong sometimes.

In an interview with Inc. Magazine, Sara Blakely (who founded Spanx), discussed growing up with a father who celebrated mistakes. She shared that, as a child, her father would meet with her once a week and ask her this question: "What did you fail at this week?"

He didn't want to know how many A's, soccer goals, or accomplishments she made. He wanted to know the mistakes. She shared that after telling him her failures, he would high-five her and smile with pride.

Blakely said: "I didn't realize at the time how much this advice would define not only my future, but my definition of failure. I have realized as an entrepreneur that so many people don't pursue their idea because they were scared or afraid of what could happen. My dad taught me that failing simply just leads you to the next great thing."

According to Inc. Magazine, Sara is "the youngest self-made woman billionaire in the world."[20]

Explore your philosophies around making mistakes. How might you loosen your grip on high expectations of yourself and of others? Let's make the world a little kinder together.

TRY THESE

1. Craft a self-compassion message you can practice saying to yourself in the moment of a mistake: "[*Your name*], you made a mistake. This is part of being human. Other people make mistakes too. What can you do to improve the situation?"

2. Make a list of things you might do if mistakes were allowed. See if you can find the courage to do something on that list.

3. Next time you make a mistake, ask yourself: "what have I learned from this?" Be grateful for that lesson. You passed another test in human school. You now realize something you didn't know before. Mistakes are how we learn and grow. There is always wisdom on the other side.

---

[20] Alexa von Tobel, "How Spanx Founder Sara Blakely Went From Selling Fax Machines to Shapewear," *Inc*, June 2023. Retrieved from https://www.inc.com/alexa-von-tobel/sara-blakely-spanx-founders-project.html.

WATCH THE CRAB BUCKET

Legend has it that a bucket of living crabs never needs a lid because if one crab tries to escape, the others will pull him back down into the bucket. I have never witnessed this myself; however, there are ongoing studies in human behavior that explore this same phenomenon that humans will hold each other back from making progress.

Among humans, the crab mentality might sound like this:

- If I can't get out, neither can you.
- If I fail, then I like it when you fail too.
- If I am miserable, I want you to be miserable too.
- If I can't be happy, you shouldn't be happy.

Here are some I have heard from clients over the years:

- I made the team, but my friends didn't and then they posted horrible things on social media about me.
- My sibling wants me to be as frustrated with our mom as she is.
- I love it when a friend gains weight and I'm not the largest in the room.
- I wish she would have something bad happen to her so she knows what it feels like.
- I hope he cheats on her just like he did with me.

Crab bucket mentality does not bring out the best in us. But it is part of being human. Sometimes we are the crab stuck in the bottom of the bucket and sometimes we are the crab experiencing success.

Think about a time when you have been a crab in the bottom of the bucket and you see another crab jump happily back into the ocean, enjoying freedom. You are stuck and they are happy. We have all had moments like this in our human experience. It is hard to be happy for someone when they are getting what you want. It is natural to feel some angst when this happens.

Also, you have likely been the happy crab and wondered why others are pulling you down. We face jealousy, snarky comments, and sabotage in these situations. You may have been the victim of crab bucket mentality when you were trying to move forward and someone kept trying to sabotage you or pull you back down.

Give this some thought and notice where you see this phenomenon in your own life. You may begin to see it in friend groups, families, organizations, and institutions.

The antidote is to climb out of the bucket and then reach back and pull the others out too. Lead the way, but don't abandon the others.

If you are a victim of being pulled back down, communicate that you aren't leaving them behind, you want success for them as well. Partner with them and maybe together you can move forward.

The undercurrent of this phenomenon is our primal longing to not be abandoned. When someone else is making progress and we feel stuck, it can bring up feelings of abandonment. Acknowledging that you feel this way is the first step in releasing this pain. Then, work to develop a plan for yourself to grow and move forward.

Let's all move forward together and help each other out.

TRY THIS

If you have a decision to make, think about what other people are suggesting that you do. What are their motives? Sometimes, people want to keep us safe from harm, make sure we are ready for the next step, or question if we are making a smart decision. Make sure you are filtering through all the advice you receive. Watch for the crab bucket phenomenon and don't let it hold you back. If you trust this is the decision you need to make, then go for it.

LIVE "AS IF"

The idea of this practice is to try on your options for size and fit. Living "as if" means identifying an option and then living as if that was your choice to see how it feels. It is like a dress rehearsal for making a decision. My children are both theater kids. The dress rehearsal before the show allows the director to see how everything feels and then adjust. The show goes better after a rigorous dress rehearsal. We can apply that same recipe for success in our lives when we have a decision to make.

Use the power of your imagination to try on your options.

1. Consider every option.
   On a piece of paper or on a whiteboard, list each option you can think of. Here are some vague examples: do it now, don't do it at all, do it in a year, do it in five years. Be specific in your options and spend some time considering every angle—you often have more options than you think you do.

2. Identify near, mid, and long-term impact.
   Under each option, imagine what life would be like for you in the near-term, mid-term, and long-term.

3. Eliminate any option that is clearly a no.

You might already be gaining clarity by this step in the process. If you can eliminate any options, cross them off your list.

4.   Live as if you made each choice.
     With the remaining options, give yourself a few days to live as if that was your choice. Walk around the world as if the decision were behind you and you were living in this new life with the effects of that decision. Notice how you feel.

TRY THIS

Substitute your situation into this example, but here is a taste for living "as if":

Let's say you are trying to decide if you should invest in taking a class. Walk around as if you made the choice to invest and the class is about to start. How do you feel? Are you feeling confident or unsure about the investment? Do you like the person you are when you signed up? Or is that person who signed up now stressed about not having any free time and the pressure of studying? Which feels more like the true you? Which feels like the you that you want to be? Does this put you on the path to becoming who you want to be? Are you proud of yourself because you signed up? Are you proud of yourself because you didn't sign up?

Role play each scenario and you will be able to tell which is the right path for you.

DECIDE WITH LOVE OR FEAR

When I was in seminary, I was losing my faith in year two. That is part of the seminary experience: you learn a lot, question everything you've been taught, and then re-build your theology. As I was in the process of developing a faith of my own, I kept seeing the book *A Course in Miracles* referenced in various places. After this happened a few times, I felt like it was a message from above and I should investigate further. I found it to be a dense, yet insightful, book of spiritual insights written in Christian language with daily practices to apply. What struck me first in this book was the idea that everything we do comes from a place of love or fear.

I wrestled with that idea and began investigating my thoughts, actions, and behaviors through that lens. I realized that a lot of what I was doing was coming from a place of fear. Fear of failure, of not being liked, of not being smart, of inadequacies or insecurities, of being wrong, of being egotistical... lots and lots of fears.

So I started a little experiment of pausing before I said or did something and shifting my mindset from fear to love. What would I say from a place of love instead of fear? What would I do if I acted from love rather than fear that someone wouldn't like me? What would it look like to fill my brain with loving thoughts instead of fearful ones? It was a miraculous shift; I could feel a change in my cells. Fear was lifting.

I realized if an action comes from a place of love, it can't be wrong. So I didn't need to live in fear anymore. If everything I said and did came from a place of love, then I would never get it wrong. And getting it wrong in any context was one of my biggest fears.

I started sharing this newfound wisdom with my friends. Most thought it was a little odd at first. Then they would circle back and tell me they were still thinking about it. Most found it made more sense to them after applying it in their lives.

Asking yourself, "is what I'm about to do coming from a place of love or fear?" can be transformational.

TRY THIS

This is a practice that you really have to test out before it fully resonates. So give it a try. Most people find that they live in more fear than they realized. Our brains like to play it safe, so it makes sense that they default to a place of fear. Work with your brain to shift toward love as the motivation for what you say and do instead of fear. When you feel the freedom from fear, you will be glad you tried it.

MAKE AN EISENHOWER MATRIX

This is a practice to help with overwhelm and task prioritization. If you are like me and everything feels urgent and important...then this practice is for us!

Make a list of things that need to be done and then use this matrix to help you make decisions about when and who will complete each task.

	URGENT	NOT URGENT
IMPORTANT	DO	DECIDE
NOT IMPORTANT	DELEGATE	DELETE

If the task is important and urgent, then do it now and make it a priority. Waiting on these tasks usually results in consequences we don't like. Procrastinating these things causes us unnecessary stress. When we feel a task is important we sometimes delay starting it to make sure we do it well, but that delay might get us into trouble. Life gets more peaceful when these tasks get done first.

If the task is not urgent but important, then decide if you want to do it now and get it out of the way, or wait until later. It might be something that needs extra energy or focused attention, so make sure the timing is right so that you can be successful. You might also decide to hand this one off to someone else.

If the task is less important but urgent, then ask someone else to do it. This is a great opportunity for us to ask for help and collaborate with someone else, which brings more connection into our lives. This is also a good opportunity to outsource something to someone who enjoys doing a task you don't enjoy. Delegating can lessen our levels of resentment and bitterness in life.

And the most liberating of all categories in this matrix is not important and not urgent = delete! Not necessary is the synonym for not important and not urgent. Give yourself some freedom by giving yourself permission to delete tasks that are not necessary.

We all get to choose how we live this one wild and precious life (as poet Mary Oliver said). So, how are you going to live it? Are the tasks on your list aligning with the life you want to live? If not, do some adjusting this week. Hand off what you can, power through what you need to, delete some things, and then do something that brings you lots of joy.

This decision matrix is attributed to President Dwight Eisenhower. It is said that Eisenhower used this matrix to make decisions in his own life and during his presidency.[21]

---

[21] Stephen Covey, et al, *First Things First* (Miami: Mango Media, 2015).

I hope this practice helps you find some calm in the storms of life. The fast pace at which most of us live is unsustainable to our mental and physical health. Explore your definitions of urgent and important; sometimes our inner critics are making us hustle more than we truly need to. Find ways to make life fun and easy—then you become a magnet for happiness.

TRY THIS

Make a list of tasks and see if you can sort them according to this matrix. What do you notice as you do this exercise? Did it seem like everything was urgent until you really examined it? Does it feel like everything is important...until you realize it isn't? Use this practice periodically to check in with your to-do list and parse through things that can be delegated or deleted.

KNOW WHEN IT'S TIME TO QUIT

Knowing when to quit can be a challenge. The fear and the stigma of quitting can often cause us to stay too long, to the detriment of our own physical and emotional health. We turn resentful; we lose passion for what we're doing; we may even say things we shouldn't say and harm our relationships. All because we worry what people might think if we walk away.

So how do we know if we should continue to carry on or if, indeed, it's time to call it quits?

Years ago, when I was in business school, we were taught something called "the law of diminishing returns." Simplified, it's a way to look at margins and profit to determine whether the results are worth the effort. And at a certain point, if the results don't justify the work put into a product or service, it becomes clear that the best decision for a company is to exit.

This same law is one we can all use to make important life decisions, like whether to stay or whether to quit. Only instead of margins and profit, think in terms of time and energy: is this project, or relationship, or client, or hobby—anything that takes up space in your life—worth the time and energy you're putting into it? Are you getting as much or more coming back to you? Are the benefits worth the effort?

There are definitely things worth enduring and persisting. There are other times when we don't have the freedom to quit. Our tolerances, risk factors, and freedoms are unique to each of us as individuals. Each of what I like to call our "quit zones" is different.

Your "quit zone" is the point at which something is costing you more than you're getting out of it. If you were to make a chart, it would be when the "minuses" column starts to look higher than the "pluses" column.

When the pluses are higher, things are good. You're satisfied, and your efforts are bringing in a high return. When the two columns are equal, ambivalence has started to kick in. Things aren't terrible, but you can feel your passion starting to slip away. And when the minus column is the taller of the two, that's when you're in your quit zone. The benefits are few, and ambivalence has turned into suffering. And that's when you'll know it's the right time: when the acceptable, healthy, wise thing to do is to quit.

TRY THESE

Determining when it's time to quit can be done a few different ways, depending on how you like to work through a problem. Here are two different practices to try:

1. Make a list of pluses and minuses, side by side, for the situation you're in. Be as honest as you can. Are they equal? Is one longer than the other? If the pluses outweigh the minuses, consider that you might be in your quit zone. And know that it's perfectly okay if you feel as though it would be best to walk away.

2. Consider this list of questions that might help you determine whether you're in your quit zone:

   - Are my results worth the effort?
   - Am I still seeing positive progress?

- Is this relationship mutually beneficial?
- Am I getting more out of this than I am putting in?
- Do I notice bitterness, frustration, impatience, or resentment creeping in?
- Is there someone else that would love this more than I do?
- Is it time for me to walk away?
- What excites me more than doing this?
- How can I honor this experience and exit |gracefully?

ASK YOURSELF FIVE WHYS

Years ago, when I worked as a business consultant, I was on a client project at a large company that manufactured medical equipment like CT scans and MRI machines.

The company was implementing a new process with the goal of improving patient care, and my role was that of a change management consultant: to help explain why the new process was necessary and important. Part of that process was something called the "Five Whys," a tool used to assist in making decisions—a progression of "whys" asked to help expose the very root of something.

Today, 25 years later, I still find myself coming back to the "Five Whys" for my own use. It's a practice I've found especially useful to help clarify what we really want in our lives.

If you have a desire for something, a decision to make, or a conflict you want to resolve, ask yourself "Five Whys" to dig deeper and deeper into your thoughts and gain the clarity you're after.

Here's an example of what this might sound like in action:

1. I'm thinking about getting a dog. Why?

2. Because I want companionship and something to take care of. Why?

3. I need a new sense of purpose and meaning. Why?

4. Because my kids are leaving for college and I feel lost. Why?

5. I love being a mother and don't know what to do with that energy. Why?

6. Because I have a lot of love to give and I need somewhere for it to go.

Here's another example:

1. I want to go back to school to become a teacher. Why?

2. My current career has lost its meaning for me and I want to help kids. Why?

3. Because I see how much kids are hurting and I want to help them. Why?

4. I can be a loving adult in their lives and can give them hope. Why?

5. I want to encourage them to achieve their potential. Why?

6. Because if more kids have hope and encouragement, they can change society for the better.

The "Five Whys" tool is an invaluable way to help you get at the root of your desires, decisions, values, beliefs, and opinions. And it might surprise you, too—often there are some very interesting insights hiding beneath the surface of your brilliant and complicated brain.

The next time you find yourself feeling indecisive or adrift, dig a little deeper. Keep asking yourself "why?" and find clarity. Clarity brings peace.

TRY THIS

What's something that you can't seem to get off your mind—a situation causing you frustration or indecision? Start by stating the issue, then ask yourself "why?" Write down the answer, then repeat the process. Keep repeating the process and digging until you come to a statement that offers some greater insight. Take a few days to ponder that last statement, and see if you feel a greater sense of clarity.

ALIGN TO YOUR MOST IMPORTANT VALUES

There's a deep longing within every human being to explore our identity, purpose, and reason for being. As we reconcile these big questions in our daily lives, we often find ourselves asking "am I doing things right?" and "am I doing the right things?"

Not long ago, I had a client struggling with just that. Among other things, she was questioning whether to continue investing time in a friendship that no longer seemed healthy. To help guide her, I had her pick four words that best represented her current values—a practice I've found to be highly effective when it comes to helping people make decisions.

She chose "family," "integrity," "health," and "peace." From there, we talked about the importance of leading from those words, and filtering every choice you make based on whether it aligns with what you know to be your values.

With those values in mind, I had her think about what that friendship meant to her. What she realized was that she felt a lack of trust in her friend, which would compromise her chosen value of "integrity," not to mention "health" and "peace." It then became clear to her what she wanted to do.

Each day we choose how we show up in the world. We may have circumstantial constraints, but we choose our values, attitudes, perspectives, and beliefs. Aligning to your most important values is a good way to be mindful of how you want to live. Selecting values for a short period of time encourages you to focus on the reality of the present moment.

As Mary Oliver asks in her poem "Summer Day": "Tell me, what is it you plan to do with your one wild and precious life?"[22] You have today. Live it according to the values you hold most important.

TRY THIS

1. Review the words in the chart on the next page and circle the ones that speak to something you want to have more of. Don't overthink it; circle any word that resonates with you. You may have 20-30 words circled.

2. Review the words you circled and place a star next to the 10 words that are most important. Now narrow those down even further by placing a rectangle around the four that you really want to prioritize in the future. These words will serve as a filter to help you make priorities and decisions that align with the things you value most. Revisit your list every year to determine which values feel most true for you as you continue to evolve.

---

[22] Mary Oliver, *New and Selected Poems* (Boston: Beacon Press, 1992).

Abundance	Decisiveness	Innovation	Protecting
Acceptance	Dedication	Inspiration	Quality
Accountability	Dependability	Integrity	Recognition
Accuracy	Determination	Intuition	Reliability
Achievement	Diversity	Joy	Religion
Adaptability	Efficiency	Justice	Reputation
Adventure	Encouragement	Kindness	Resourcefulness
Alone Time	Entertainment	Knowledge	Respect
Altruism	Enthusiasm	Laughter	Responsibility
Animal Rights	Entrepreneurship	Lawfulness	Restraint
Anti-Racism	Environment	Leadership	Righteousness
Artistry	Excellence	Learning	Security
Authenticity	Exhilaration	Leisure	Self-Control
Authority	Experimentation	Liveliness	Self-Love
Autonomy	Exploration	Love	Self-Respect
Awareness	Fairness	Loyalty	Selflessness
Balance	Faith	Management	Service
Beauty	Fame	Meaningfulness	Sincerity
Bliss	Family	Mentorship	Social Justice
Boldness	Finances	Modesty	Socializing
Bravery	Finesse	Naturalness	Spirituality
Calmness	Forgiveness	Non-Conformity	Spontaneity
Caring	Freedom	Non-Violence	Stability
Challenge	Friendliness	Openness	Status
Change	Friendships	Optimism	Stewardship
Charisma	Fun	Organization	Strength
Charity	Generosity	Originality	Success
Citizenship	Goodness	Patience	Sustainability
Clarity	Gracefulness	Peace	Teamwork
Cleanliness	Gratitude	Persistence	Tidiness
Cleverness	Growth	Personal Development	Timeliness
Coaching	Happiness	Personal Expression	Tolerance
Comedy	Hard Work	Planning	Tradition
Community	Harmony	Pleasure	Transparency
Compassion	Health	Poise	Travel
Competency	Honesty	Popularity	Trust
Conformity	Honor	Positivity	Truth
Consciousness	Hope	Power	Understanding
Consistency	Humility	Pride	Vivaciousness
Contribution	Humor	Problem-Solving	Wealth
Courage	Imagination	Professionalism	Wellness
Creativity	Independence	Profit	Willingness
Credibility	Influence	Promise-Keeping	Wisdom
Curiosity	Ingenuity	Prosperity	Worship

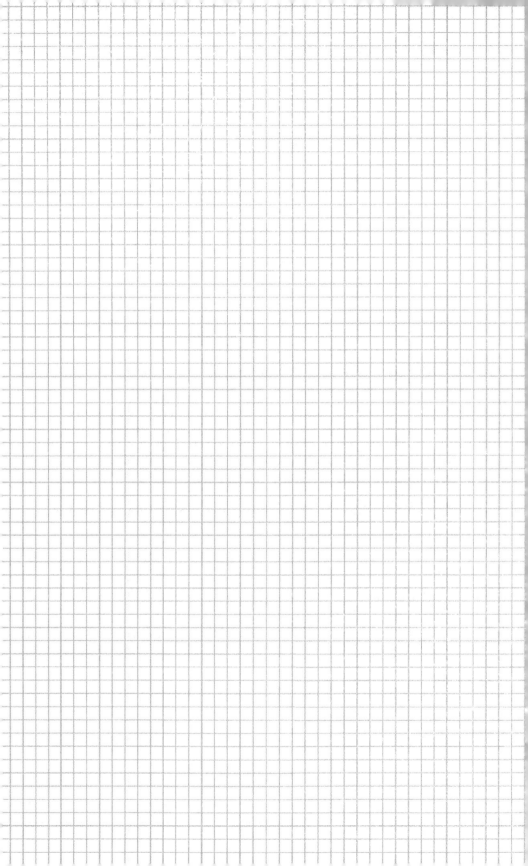

FOSTER RELATIONSHIPS

As humans, we are hardwired for connection. We literally have a primal need to feel like we belong and matter to someone. This is why loneliness is so detrimental to our health and well-being.

Fostering relationships comes easy to some of us but can be difficult for others. The practices in this section are intended to give you some ideas for how to foster relationships with people at work, school, home, and throughout your life.

These practices help us get better at making people feel loved and important to us. When we pour out love, it comes back to us. If your intention is to make people feel loved and that they matter, you will feel loved and realize you matter too. Love begets love. And I don't mean romantic love here, I mean agape love: the love we have for each other because we are human beings on the Earth at this moment together.

We are all trying to figure out what it means to be human and how to do this thing called life. We are all new at this. So let's be a little gentler with ourselves and others. Share, listen, reach out, validate, communicate, repair, and send love. You and every human on this planet deserve to feel loved. It starts with us. I hope these practices help you deepen your connection with others.

KEEP A "KEEP IN TOUCH" LIST

My friend Tina told me about her "keep in touch" list. She created a list in the notes app on her phone. It's a list of everyone in her life that she wants to remember to check in with. It includes a variety of people: childhood friends, college friends, former coworkers, extended family, people she met through activities, and even her current-day close friends and relatives.

She started the list during 2020, when the pandemic had made her feel isolated. She wanted to remind herself of just how many people meant something to her, and how easy it would be to feel less alone and closer to them just by making more of an effort to reach out.

Once she started making a habit of connecting more with the people on that list, she quickly realized how much happiness it brought her; her world grew bigger when she heard more from all the people she loved.

It's a habit she continues even now, years later. She picks someone from the list each week to check in on (one week, I was the lucky recipient!). I loved this idea, and after seeing how much it lit her up, she inspired me to make a "keep in touch" list of my own.

Like my friend, I've also found a lot of joy through a regular practice of reaching out to those people who have had a special place in my life. It's such a simple act, yet one that's so easy to overlook during the busyness of our days.

If we're not careful, we can end up going years without connecting with some of our loved ones.

I've found that it doesn't need to be much—even a short "just thinking of you today!" is enough. That's all it takes to give a shot of happiness to both you—the sender—and your recipient (that's double the joy in one message!).

Making a "keep in touch" list is a great way to be proactive, and to gently remind yourself that you're not alone. Your world is bigger than you realize.

Plus, reaching out to someone on a regular basis will remind you of all the people who bring you joy. Just like you do for them.

TRY THESE

1. Go through the contacts on your phone, social media friends, address book—anywhere you can reference people you know. Write down everyone you'd love to hear from, even if it's the friend you already text with every day. Once you have your official "keep in touch" list, put it somewhere you can easily refer to it.

2. Pick a cadence that feels best for you (i.e. once a month, once a week, or even once a day) and choose someone from that list to reach out to. Send a text, a social media message, an email, or even a greeting card—whatever feels most doable.

3. Your message doesn't have to be long or complicated. It can be a simple: "Hi! You just popped into my head. How are you?" You could send someone:

   - A story or a joke you've run across that reminds you of them
   - A picture of the two of you together
   - A memory you have of them that made you smile

HELP OTHERS KNOW YOU

As a parent, one of my favorite things about the annual open house at my kids' elementary school was seeing the "About Me" projects lining the hallways: little questionnaires filled out by each child, usually accompanied by a self-portrait they'd colored. With categories like "favorite food," "favorite movie," and "what I want to be when I grow up," it was such a sweet way to introduce themselves and help others get to know them.

We're less apt to do this as adults...even though it's just as important. A client recently told me that in conversation with her children, she shared that she always wanted to be a professional figure skater—something they were shocked to find out. She went on to share that it's a dream she'd had ever since the sixth grade, when she'd almost qualified for a major competition. A story they'd never heard.

It's no surprise that our aspirations, dreams, stories—all the things that make us so unique—can get buried and forgotten by the day-to-day motions of living our lives. There's often no time to sit around and tell our stories. Either that, or it never crosses our mind to do so.

Yet it's so important to know each other's stories. By sharing them, you're able to find that team of supporters who can encourage you, or others who share your same interests.

If you could finish the following sentence, what would you want others to know? *"If you really knew me, you would know...."*

Now take it a step further. *"If you really, really knew me, you would know...."*

Now, one more. *"If you really, really, really knew me, you would know...."*

Those statements can help you consider: Are you able to be your true self with the people in your life? Do they really know you? And, on the flip side, if your loved ones were to do the same exercise, do you really know them?

While this exercise can help you be more authentic with others (and vice versa), it can also help you honor yourself. It's a great way for you to uncover the hopes, goals, doubts, interests, struggles, frustrations, fears, disappointments, and dreams that may be buried deep beneath the protective armor you put on to go out into the world.

TRY THIS

Write down your answers to the following questions. Notice, without judgment, what arises in you as you think about these prompts. And when you're ready, you might consider sharing some of your answers. Perhaps something on your list might help others feel less alone (you don't have to share with anyone; just take time to appreciate how deep and complex you are. There is a lot to know about you.).

- When and where are you happiest?
- What are you passionate about?
- What do you fear?
- What is your dream career?
- What makes up your ideal day?
- Where do you hope your future takes you?

- What were you like as a child? Have you changed? If so, how?
- In what type of situation do you feel like you're at your best?
- What is something you'll never regret?
- How do you hope others see you?

SHARE THE KIND THOUGHT

I was at a dinner with a large group and was seated across the table from a woman whose hair and makeup looked incredible. Then I realized—if I'm thinking it, I should be saying it. So even though it felt a little awkward, I did just that: I spoke up and told her. She shared that she was feeling unsure of herself; she'd recently had a baby and was feeling less than confident about getting dressed up.

We know to say "thank you" and share everyday kindnesses with others, but we don't always remember to tell those close to us all the little ways we appreciate them and feel grateful for them—to offer them the loving little boost they just might need in that moment.

Try sharing more compliments with your loved ones and people you encounter during your day. Putting kindness out into the world means there's more kindness to go around. And that's always a good thing.

So if you think someone is doing a good job, or that they always know how to make you smile, or that they're a great friend, or that you love them, don't just think it. Say it.

TRY THESE

Think about each person you'll see this week and have a phrase in mind that you might say to express your gratitude or appreciation. Here are some ideas to get you started:

- "I'm glad you're here."
- "What can I do to help you?"
- "I enjoy spending time with you."
- "I admire your ability to…"
- "You always make me smile."
- "I want to hear your story about…"
- "You're so understanding."
- "Your laugh is contagious."
- "I'm so proud of you."
- "You have great ideas."
- "You're a great listener."
- "Thank you for being kind to me."
- "You're so thoughtful."
- "Thank you for being our truth-teller."
- "You brightened my day."
- "I'm glad I know you."
- "I can be myself around you."
- "You're so creative."
- "I love your sense of style."
- "Thank you for sharing that with me."
- "Being around you inspires me."
- "You make things so fun."
- "I'm lucky to have you in my life."
- "I like your perspective."
- "Your generosity is inspiring."
- "You bring such joy to me."
- "You mean a lot to me."

WAIT WHEN YOU LISTEN

As a mom of two teenagers, I've noticed they enjoy being around me if I talk less and listen more.

When I bite my tongue and avoid offering solutions, opinions, and ideas, they seem much happier (my tongue might bleed sometimes, but it works!). They like having me around a whole lot more when I'm not trying to tell them how to live their lives. This helps make peace around our household more possible.

I often see this in my coaching practice as well. I notice that the more I listen to clients, the more they end up finding their own solutions—and feeling more empowered along the way.

Every human being wants to feel seen, heard, and loved. And when we speak up too quickly, it might feel like we aren't allowing for those basic desires to be met. When we interrupt someone, it might seem like we don't care. When we share what we think they should do, it might feel like we don't trust them enough to figure it out for themselves.

A practice I like to teach clients—and to use myself—to help us become better listeners in all of our relationships is the acronym WAIT, which stands for Why Am I Talking?

WAIT is a great reminder to choose your words and timing wisely while in a conversation with someone. To let someone put the period on the end of their sentence. When you get the urge to jump in, remind yourself: "WAIT."

WAIT can prompt you to consider the following questions:

- Am I really paying attention to what they're saying?
- Is it my turn to talk or can I listen a little longer?
- Is this a good time to ask a question and show my interest?
- Do they feel understood by me?
- Am I trying to control the situation?
- Did they ask for my advice or opinion?
- Am I being overly helpful?

Sharing how you feel is always important, but if you want to strengthen a relationship, you might want to try talking less and listening more. People love you when you listen to them. They feel loved, respected, trusted, and valued. That's a win-win—you're loved and you're making someone else feel loved, too.

TRY THIS

Try writing WAIT somewhere that you can see it for an entire day—or, even better, an entire week. If you really want to practice it, you can even write it on the back of your hand. Every time you see it, remind yourself of what it means. Then, put it to use by practicing it with anyone you enter into conversation with.

FIND COMMON GROUND

We love our friends and family, but sometimes they hold drastically different beliefs than ours, and carrying on a meaningful conversation can make us feel like we're walking on eggshells. That's why gatherings like Thanksgiving can so often feel fraught and filled with disagreements.

We want to continue deepening our relationships with loved ones, but finding topics that don't bring on disagreement can be downright challenging. This is why I've found it helpful to be proactive in finding common ground, and have a few easy conversation starters all prepped and ready to go.

Conversation starters are a great strategy to help encourage meaningful dialogue—they can even help you walk away feeling like you learned more about your loved ones, and strengthen those bonds even more.

When we hold the intention of connecting with someone rather than trying to correct their thinking, we deepen our relationship with them. Remember that our relationships with loved ones are more important than being right about something, and that they will listen to you when they feel loved and safe. If they feel like they're under attack, their brains cannot receive your opinion or contribution.

Start by establishing love and respect first. These prompts may help.

TRY THESE

Here are some great conversation starters to help you connect with your friends and family, and stay safely on common ground.

- Who has had the greatest impact on your life?
- What is the most beautiful place you have been to?
- Do you have any travel you are hoping to do soon?
- What is your happiest family memory?
- What has this family taught you?
- What helps you when you are stressed?
- What is your day like? Will you walk me through it?
- What are you looking forward to?
- What is your favorite thing to do that makes you lose track of time?
- What gives you hope?

EXPRESS YOUR DISAPPOINTMENT

Years ago, I had a girls' trip planned when one of my friends had to cancel. Her son was sick and she needed to stay home with him. Thinking that I could still help her feel included, I sent her a few videos while on the trip. Unfortunately, they didn't have the effect I'd hoped; instead, she felt sad when she watched them. Seeing all the fun we were having without her made her feel isolated and excluded.

I know this because she was brave enough to tell me. Instead of holding that hurt in, she came to me and told me how she felt. And it strengthened our friendship. She had a chance to express how those videos made her feel, and I had a chance to explain why I'd sent them. She never considered that I did it as an act of love and inclusion; and I didn't consider that they would make her feel even more excluded.

Disappointment is inevitable in our relationships. And expressing that disappointment in a compassionate, caring, constructive way is a foundational skill in maintaining healthy relationships. It's important that both individuals feel seen, heard, understood, and most importantly, loved.

Expressing disappointment may cause you to fear that the person will get angry with you or abandon you. But your feelings matter, and if the relationship is important to you, it's worth finding the courage to express yourself. If you don't, that disappointment gets swept under the rug again and again and again, until that small pile becomes a mountain just waiting to trip you.

Before you express your feelings, you can always begin by saying something to help the other person feel safe and less defensive. It also helps to offer a solution for what you would like to happen next—to offer an alternative to the resentment and bitterness that could otherwise become toxic to your relationship.

TRY THESE

1. Practice the following prompts as ways to help you express your feelings. If these don't feel accurate, develop a few phrases on your own so that you can become more comfortable with sharing how you feel in a compassionate manner.

    - "I feel disappointed and I need to tell you why."
    - "I understand why you made the choice you made, but I feel disappointed and hope that next time you will talk to me first."
    - "The way you were behaving made me feel disrespected and it hurt me deeply."
    - "What you did yesterday made me feel uncomfortable and I need you to understand why…"
    - "I know you didn't mean to hurt me, but I want to explain why it hurts me when you do that."
    - "This may not seem like a big deal to you, but it is a big deal to me and I want to tell you why."
    - "You may not have intended to disappoint me, but you did and it made me feel like I didn't matter to you."

- "I'm struggling to understand what happened between us and I'm disappointed that we haven't talked about it since it happened."
- "I love you and I am disappointed in what happened between us today. When is a good time for us to talk about it?"

2. Try to recall a time when someone disappointed you and you chose not to share your feelings with them. How might it have gone if you'd used one of the prompts from above? Walk back through the situation, playing out how you might have used compassion and care to share how you felt.

MAKE A U-TURN

Sometimes while driving, I forge ahead so mindlessly that I miss a turn. Then my navigation system kicks in and brings me back to my senses by saying: "Rerouting...turn around...take the first available U-turn." Making a U-turn puts me back on track so I can get where I need to go.

An effective practice to help us get back on track when we're stressed, angry, or in times of conflict is one I like to call "making a U-turn." It's taking the time to stop forging ahead and intentionally turn around to figure out how we're contributing to the situation. U-turns can offer us the self-reflection and self-awareness needed to take accountability and give us a better chance at fixing things.

Make a U-turn to explore the source of stress by asking yourself: "Am I making this more stressful than it needs to be? How can I minimize my own stress level?"

When you notice you are blaming someone else, make a U-turn to examine your personal responsibility in the matter: "Did I do everything I could in this situation to help? What can I do to move toward peace with this person?"

Making a U-turn can be effective when you're angry, too: "What caused my response? Is there something I'm afraid of?"

Is someone distancing themselves from you? Make a U-turn to reflect on your behaviors: "Did I do something that would cause them to question my loyalty? Have I been contributing wholeheartedly to our relationship?"

When someone disappoints you, make a U-turn to consider your expectations of this person: "Was I expecting them to be someone they are not? Are my expectations of this person within reason, based on what I know to be true about them?"

After the self-reflection a U-turn offers, you may feel stressed, angry, disappointed, or that blame is still warranted. What's important is that you paused to consider your responsibility in the matter—which is doing your due diligence in maintaining your relationships. If you decide you've done everything you can, then you can move forward in good faith knowing you took the time to examine the circumstances.

Making a U-turn aids in self-reflection, which leads to greater self-awareness, which builds greater self-compassion, which builds greater compassion for everyone. That's a long journey—but one that always leads to peace.

TRY THESE

1. Is there something that's causing you stress at the moment? Make a U-turn to examine what you can do to minimize it.

2. Is there a relationship that's been a source of conflict recently? Make a U-turn: ask yourself what role you play, and what you can do to move toward peace.

HONOR OTHERS
THROUGH VALIDATION

A teen client of mine once shared how frustrated she was becoming with her parents. She found that often, after venting to them about something, they would go right to finding a solution. Her parents were trying to be helpful, but instead, she was left feeling unheard.

She wasn't looking for a fix to the problem; what she needed was validation.

Validating someone means that you acknowledge their experience without fixing it or negating it. Fixing or negating—instead of validating—sounds like any of the following phrases:

- "It could be worse."
- "You're overreacting."
- "You need to get over it."
- "You're being too sensitive."

Validation is the acknowledgment of someone else's feelings and experiences. It conveys respect and acceptance of the other's feelings, and helps build understanding and closeness within a relationship.

When people you love feel afraid or hurt or angry, of course you want to help relieve that feeling. But the most helpful thing you can do is listen to their perspective, imagine what it's like to be them in this situation, and allow them to fully express themselves. Once someone feels validated, their negative feelings tend to diffuse a bit; they feel better when they're able to share them with someone they trust.

Validating someone doesn't mean you agree with them; it means you heard what they said when they expressed their feelings. And even if you disagree, you're still respecting and honoring them—without minimizing their feelings.

The next time someone is venting to you, or sharing a difficult emotion with you, take the time to pause and consider a more empathetic approach. Sit in those emotions with them, without jumping to a solution. Hold your own filters and experiences back, and ask yourself: "what is it like for them?"

TRY THESE

Here are some helpful ways to help someone you love feel validated:

1. Give them your full attention. Look them in the eye, engage in the present moment, observe what they're feeling, give nonverbal reactions to what they're saying, and resist interrupting them until their words come to a full stop.

2. Match their tone. Tune in to what they're feeling and respond with body language that matches their tone. Adjust your expression, gestures, and eye contact according to what would be most supportive to the person talking to you.

3. Silently process what you hear. As you listen, summarize to yourself what they're telling you. Imagine you have a play-by-play commentator in your head who's reporting on what's happening. Silently

fill in the blanks: they're feeling _____, they want _____, they said _____, they did _____. This will keep you engaged and give you a better perspective on what they're feeling.

4. Resist the temptation to fix it for them. Most of the time, the people close to you just want to be heard. If they want your opinion or solution, they'll ask you for it. If they don't ask, don't offer.

5. Stay curious. If you aren't sure what they're feeling, ask them. If you aren't sure what they want from you, ask them. And if you disagree with them, stay quiet a minute longer than you want to (a helpful image is that of a puppy being trained: tell yourself, "stay.. stay...stay..." as a reminder to stay quiet and keep listening.).

6. Validate their emotions. Watch for cues that indicate they're now ready for you to talk. Wait for a pause in the dialogue and then proceed. Here are a few helpful phrases to use:

   • "It makes sense that you feel that way."
   • "Of course you feel _____."
   • "I get that you feel _____."
   • "It seems like you feel _____."
   • "This has to be hard for you right now."
   • "I would feel that way too."

REPAIR RIFTS

In relationships, we naturally have drifts and rifts. Author Shasta Nelson has written multiple books on friendships and she describes a drift as: "when two people have less in common due to life changes or personal preferences. There's typically no big break-up or blow-up, it's just two people moving apart."[23]

She describes a rift as: "when an event or behavior causes damage to our relationship leaving us hurt, angry, or confused for what we'd consider a grievance or mistake."

I have noticed drifts in my life with friends I went to college with, people who were parents of my children's friends that changed schools, graduate school friends, former coworkers, cousins I rarely see now, and neighbors I've lost touch with. These are all very normal as our lives change seasons, locations, jobs, neighborhoods, etc. Allowing people to drift away without guilt is a peace-giving way to live. There wasn't an issue between us, our lives just took different paths. I'm grateful to all of the people who have walked with me through various seasons of life. I have fond thoughts when I reflect upon them.

---

[23] Shasta Nelson, *Frientimacy* (New York: Seal Press, 2016).

Drifting apart doesn't mean the love stops, just that the contact drifts away. Drifts are a normal part of life.

Rifts are another story. Rifts are times when I have messed up in our relationship or the other person messed up and we haven't yet discussed what happened. Rifts deserve repair. If we don't repair a rift, we carry a toxicity in our bodies about that relationship. When we think of that person, we may feel guilt, remorse, or disappointment.

Repairing a rift sets both parties free. Repair liberates us from the pain of the rift. But healing a rift can take some courage. It is hard to bring these things back up, but it is also hard to carry the yucky feeling of thinking about the rift. This is a case where we have to weigh our difficult. See the Table of Contents for that practice.

Rifts deserve repair. In working with many people suffering from rifts in their lives, I highly encourage all of us to repair rifts because there is such peace and freedom on the other side of the awkward moment. It is hard to bring up old hurts, but it is a gift you give to yourself of a clear conscience.

Writing a letter is good for repair if you are too worried about the in-person conflict that might arise. Write from a place of appreciation for the relationship, sadness for the outcome of the rift, and an apology that shows your responsibility for your role in the rift. You may never hear back from the other person, but at least you clear your conscience of the tension when you think about that person.

If you have a rift from your past that is way overdue for repair, you might decide that repair isn't possible anymore. The person may be deceased, it might be too complicated to re-contact them, or you might not know how to reach them anymore. Allow yourself to close the file on this relationship by replaying the rift and seeing if you can view it differently this time. Can you see each person's responsibility in this rift? Can you have compassion for the other person as well as yourself? You might need to write a letter that you don't send, or talk out loud as if that person was there with you, or confide in a friend about this rift. Describe what you wish you would have done differently, why you did what you did, and close with sending this person love and well wishes. You might use something like "may they be well, may they be happy, may we both have peace about this and feel a sense of repair."

Making mistakes is part of being human. We do it every day. Allow yourself to make mistakes. Really good people make mistakes and then they repair the damage. It's the repair that really matters. It is never too late to make a repair.

TRY THESE

1. Consider the people you have drifted away from that were once an important part of your life. Send loving gratitude to them now—bring their image to mind and then envision them surrounded by love and goodness.

2. Consider those with whom you have encountered a rift. How could you repair this? Decide to take the steps to make a repair or decide that you won't continue to torture yourself by over-thinking this rift. You have options: Release it. Repair and reconnect. Repair and release. You decide what is best for you.

BEAM LOVE

I had a client once who was devastated by a rift in the family. She had done something that her sister couldn't forgive her for. Her sister had not spoken to her in years. My client had tried to reconnect with her, with no success. She felt powerless and didn't know what else to do.

I took her through a powerful practice to help those who seek peace when it comes to a relationship: it is one known as the ancient meditation of Metta, but I refer to it as "beaming love." Place your hands on your heart, close your eyes, and send that person the following thoughts:

May you be calm.
May you be happy.
May you be healthy.
May you be loved.

When you send love to someone through those thoughts, you feel compassion for them. You carry that feeling; it stays with you. Softens you. Helps you feel connected to them. To some, it may sound like a strange thing to do, but I've seen it work time and time again.

My client did this practice daily and after a few months, her sister reached out to her and they were able to reconnect. We can't explain why this thinking exercise touched her sister's heart, but it did. It also happened once when

I was teaching the practice in a class and I noticed a woman suddenly leave the room. She explained after the class that her husband was overseas for an extended period of time and unable to call home frequently. Seconds after she tried the practice, he called out of the blue, just to say hi.

Even if the practice of sending love seems uncomfortable or unfamiliar, it certainly can't hurt to try. No matter what, you're putting more love out into the world. You're contributing compassion and peace to others through a cycle that can truly change your life and the energy of those around you.

I like to use this practice to reset when I'm having a bad day. Not only do I send silent love to my family and friends, I'll even try it on people at the grocery store or the gas station. More often than not, someone will smile at me, like they can feel the warmth being sent their way.

Sending love is a great maintenance exercise—a way to keep your compassion skills in shape. After doing it a few times, you'll find that it becomes more natural, bringing you peace, sending out good energy, and maybe even drawing someone you love closer in the process.

TRY THESE

Close your eyes, place your hands on your heart, and practice sending love to the people listed below.

1. As your loved ones depart to begin their day, send them these thoughts:

   - May you be calm.
   - May you be happy.
   - May you be healthy.
   - May you be loved.

2. As you fill up your car with gas or buy your morning coffee, send these thoughts to a person whom you see, but do not know:

   - May you be calm.
   - May you be happy.
   - May you be healthy.
   - May you be loved.

3. As conflict arises with someone, or if you are ruminating on an old pain or betrayal, bring that person to mind and send them these thoughts:

   - May you be calm.
   - May you be happy.
   - May you be healthy.
   - May you be loved.

4. To a loved one who is away at college, on a business trip, or living far away, bring them to mind and send these thoughts:

   - May you be calm.
   - May you be happy.
   - May you be healthy.
   - May you be loved.

5. To people who are suffering from pain, in the hospital, or feeling hopeless, bring them to mind and send them these thoughts:

   - May you be calm.
   - May you be happy.
   - May you be healthy.
   - May you be loved.

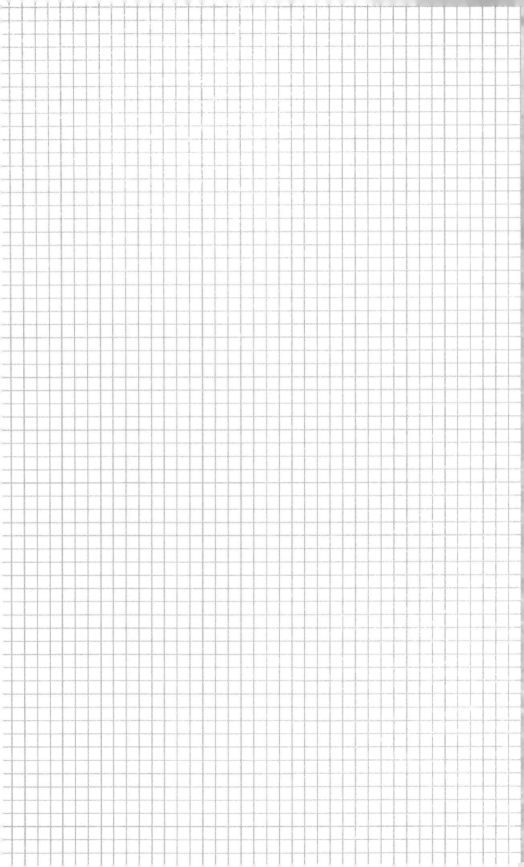

WORK WITH
YOUR WIRING

My dream is that practices like the ones in this section will become part of our education system. I long for children to learn these at a young age. Young people know more about how their iPhones work than how their brains work. Learning how to manage your brain and work with your inner wiring is a fundamental part of navigating what it means to be human.

Learning about my inner roommates was a game-changer in my life. I could begin to love all of me instead of fighting with parts of me. Some of those parts are afraid, annoying roommates, but they will always live with me and they respond really well to loving care. They just want to be heard and seen. When I love those painful parts of me, inner peace comes quickly. Understanding how our brains work should be one of the first things we learn in our lifetime. My clients in their 80s tell me that knowing this information much earlier would have changed the trajectory of their lives. They could have experienced more freedom from negativity, more joy, more loving relation-

ships, more fulfilling career choices. Knowing your brain is knowing how to live a good life.

The practices in this section can change your life. I hope you will spend time in these pages and let these practices soak into your being. They may resonate differently over time as you become more familiar with the unique way your brain works. Return to this section often and review the practices. One day they will click and you will realize you can take your brain where you want it to go instead of feeling controlled by it. You can live the life you dream of, especially if you learn to work with your wiring.

MEET YOUR ROOMMATES

In Michael Singer's book *The Untethered Soul*, I was introduced to the idea of inner roommates and it clicked with me that the voice of criticism in my head was just an annoying inner roommate: following me around the house, commenting on everything that I did in an overly critical manner. As a home-owner, I would likely ask that roommate to find another place to live, but our inner roommates live rent-free in our heads for our entire lives.

Singer writes:

> *"In case you haven't noticed, you have a mental dialogue going on inside your head that never stops. It just keeps going and going. Have you ever wondered why it talks in there? How does it decide what to say and when to say it? How much of what it says turns out to be true? How much of what it says is even important? And if right now you are hearing, 'I don't know what you're talking about. I don't have any voice inside my head!'—that's the voice we're talking about...There is nothing more important to true growth than realizing that you are not the voice of the mind—you are the one who hears it."*[24]

---

[24] Michael Singer, *The Untethered Soul* (California: New Harbinger Publications, 2007).

In the 10 years since reading Singer's words for the first time, I have practiced becoming the observer of my inner roommates and offered this practice to my clients. For most of us, this awareness has resulted in some rearranging of our internal power structures.

I realized that I had given my inner critic the most power in my mind and allowed it to be the primary voice I listened to. And yet, there was a beautiful encourager whom I had moved down to the basement long ago and forgotten about. I realized that I needed to rearrange my house and move the encourager to the big room and the critic to the basement, to be heard from only when I truly need to improve something.

Who lives in the House of You? You are the watcher and observer of these inner roommates. See if you can name some of them. In my house, there is a critic, encourager, worrier, fun-lover, risk-taker, spiritual-seeker, academic, laughing-enthusiast, protector, creative-explorer, self-doubter, compassionate-coach, and many others I continue to uncover. These are all parts of me, and I am learning to love all my roommates and their idiosyncrasies. And even though some of the more aggressive ones take over sometimes, it is up to me to keep the house in balance. Periodically, I have to call a figurative kitchen table meeting where I gather the roommates and review the house rules. The newest house rules are: the critic must remain silent if I wake up in the middle of the night, the encourager needs to increase her volume because it is hard to hear her, and the fun-lover gets to run the show in the summer months.

What rules might you need to review with your inner roommates this week? Who is running the show in the House of You?

All of our inner roommates are an integral part of us. They make up the complex, beautiful human that you are. Naming your inner roommates is a practice that helps you remember that you are in charge of the house. You make the rules. You decide who gets to speak up and when. You assign who gets to have a prominent role and who is less active in the house.

You own the house, so make sure your inner roommates are behaving the way you want them to and being helpful. Your soul deserves a peaceful home.

TRY THESE

1. Name your inner roommates if it helps you to personify them. What rules do you need to put in place in the House of You?

2. Observe and watch your inner roommates. When you are driving, working, trying something new, in the shower pondering life, or having a conversation, ask yourself: What part of me is showing up right now? What does that part need? Is that part of me helpful or harmful at this moment?

WATCH FOR CATTLE PATHS

My grandpa was a cattle rancher in the Flint Hills of Kansas. Growing up, I loved spending summers on the ranch with him. Often, he'd take me along with him on horseback across the vast acreage of pasture to check on his cattle. Even with all that land, the cattle would always stay on the same path, walking the same route from their shady spot to water, over and over again. They'd create deep ruts in the earth, walking head to tail, mindlessly following one another day after day.

Our brains get ruts like this, too. Neurologists call them "neural pathways." When we repeatedly think the same thought, it becomes hardwired into our default thinking. We form our belief systems that way—the more we reinforce a belief, the deeper the path becomes in our brain.

Not all of those deeply ingrained thoughts serve us, though. And once they're hardwired in, they become much harder to let go of.

The good news is, we can create new pathways by thinking new thoughts— what's technically known as "neuroplasticity." We can actually rewire our brains, forming new neural pathways and overcoming some of those long-held beliefs about ourselves that may be holding us back.

I had a client come to see me about her difficult relationship with her mother. She'd always thought it was her fault: she believed she was a bad daughter.

Together, we worked on those long-held thoughts. What if she could try out a new thought—create a new neural pathway?

We chose the thought: "I was a good daughter, and my mother was incapable of being the parent I needed." She repeated it to herself daily and wrote it in her journal. Within a few weeks, she felt relief as she started to believe that thought. A few weeks later, she could fully embrace it and was on a new path toward healing.

By assessing our thinking patterns, we can notice if we have neural pathways that sound like self-criticism, negativity, or frustration and make an intentional effort to try out some new thoughts. To stray away from those deeply rutted cattle paths and build new pathways. And to enjoy our journey more.

TRY THIS

What long-held beliefs have become ruts in your brain? Try counteracting those thoughts by creating new paths: keep repeating the opposite belief. Work at it daily for a few weeks and see how it feels. Even if you don't believe it, think it and know that it needs time to form. Here are a few examples:

Old path: "I'm not good enough."
New path: "I am enough."

Old path: "I don't have anything to offer."
New path: "I'm growing and learning."

Old path: "I'll never be successful."
New path: "I'm redefining what success means for me."

Old path: "No one cares about me."
New path: "I am loved, lovable, and loving."

Old path: "I can't do anything right."
New path: "I'm doing better than I think I am."

IMAGINE THE POSSIBILITIES

Benjamin Zander is the founder and long-time conductor of the Boston Philharmonic Orchestra. He also taught at the New England Conservatory of Music and created the Boston Philharmonic Youth Orchestra. He has an exuberant personality and passion for helping people fall in love with classical music. In his book *The Art of Possibility*, written with his wife Rosamund, he teaches us the power of imagining the possibilities in our lives.[25]

Zander's philosophy is to live as though anything is possible. As a teacher, he noticed that highly talented students were dimming their giftedness to meet the grading criteria of the professors. He saw them play it safe, stop taking risks, and play their instruments more timidly instead of playing from their souls. So, he designed a way to stretch the students into their creative potential.

At the beginning of each school year, he assigned a letter-writing project to his students. They were to date the letter as the last day of classes in May and the letter was to begin with: "Dear Mr. Zander, I earned my A because..." Then they were to explain who they had become as a musician during this school year and what outstanding things they had accomplished. He wanted

---

[25] Benjamin Zander, *The Art of Possibility* (New York: Penguin, 2002).

them to dream big and stretch beyond what they thought they could do. If they achieved that, then they received a guaranteed A in the course.

If they turned in a letter with something easy to achieve, he gave it back to them and told them to stretch themselves further. Zander says in his book that almost every student reached their goal. Many surprised themselves. They played pieces of music they once thought were impossible for them to play. They guest-conducted symphonies. They were invited to play in famous concert halls. What began as dreams became their realities.

Zander describes that writing down their goals created the vision of possibility in his students. He watched them transform into the person they hoped they could become. He says that writing the letters "changed the whole atmosphere of the class" and that students began "floating into the room" instead of walking in with dread. They were lighter because they were leaning into their possibilities rather than limits. They recognized their own potential.

What areas of your life might need a dose of the spirit of possibility?

I first read Zander's book 20 years ago, when I was diagnosed with multiple sclerosis. I picked it up in the airport bookstore on our way to Arizona. My husband and I were going for a long weekend to sit in the sun before I started a medication that was likely to have tough side effects. As I read Zander's thoughts on the power of believing in possibilities, it filled me with hope and our mantra became "imagine the possibilities." When I would get worried about what was ahead, Rob would say: "imagine the possibility that they find a cure." When I was afraid of the medication, Rob would say: "imagine the possibility that it works with no side effects." Throughout our marriage, we have continued to use this phrase when one of us feels stuck or worried.

I encourage you to look up Benjamin Zander's fantastic TED Talk online by searching for the title "Benjamin Zander The Transformative Power of Classical Music."

TRY THIS

When you notice that you are preparing for the worst, see if you can challenge yourself to imagine the great possibilities. Our brains like to imagine the worst-case scenarios, and we forget to consider the best-case scenarios. If you are worrying about something, experiment with turning the worry into positive possibilities. If you are seeking a sense of purpose, allow yourself to imagine the possibilities and see what begins to align for you. If you are afraid of taking a risk, imagine that it goes amazingly well. If you are afraid to fall, imagine that you fly. Explore the possibilities as a practice, and then your brain will start to go to positive places automatically when a new idea arises.

MANAGE NEGATIVITY BIAS

Ever wonder why you feel so negative some days? Or why other people seem stuck in negativity?

It is because we are hardwired for negativity. By design, negativity can be a helpful quality—our brain's job is to keep us safe and alive. It believes that if we remember everything that we do wrong, we are more likely to get it right next time. It is an internal feedback loop that says: "that is bad, so avoid it," or "you screwed that up, don't do it again." It can be helpful, but it is harsh.

The tendency of our brain toward negativity was helpful in our caveman days. If I didn't have an inner critic screaming in my head, "you are running too slow!!" I would have been eaten by a saber-toothed tiger. Survival of the fittest might be re-written as survival of the most negative. Negativity can keep us safe. It can also keep us playing it too safe.

Negativity isolates us and makes our world small. We keep shutting out people and ideas until we are left alone with nothing. The fear center of our brain likes us alone with nothing to do because its job is solely to keep us safe. It counts that kind of existence as a job well done. For many of us, a negative, isolated, non-inspired mindset leads to feeling depressed, sad, irritable, judgmental, angry, and low-energy. Safe from saber-toothed tigers, but really unhappy.

We can manage our negativity bias by catching ourselves with it. Notice when you feel like a negative cloud is floating around with you everywhere you go. Notice when you think the world is a dumpster fire. Notice when you think everyone is wrong in their thinking. Notice when your energy is low and you are irritable. We shift out of this negative bias by noticing it and deciding we don't want to live like that. When people come into my office and say, "I don't like feeling this angry all the time," I know they have a negative inner critic that needs to be reined in. That voice of their inner roommate has become too loud and too harsh. Negativity erodes our self-worth. After we decide that everything in the world is wrong, we also see everything about ourselves as wrong.

The world is a beautifully complicated place, and humans are beautifully complicated creatures. See it all through a lens of love, not fear, and the negativity will start to lift. Negativity is fear. Address what you are really afraid of and then the negativity will diffuse. You can control your brain when it becomes negative; begin practicing today and it will quickly get easier to shift into a more hopeful state of mind. We train our brains like we train puppies to sit. Through repetition. And treats. Shift out of negative thinking into hopeful thinking and the treats begin to flow to you. Life can be big and glorious, and you deserve to live unafraid.

TRY THIS

When you notice someone else being negative, wonder to yourself: "what are they afraid of?" That will help train your brain that negativity is really fear. Most humans are afraid of rejection, failure, judgment, being alone, losing power, or not mattering. These are valid fears, but unchecked they can feed our negativity bias. Notice this in other people. Then notice it in yourself. Identify the deeper fear that is underneath the negativity. Bring it up to the surface and love yourself through it. Assure yourself that you don't need to live in fear. You can push back the negativity. You are a beloved human who deserves peace, joy, and love.

USE "AND" STATEMENTS

Sometimes when I'm working with a client who is experiencing conflict with a family member, they will interrupt their criticism of that person with: "I shouldn't be saying this, I really love her" or "he is a really
good person"—they feel a need to soften their criticism with a disclaimer.
My response is, often: "let's play with the word 'and' here. I understand
that your relationship is stressful right now AND you really love her.
I hear that he is an intense father AND he is a really great person."

Two things can be true at the same time. We are all complicated human beings. I think we need to make more room for AND in our lives.

We can love people and be frustrated with them.
We can have great memories of someone who has died and horrible memo-
    ries of that same person.
We can be having the time of our lives in college and miss home too.
We can feel happy in the mountains and on the beach.
We can love the person we are dating and miss things about our ex.
We can be rooted in one religion and explore the teachings of other religions.
We can agree with something in one political party and something in
    another party.
We can have one career and then go back to school to become something else.

It is important to make room for all of our feelings, opinions, interests, and people. Our world might be a lot more loving if we all gave each other permission to be curious, change our minds, and explore new options.

Be all the things. Feel all the things. Explore all the things.

TRY THIS

Pause for a few minutes and play with these fill-in-the-blanks:

I am _____ and _____.
I can do _____ and _____.
I believe _____ and _____.
I want to _____ and _____.

Was it easy or hard to fill in those blanks?

Some people might discover they have some rigid thinking in their brain that sounds like an adult saying: "you have to pick one lane and stay in it." Or you might hear your inner critic say: "you can't do/be/believe/want both of those things." You might have grown up in a faith that said there is only one truth and everyone else is wrong. See if you can help your brain accept a little more nuance this week. As I see so much division in our country, I think the word AND might bring a little more compassion into our conversations.

You can be strong and kind. You can be smart and silly. You can be confident and likable. You can be successful and humble. You can be wealthy and generous. You can be one thing today and something else tomorrow.

KNOW YOUR TRIGGERS

A client of mine had major surgery when he was young that kept him from being able to participate in youth sports. Now a young adult, he has an intense fear of weakness. He even works out to the point of exhaustion, just to prove to himself that he's not weak. All because of how devastating and traumatic that surgery and its after-effects were for him as a kid. Weakness, for him, is what's known as a "trigger."

Do you ever have a strong reaction to someone's behavior and you're surprised by how deeply it affected you? Likely, their behavior hit upon one of your triggers.

Any event that threatens your primal need for safety will be deeply hardwired into you, causing your amygdala to light up—be triggered—any time something makes you feel a similar way.

Triggers are points of internal emotional stress. People sometimes bump up against our stress points and we're surprised by how much it hurts. Think of it as a cut on your finger that you accidentally spill lemon juice on. It stings. You're suddenly reminded that the cut is there.

Triggers are those cuts; they're wounds from the past we might not think about, but really hurt when someone hits one. They also remind us there's still some healing needed in that area.

Our subconscious is like a sponge—it soaks up the events that have a large emotional impact. And that's where triggers come from. They indicate areas of pain that are still raw for us—signs that we're experiencing the past in the present moment. Many times, they're related to areas of past trauma, deep hurt, shame, or judgment. They're unhealed emotional wounds that are still tender to the touch.

A trigger signals our nervous system to sound the alarms that we are in emotional danger or that something feels threatening to us. And while it may feel like we are angry when we are triggered, often, there is real pain that lies underneath that anger.

Here are some common triggers in our lives:

- Being judged or criticized
- Feeling excluded or forgotten
- When someone repeatedly corrects you
- Feeling taken advantage of
- Being ignored or interrupted
- Noticing that you're being manipulated
- Someone trying to control you
- Your boundaries being ignored
- Being belittled or dismissed
- Someone treating you with disregard or disrespect

It is natural to feel emotionally threatened by these kinds of behaviors—they hurt. None of these things feel good. If you have been subjected to these repeatedly, you are more likely to be emotionally triggered when they occur.

Many times, our triggers are open wounds from our past that were never tended to. If you were often manipulated as a child, then another adult manipulating you today brings up that old pain. If you were a child who was often interrupted, then today as a parent, you might snap angrily at your child when they interrupt you.

It is important work for us to understand and heal our triggers. Hurt people hurt people. If we can tend to our own wounds, we are less likely to inflict pain upon someone else.

Triggers are an invitation to look inside yourself a little deeper. Even naming a trigger is a huge step. If you can recognize it, then you can work at becoming more of an observer. Just knowing why you feel the way you do is an extremely helpful way to start coaching yourself with compassion through triggering events.

Try to see your triggered moments as a message that this tender part of you needs extra compassion and love. Be gentle with yourself and with everyone you encounter. We are all walking around with tender areas from past pain.

TRY THESE

1. To help uncover what triggers you may have, ask yourself the following questions:

   - Is there an area where you feel extra defensive or easily offended?
   - Does someone do a certain thing that they think is benign but that really upsets you?
   - Does something really get to you and you aren't sure why?
   - Is there an insult or criticism that hurts you deeper than others?
   - What makes you angry in the moment, but when you reflect later, you realize you overreacted?
   - What makes your blood boil?

2. Give yourself the healing love and kindness you've longed for. The next time you notice that you feel triggered emotionally, try this self-compassion prac-

tice: place your hand on your heart and say to yourself, "[*your name*], you are triggered right now by
[*the person/words/behaviors/setting*]. You are safe and
I am with you. This is coming up now to be healed.
Let's send love to the wound and remember that you
are loved, lovable, and loving."

FILE IT WITH CARE

I notice a lot of my clients have regrets over decisions they have made in the past. They will tell me the story and I often respond with something like: "you have filed that away in the bad decision file, but I think we need to consider seeing it differently."

We make life decisions and then afterward, we decide if it goes in the "good decision" file or the "bad decision" file.

Which file is bigger in your figurative filing cabinet?

Maybe it is time to re-file some of those memories.

We get to decide if we made a bad decision or a good decision. What might look like a bad decision at first could have actually helped you get to where you are today. What might have hurt in the short term, helped you in the long term.

I started my private coaching practice in a small office above an Italian restaurant in Kansas City in 2017. The office had a waiting area and a room that fit two chairs and a bookshelf. It was cozy and my clients and I loved that quirky space. But as my practice grew, I wanted to be able to host classes and group workshops. So, after three years in that cozy nook, I took a leap of faith and rented a large commercial retail space. The new space was set up for two counseling offices and a workshop area to host large groups. I tripled my operational expenses, purchased tables and chairs, and was counting on full classes to offset the cost. I moved into that new space on March 1, 2020. Before I could host my first class, the world shut down due to COVID-19.

My inner critic had a heyday, telling me this was a horrible business decision. I was on the hook for tripling my expenses and had no way to increase revenue because people were mandated to stay home. My vision for building a community of learning, growing, and exploring new topics together vanished in a matter of days. And, I was bleeding money.

I filed this decision in the "big mistake" file. Every time I walked into the beautifully decorated, set-up-for-classes office, I reminded myself how much it was costing me and how stupid I was to take on this large expense. Every day, I kept adding more evidence to the "big mistake" file.

In August of 2020, I decided that I needed to generate revenue somehow, so I started an online group, the Compassion Fix Community. I lectured via Zoom on a new topic every month, and weekly we met to dive into deep, compelling, rich discussions about that topic. Three years later, this group is still meeting weekly and we've added new members over time. The people in the class are some of the most amazing humans I have met. They have undergone transformations that amaze all of us. It has been a gift to host that group and watch our lives change for the better as we learn together.

I think I filed the office move in the wrong file. It actually wasn't a "big mistake." Signing that lease led me to create something amazing. Plus, I loved Zooming in that beautiful space. I loved that I believed in myself when I signed the lease. I am proud of myself for taking the leap of faith. What if it was actually one of my best business decisions, not my worst business decision?

Can you pull out the "bad decision" file and revisit some of those memories now? How did those things serve you?

Our brain defaults to reminding us of our mistakes in hopes that it keeps us safer in the future. We are wired to recall mistakes. It helps us survive. But we can work with our brain to find the nuance in the situation. Almost always, good can be found in everything. We have to help our brain see it. Give some thought to your inner files and be sure you file things carefully.

TRY THIS

Bring to mind a decision that you have told yourself was a bad decision. What good came of it? What did you learn because of that decision? Can you stop beating yourself up about it now? Pull it out of the "bad decision" file and move it to the "I learned a lot" file.

WORK WITH YOUR SUBCONSCIOUS

Our subconscious brain runs automatically and continuously to keep us breathing, moving, and safe. We don't have to think about breathing; it just happens for us. If we pause and become aware of our inhales and exhales, then we realize how much we can control our breathing. We can speed it up, slow it down, hold it, make it audible, and shift the airflow from our nose to our mouth. We breathe without thinking about it, but with awareness we can also adjust it.

In our daily busyness, we take our subconscious mind for granted, but it can be a powerful practice of transformation in our lives.

Imagine a garden where everything thrives and grows—this garden is similar to your subconscious mind. When you were a baby, your subconscious brain was soaking up every experience and observation. Repeated experiences and observations became beliefs. Experiences that had emotional pain or joy were even more deeply planted. Through trial and error, you figured out how to go downstairs safely, how to not spill your drink, and how to please the people around you. Your subconscious mind held onto how to do these things and, over time, they became automatic for you.

You also soaked up the opinions of the adults you heard talking, the words of kids on the playground, and the preferences of your teachers. These thoughts were planted in the garden of your mind and have grown into adult beliefs. Now, as adults, we have to tend to the garden of our subconscious and we may need to make some adjustments.

Are there new thoughts you want to entertain or explore? Are there other sides to a story you want to understand? Do you no longer agree with something you once believed to be true?

You have the power to literally change your mind. I hope that you feel empowered reading that sentence, but if it feels a little scary then I officially give you permission to change your mind—this is your life and it is yours to live.

Weeds grow as quickly as flowers in our subconscious minds. Remember, it is incredibly fertile ground in there. We can't leave it unattended. Plant the stuff you want to grow, and pull out the weeds that block your progress.

Life is beautiful and hard—often at the exact same time. If your subconscious is full of positive, peaceful, life-giving beliefs, then your automatic system will default to hope and help you get through the tough times.

TRY THIS

If there is something you long for or want, then plant the thought (write it down or say it out loud to plant it even deeper), water it by imagining how you will feel when you get it, and then repeat that thought-emotion combo every day. Your subconscious soil will go to work helping that idea grow and become a reality in your life.

Harness the power of your own brain. You get to choose what gets planted from here on out.

REWIRE YOUR WAY
TO RESILIENCE

Many years ago, my husband and I were struggling with infertility. During that time, I would fall into deep holes of self-pity; I'd find myself thinking that I was the only one having difficulties getting pregnant and spiral even further down.

I wish I could go back and talk to that long-ago Ginger and teach her what I now know: that in reality, there were millions of women going through the same thing at the same time. By stopping to consider that, and having compassion not only for myself, but for those who were also living through the same experience, it would have helped me be more resilient. Whereas self-pity—"I'm the only one"—brings about isolation, compassion for others brings with it resilience: the ability to better face whatever difficulties come your way.

Some of us are naturally more resilient than others, but with a little brain work, we can all become more resilient.

Having resilience means you're more equipped to recover from difficulties. It can be both learned and strengthened by training your brain to remember that you are not the only one facing whatever it is that you are facing—you are not alone. Reminding your brain of that will help you move out of isolation and be better prepared the next time a difficult situation arises.

Compassion for others and resilience go hand in hand: when we see our current adversity as part of a human experience and recognize that others have felt how we feel—and survived—it gives us hope that we, too, can survive. When we have compassion for others, we become more resilient.

You're capable of learning resilience just by reminding yourself that others feel the way you do. Resilience brings readiness and, most importantly, hope. We cultivate hope in knowing that our current pain is temporary and that the future will bring brighter days.

TRY THIS

To build resilience, try this simple self-talk exercise: "[*this experience*] is hard for me. I am sad for the many things I am losing/missing/grieving. But I'm not the only one struggling with this. People around the world are also feeling what I'm feeling." End by making a plan: "I think I need to go on a walk and then call a friend." You are pulling yourself out of self-pity and isolation into compassion and resilience.

Remember: you are learning how to do this, and it will get easier with time. Give yourself self-compassion and patience; know that you are becoming competent at creating new neural circuitry for resilience.

GET YOUR DOSE

If you know you need to feel more awake, you think: "caffeine."
If you know you need to feel happier, think: "DOSE."

Just like caffeine is a chemical that helps us perk up, DOSE is an acronym that can help you remember the four neurochemicals our brains produce to help us feel better: dopamine, oxytocin, serotonin, and endorphins.

If you want to be happier, you can help yourself more than you know just by stimulating the brain to make more of its feel-good DOSE hormones. How do you do that? There are a number of behaviors and activities that can help. Here are a few examples:

Dopamine is released when we:

- are excited about something (ordering your favorite take-out food)
- accomplish a task (organizing a closet)
- discover something new (unlocking a level in a video game)
- see improvement in ourselves (taking an art class and noticing your skills growing)

Oxytocin is released when we:

- feel loved (by a pet or person)

- feel safe (being held in the arms of someone you trust)
- bond with another person (looking into the eyes of someone you love)
- care for someone we love (tucking a child into their bed)
- take compassionate action (seeing someone fall and helping or comforting them)

Serotonin is released when we feel:

- that we matter to someone (being recognized for your contribution)
- an inherent sense of worthiness (knowing you are enough no matter what the circumstances may indicate)
- a sense of life purpose (your existence is important to someone)
- satisfaction with life as it is (you are living a meaningful life)

Endorphins are released when:

- we push ourselves further than we thought we could (new strength or endurance found during exercise)
- we feel pain from something fun (we laugh so hard it hurts)
- we feel relief that something we thought would hurt actually didn't (a difficult conversation with a friend goes better than you thought it would)
- something we were afraid to do goes really well (you make a presentation you were nervous to give)

When I need a lift, I go for a walk just to get the endorphins. Or, I'll cuddle with my dog intentionally, knowing that it will produce oxytocin. When you need a lift, stimulate the happy chemicals in your brain by getting a DOSE.

TRY THESE

Here are some of ways to get your DOSE:

1. Dopamine

    - Make a to-do list and check off each item as you complete it
    - Create something—like writing, music, art, or a floral arrangement
    - Eat your favorite meal
    - Go to bed early
    - Buy yourself something new
    - Work in your yard or garden
    - Clean something
    - Set long-term goals for yourself

2. Oxytocin

    - Place your hand on your heart, close your eyes, and take a few deep breaths
    - Wrap your arms around your chest and give yourself a hug
    - Write a letter to yourself filled with admiration
    - Make a list of all the things you love
    - Wrap up in your favorite blanket
    - Cuddle with a person or pet
    - Connect with a friend
    - Listen to slow-tempo music

3. Serotonin

    - Sit in the sun for 10 minutes
    - Put yourself in situations where you know you will be confident

- Give yourself a pep talk
- Take a cold shower for 2-3 minutes
- Declutter your space
- Eat more foods with folate and Omega 3 (fruit, fish, eggs, leafy greens, avocados)

4. Endorphins

- Walk outside for 20 minutes
- Listen to music and dance around the kitchen
- Meet up with the friend who always makes you laugh
- Watch a hilarious movie or silly online videos
- Eat dark chocolate or spicy food
- Push a little further when you want to quit
- Celebrate after a difficult task is completed
- Work hard on a project at school, work, or home

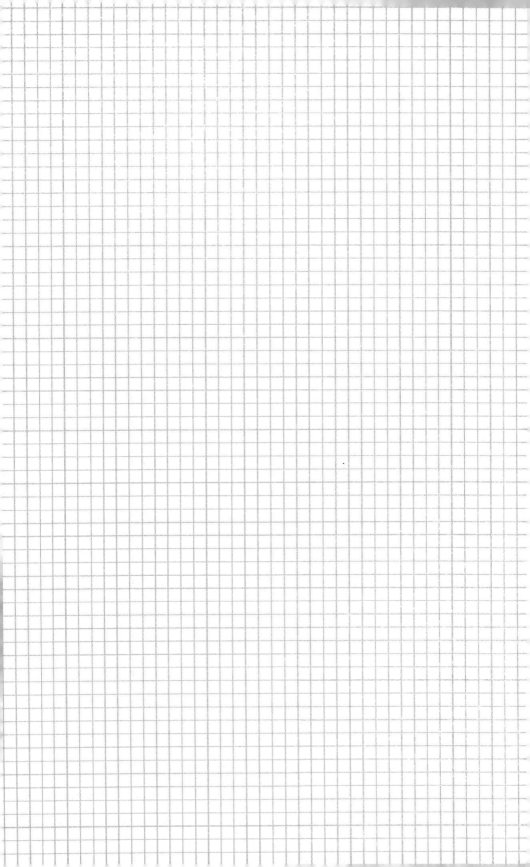

TRUST YOURSELF

In the first draft of this book, this section didn't exist. These practices were placed among the other sections. And yet, I kept feeling that this needed to be a section of its own. And while that was stirring in my brain, I attended a webinar on anxiety and came away pondering the idea that a lot of anxious thinking is due to a lack of self-trust.

This certainly feels true in my own life. If I trust that I can figure it out, no matter what happens in life, then my anxious thinking is reduced dramatically. I started talking with my clients about self-trust and testing out these practices. Over time, it became clear to me that practices to help with trusting ourselves needed to be a section in this book.

I hope you will read through these now, and then return to them as needed. Developing self-trust can take a while. There are so many factors in our early years of life that cause us to begin doubting ourselves, and that doubt never seems to let up. Life gets more complicated, we make mistakes, we doubt our decisions, and the cycle continues. But what I know to be true is that you have an inner compass of sage wisdom inside you.

Trust your intuition, your inner knowing. Develop a relationship with it. Have your own back. Believe in yourself. I hope these practices help you and me continue to grow in trust. We can do this together!

REMEMBER YOUR TRACK RECORD

Christine, a client of mine, wanted to start her own business, but was crippled by the fear that she wouldn't be successful.

Together, we did a simple exercise I love to help turn self-doubt into self-confidence: we looked at track records. I reminded her that she'd had a stellar track record at the large company where she'd most recently worked. She'd managed several major projects that all turned out to be successful; she'd planned a number of big events that went off without a hitch. She'd garnered high marks from everyone she worked with. Once she remembered her past success, she began to believe she could be successful again.

Of course, we have setbacks and challenges in our lives. That's part of the human experience. However, in my conversations with people, I notice that we often forget our track record of successes. When I ask someone to name a time in their life that went better than they thought it would, they often light up as they tell me the story. They forgot what they had accomplished, and it felt good for them to remember the success. Revisiting their track record gave them confidence for their next challenge.

The next time you're doubting your abilities, try reflecting upon your own track record. Go all the way back—to high school, or even younger. Review your entire life: everything that you've taken on, and everything you've done well. I bet that there's far more evidence of success in your past than of failure.

We so easily forget the wins and so often obsess over the losses...the one C on the transcript, or the one bad review, or the one tiny mistake. How many A's or great reviews or smart decisions have you forgotten about? Your track record is better than you think it is.

Look at the evidence to date. You've done well. You figured it out. You pressed on. You achieved success. You are more capable, smart, and equipped than you think you are.

TRY THIS

Take a piece of paper and write "My Track Record" at the top. Make a list of your past achievements and keep it somewhere you can easily access during times of fear or self-doubt. Don't be shy: everything and anything counts, whether it's raising kind human beings, being a good friend, or achieving success in the workplace. Include things like:

- Degrees and academic achievements
- Leadership roles
- Great moments in athletics or performing arts
- Things you created
- Groups you brought together
- Gatherings you hosted
- People you helped
- New places you moved to
- Trips you took
- Friendships you formed
- Invitations you received
- Awards and honors over the years

What else comes to mind? Keep the list going!

TAKE TWO MINUTES TO BUILD SELF-TRUST

When I find myself filled with self-doubt and wanting to give up on something, I help myself by doing something that, at first glance, might seem strange: I set a 30-day challenge to make my bed every day.

So often, we make grand promises to ourselves (like starting a diet or looking for a new job), only for our self-critic to say: "you're never going to stick to this." And just like that, we find ourselves giving up.

What it really means when our self-critic kicks in is that we don't trust ourselves to keep our own promises.

Don't despair: you can and will make good on your promises with a simple practice that will help rewire your brain and build trust in yourself. Start with a really, really small habit—like making your bed—that takes you no more than two minutes, and do it every day for 30 days.

Promise yourself something small, and when you find yourself completing it, you'll build the trust you need that you'll keep your own promises.

To help build trust in yourself and hit those bigger goals later, here are some examples of two-minute habits you can start now:

- mindful breathing

- tidying up
- flossing your teeth
- having a glass of water first thing in the morning
- taking a vitamin
- putting your keys in the same place

By making a habit of doing something simple, you're teaching your brain: "I can keep a promise." And—bonus—not only will you build confidence in yourself, you'll also feel better; our brains release the feel-good chemical dopamine into our system anytime we feel a sense of accomplishment.

A lot of magic can happen just by committing to two minutes. Research shows that meditating for two minutes every day has more value than meditating for 30 minutes once in a while.*

I know that for me, the two-minute practice has also helped me feel less overwhelmed so that I can continue to move forward with confidence. Two minutes seems like a small commitment; often, that's all we need to get started. And we all know that getting started is the hardest part.

TRY THESE

1. Begin by making a list of the things you'd like to start doing. Some examples: getting up earlier, paying bills on time, meditating, exercising, eating healthier, writing every day, going to bed earlier, making the bed, staying organized, walking the dog, cleaning your car, etc.

2. Now, explore how you could do the things you want

---

* Jon Kabat-Zinn, the founder of mindfulness-based stress reduction (MBSR), shared this in a class in which I participated.

to start by committing to only two minutes of that activity. Here are some examples:

- I will set my alarm for two minutes earlier tomorrow morning.
- I will take two minutes to pay one bill every day.
- I will set a timer on my phone to meditate for two minutes.
- I will run in place for two minutes.
- The first two minutes of my meal will be spent eating vegetables.
- I will write in my journal for two minutes.
- I will make the bed in two minutes.
- When I feel too tired to hang up or fold a clothing item, I will remind myself that it will take less than two minutes to put it where it belongs.
- If I am tempted to put off a project, I will set a timer for two minutes and work on it until the timer goes off.

CHECK YOUR BAROMETERS

Barometers measure atmospheric pressure in the environment and help us predict changes in the weather. They allow us to understand more fully what's happening and prepare ourselves accordingly.

Each of us has our own built-in barometers, too, yet so often, we forget to check them.

I live with a diagnosis of multiple sclerosis, and I'm grateful that it gives me the push I need to ensure that I'm checking my barometers. I know now to watch for signs that I'm getting too stressed, overworked, and fatigued— over the last 20 years of my MS, I've learned to watch for those warning signs and make the necessary adjustments. A few bad relapses have taught me that if I don't pay attention to the little whispers, my nervous system will end up screaming to get my attention.

Knowing your personal barometers means checking in with yourself to understand what's going on and better prepare for what's coming. Your body will often send you messages that something is off through things like fatigue, headaches, and gastrointestinal issues. Your emotions do, too. If you are irritable, or snapping at people, or more frustrated than usual, those could all be signs that you need to do a self check-in.

Think of our built-in physical, mental, and emotional barometers as instruments to measure the pressures of our lives; they help us better understand the effects of the challenges we're weathering—and let us know when there is a serious storm brewing, too.

Our barometers can also let us know when we're in a low-pressure system, too: when lingering boredom or ambivalence might signal that it's time to stretch ourselves or embark on something new.

Do you have a method for checking in with yourself to prepare for what's coming? How do you gauge your inner pressure and tension? What are the signs that the pressure within your mind may lead to a storm? What dissipates pressure in your life—joy, laughter, a sunny day? What indicators help you to know when enough is enough?

These are all important questions to consider; if we don't pay attention to our inner barometers, we may not see what's coming and may be devastated by the results.

TRY THESE

Here is a series of questions to consider that can help you check your barometers. Keep these in mind on a regular basis, so that if something changes, you have the notice you need.

1. At home:

    - What is working well in our home right now?
    - Are conversations healthy and uplifting in our home?
    - What does the most unhappy person in our home need from me?
    - Are household duties well balanced among the residents?

- What are the indicators that something needs to be adjusted?
- Are current schedules life-giving or challenging?
- Do all residents feel seen, heard, and loved in our home?
- Is there a conversation that needs to occur and how can I help to start that dialogue?
- What do I need to do to feel more peace at home?

2. At work:

- What parts of my work do I love?
- Which projects cause me the most stress?
- Which people trigger tension in me?
- What would it take to do more of what I love?
- What needs to happen to reduce tension in my work relationships?
- What indicators tell me that I need to take a break?
- How will I know when it is time to find a new job?

3. For your physical well-being:

- Are there indicators telling me I am not paying enough attention to my health?
- What happens when I don't get enough sleep?
- How do I know when I need to adjust my nutrition?
- How do I feel when I drink more water?
- What good comes from exercise and movement?
- What pain in my body needs to be addressed?
- How do I quiet my racing mind and worried brain?

- What happens to everyone around me if I don't care for my physical and mental health?

4. For your spiritual well-being:

   - Is the pace at which I am living right now sustainable?
   - Do my work and relationships feed my soul?
   - Do I feel aligned with a meaningful purpose?
   - How do I know my work matters?
   - Am I an instrument of peace, encouragement, and compassion to those who surround me?
   - Am I living my potential?
   - Am I someone that I admire and respect?

CONSIDER YOUR DNA

One Memorial Day weekend a few years ago, I went with my family to visit the cemetery where four generations of my relatives are buried. It's a beautiful place, situated in the Flint Hills of Kansas between two rolling pastures.

I listened as my mother told my children stories about each generation, much like my grandfather had done with me. There were stories of wars, diseases, and tragedies; of marriages, miracles, and fond memories. Generation after generation, we come back to remember our ancestors and share these same tales.

As I stood at the graves of my grandparents, I thought about all they had experienced in their lives. They grew up as children of the Depression era and went on to become farmers and cattle ranchers. Life for them was often hard.

As we remember those family members who came before us, it's also important to remember that their experiences live on through us and affect us in ways we might not fully understand.

There's a relatively new area of science called epigenetics, which suggests that the lives of your ancestors are imprinted onto your DNA. The stress they endured, the choices they made, their experiences, their worries—even their thought processes—all of it has made a genetic mark on your DNA.

Epigenetics tells us that behaviors and tendencies can be passed down for generations. Scientists continue to study which biological markers can cause genes to switch on or off, and how that switch is passed down in our DNA structure.

For example, a relative who lived through the Great Depression and experienced great financial stress may show up in you as an irrational fear of running out of money. As a coach, I take into consideration the effect epigenetics might have when a client can't find a cause for deep fears or behavioral tendencies.

To better understand ourselves, it helps to consider the generations that came before us and what they may have experienced. You may have been shaped by them more than you realize.

If you were adopted or don't know your biological ancestry, consider the influence of the people in your adoptive or foster families. Their experiences shaped you as well, which impacts the DNA you pass on to your children.

Pause today to think about what you might be carrying from the generations who came before you. It may help you become more intentional about living life from a place of self-awareness, interconnectedness, and hope.

Above all, give yourself grace and know that some things are out of your control.

TRY THESE

1. Think of a few family members from a prior generation whom you admire the most.

   - What do you admire about them?
   - How are you similar in your personalities, motivations, and desires?
   - How do you imagine they would guide you today?

2. Consider which family members have had the greatest influence upon you.

- What are you grateful to have learned from them?
- What did they teach you?
- What would they want their legacy to be?
- How would they want you to live your life?

3. Go back a generation or two in your family.

- What themes come to mind? (*Examples:* hardships, scarcity, family dynamics, illnesses, country of origin)
- What have these generations survived?
- What brought them joy?
- What would they want their legacy to be?

MOVE FROM DISCIPLINE TO DEVOTION

One year, I noticed there were several areas of my life in which I thought I needed more discipline—eating, exercising, writing, finishing home projects, staying organized. And yet, I noticed resistance to the thought of "discipline." It felt so punishing. Like I was doing something wrong.

I started thinking a little deeper about what would motivate me to do these things—I knew I would feel better, but I needed to stop punishing myself.

That's when a realization hit me: maybe it was devotion I needed to seek, instead of discipline. If I was devoted to my health, I would make better food and exercise choices. If I was devoted to helping people, I would write more to share my work. If I was devoted to order and calm in my home, I would finish house projects and stay organized.

And that's when I decided to move away from being disciplined and try to be devoted instead.

"Devotion" has a hopeful, inspiring tone to it. If we feel like we have to "be disciplined" about something, that's not a compassionate attitude—it's hard and heavy and brings to mind deprivation and punishment.

Devotion is driven by hope; discipline is driven by failure. Discipline feels like a push: what do you have to do? Devotion feels like a pull: what do you want to do?

Being devoted is also more self-compassionate, and research shows that when we take a compassionate tone with ourselves, we're more likely to achieve our goals.[26]

If you have a goal, see if you can't shift your thoughts. Ask yourself:

- "What do I value?"
- "What am I devoted to?"
- "Why is this important to me?"

Looking at your goal through the lens of devotion may help you get to the bigger thing—like being healthy versus losing weight, for example.

From the opera singer Luciano Pavarotti: "People think I'm disciplined. It is not discipline. It is devotion. There is a great difference."[27]

The idea of being devoted, rather than disciplined, may help motivate you more, help you accomplish more, and help you be a whole lot nicer to yourself along the way.

TRY THESE

First, consider what you're already devoted to. Then, think of a few goals you have, and the tasks you feel you "should" do in order to fulfill them: the things that make you feel like you lack discipline. Can any of the things you're devoted to help pull you toward those goals? See if you can work toward authentic desire instead of obligation, and let the "should's fade away.

---

[26] Elizabeth Sanders, "To Reach Your Goals, Embrace Self-Compassion," *Harvard Business Review*, February 2022. Retrieved from https://hbr.org/2022/02/to-reach-your-goals-embrace-self-compassion.

[27] Luciano Pavarotti and William Wright, *Pavarotti: My Own Story* (New York: Grand Central Publishing, 1982).

1. What are five things or people you know you are devoted to?

    -
    -
    -
    -
    -

2. Old thinking: I should _____.
   New thinking: I am devoted to _____.

3. Repeat step two for each of the five things or people you are devoted to.

ADJUST YOUR TRUTH-TELLING

From a young age, we're taught to always be truthful. The reality is, that's not always the best course of action. You actually don't always have to tell the truth. Depending on the situation, self-protection is just as important. Discernment is not dishonesty.

Sometimes, even though it doesn't feel like it, you might actually be strengthening your relationships when you hold back the truth. Laying it all out can be overwhelming, especially for new relationships. It can also leave you feeling vulnerable and emotionally raw.

A client once taught me a metaphor she had learned to help determine the level of vulnerability that felt best with different people in her life. Imagine each relationship as that person visiting you at home. Would you feel most comfortable if they stayed outside on the sidewalk? Would you want them to stay on your front porch? Would you invite them inside your doorway? Would you invite them all the way in to sit down and talk?

The truth is not something you have to give up the moment you meet someone, but rather something earned as your relationship grows stronger and you're able to be more vulnerable.

If holding back a truth feels dishonest, think of it as discernment rather than dishonesty. Discernment is being thoughtful about when to share the truth.

In my experience, there are three levels of truth that are important to discern:

- Being truthful with acquaintances.
  Tell acquaintances enough truth to maintain optimal connection—share less to keep your distance, but share more to draw them closer. Reveal truth slowly as you are getting to know someone; test how much they can handle at any given time before deciding how to proceed.
- Being truthful with loved ones.
  Tell loved ones as much truth as you can. Lying to please someone means giving up the chance to connect with them; it always pushes us away, even when we think it will bring us closer. Truth leads to healing, but it can also rock the boat for a bit. You get to decide whether it is worth telling the truth versus tolerating the distance in the relationship.
- Being truthful with yourself.
  This is the most important truth-telling of all. Dishonesty with yourself can be catastrophic. Telling the truth about your childhood, disappointments, feelings, desires, etc. will free you from the burdens of lying to yourself. Then you'll be free to move forward and begin to trust yourself again.

These clearly don't cover all circumstances and scenarios—truth-telling and preparing to tell someone the truth are unique, soul-searching processes.

We each have to decide how much truth to tell based on the relationships we desire. I've seen the truth bring people together, and I've also seen it end relationships. No matter what, it's up to you to determine what feels right. It isn't always an easy decision, though; consider talking it through with people you trust, like a therapist, mentor, coach, or loved one.

TRY THIS

Take some time to consider your truth-telling behaviors. If you notice some areas where you lack honesty, spend time asking yourself why. Explore what you are afraid of when it comes to telling the truth. Do not judge yourself too harshly, however; instead, observe how the truth could benefit your relationships or where it might not be necessary. And remember, you always know the best answer. Trust yourself.

Here are a few areas to consider:

How truthful should I be with acquaintances?

- What does this person really need to know?
- How will it benefit our relationship?
- Will I regret not sharing this if our relationship gets deeper?
- What is the best time to say what I want to share with them?

Am I truthful with loved ones?

- Do I tell white lies to avoid getting into trouble or disappointing someone?
- Am I afraid of telling people something they won't like to hear?
- Do I ever say I'll do something and then not follow through?
- Do I ever say things like "I'm fine" when I'm not really fine?

Am I truthful with myself?

- Do I make promises to myself that I don't keep?
- Is there something I'm afraid to know about myself?
- Am I hiding something from myself?
- Is there a question I'm afraid to ask myself?

REFLECT ON "UNTIL" MOMENTS

I was talking to a client in her 70's and she shared this story with me: "I believed that prayer worked until I was 14 years old and caring for my dying mother. As I was growing up, I was taught to pray and that my prayers would be answered. But when she got sick, I started praying at least every hour for God to save her, remove the disease, help her live, keep her alive, don't let her leave me all alone. None of it happened. I lost my precious mother when I was only 14. As a child, I believed in prayer until I couldn't anymore."

In our lives, we all have these "until..." moments:

- We believe things until they no longer ring true.
- We think about things one way until we learn more.
- We reject ideas until we open up and get more curious about them.
- We neglect ourselves until we learn to befriend ourselves.

Spend some time thinking about your "until..." moments in life. These are important pivots, evolutions, and growth areas that are worth honoring. Remember that we are all souls here in human school, learning every day how to do this thing called life. We are students, growing and learning, then growing and learning some more. Spend some time thinking about all that you have learned so far.

What have you started, stopped, or paused doing/thinking/being/saying because you learned something new?

The Jewish Talmud says: "Every blade of grass has its angel that bends over it and whispers, 'Grow, grow.'" I think this holds true for us too. Notice your own whispers of growth this week.

I _____ until...

Here are some verbs to fill in the blank to help you get started: I agreed, allowed, ate, believed, built, collected, compared, danced, defended, deserved, did, didn't, disagreed, dreamt, enjoyed, expected, feared, fit in, followed, had, hated, helped, ignored, invited, judged, kept, knew, laughed, lied, liked, listened, lived, loved, made, managed, needed, neglected, numbed, observed, offered, opened, paid, participated, passed, performed, played, promised, provided, qualified, questioned, quit, raised, recommended, refused, rejected, related, required, resisted, said, served, spoke, studied, thought, told, tolerated, trusted, underestimated, understood, upheld, used, waited, wanted, was, wished, worked

Some of these pivots come from hard-won wisdom. Some might reflect a disappointment, some might be transformed into something better, and some might remind you of your endless inner strength.

TRY THESE

1. Read through the list of words above slowly and notice the words that resonate with you or bring to mind a memory of a pivot in your life. Maybe write down the story of what you used to feel until you experienced something different. This exercise can help you connect some dots in your life. It can often be a missing piece in a puzzle you are trying to solve.

2. One of the women in a class I led through this exercise suggested using this "until..." list to start conversations with her friends and family the next time they are together. She is going to invite them to share their own pivot moments. Brilliant! We can do that too. It will likely lead to some great conversations and more meaningful connections with those we love.

BE YOUR FAVORITE SELF

From inspirational TV shows to books to Instagram-ready quotes, we hear a lot about how the path to happiness is "being your best self." What exactly does that mean, though: "best self?" Best to whom?

We already have so much pressure on us. So often, we feel like we're expected to be the best parent, the best spouse, the best friend, the best employee, and on and on. Our "best self" can feel like yet another thing we need to chase.

It is true that to find peace and joy, we must start by looking within. But we are also vastly complex individuals. So many versions of us exist through our lifetimes. How can we possibly pick the "best?" We all experience different chapters of life, with groups of people, environments and circumstances that change over time.

What's important is how you view yourself. Which version of you do you like the most? Which version feels the truest to you? Instead of being "your best self," are you being "your favorite self?"

I often use "my favorite self" as a journal prompt: "For Ginger to be her favorite self, this needs to happen today...." Then I can brainstorm ways that my favorite self might be able to show up through all the daily obligations, events, and activities on my schedule.

To identify your favorite self, think about those times when you are in your element, your true self, proud of yourself, and most authentically you. Strive to do whatever it takes to be your most favorite version of you.

TRY THESE

1. To identify your favorite self, ask yourself a few of these questions:

    - Where did you feel like you were most thriving?
    - When did you feel most proud of yourself?
    - When were you in a role most aligned with your strengths?
    - When did you most feel like you were living your full potential?
    - When did you most feel like you were living in line with your values?
    - When could you most feel yourself stretching and growing?
    - When were you working on projects you cared about?
    - When do you feel the most alive and authentically you?
    - What does it mean to be "in your element?"
    - When are you most engaged with life?
    - When are you in your most natural state—not pretending to be someone else to please others?
    - How would you describe you at your best?
    - What words would you use to describe your "truest essence?"

2. Now visualize that version of you in the future: where are you? What are you doing? How did you get there? Who are you with? How do you feel in-

side? Keep that visual in mind and challenge yourself each morning by asking: "how can I be my favorite self today?" See if you can't find opportunities every day to work a little more toward being your very favorite self.

SAY "NO" MORE OFTEN

A number of my clients struggle with saying "no." They worry that they will hurt somebody, when often, they only hurt themselves.

Recently, I spoke to a group of physicians. One talked about burnout; often, she had to catch up on paperwork when she got home instead of saying no to coworkers in order to have time to do it while at work. Sometimes it was another person asking a question that could easily be looked up, or a shift she felt like she had to cover when someone else didn't show up.

The reality was, she could and should have said no. Her coworker could try to figure out the answer herself; she could check in later with her. Someone not showing up wasn't her responsibility; they had an HR department who could figure that out. She needed to say no in order to say yes to her health and well-being. No to burnout. Yes to taking proper care of herself.

There are a number of other service-oriented people I talk with who struggle when it comes to saying no to commitments, projects, events, and opportunities. The important thing is to realize that you're actually saying yes. Yes to your own time. Yes to your health. Yes to your emotional well-being. Yes to your family. Yes to your interests. Yes to you.

I love what inspirational author and speaker Iyanla Vanzant has to say about this: "You have a right to say no. Most of us have very weak 'no' muscles. We feel guilty for saying no. We get ostracized and challenged for saying no, so we forget it's our choice. Your 'no' muscle has to be built up to get to a place where you can say, 'I don't care if that's what you want. I don't want that. No.'"[28]

Even Apple co-founder Steve Jobs was a proponent of saying no: "I'm actually as proud of the things we haven't done as the things I have done. Innovation is saying no to 1,000 things."[29]

Whether you want to take more time for your well-being, time for your family or friends, or time to pursue your own interests and goals, "no" is always a great way to start.

TRY THESE

Here are 36 ways to say no. Read them, practice them, then challenge yourself to use one this week. With time, they'll get easier and you'll find yourself happier and more peaceful doing the things you really want to do.

- No, I'm not able to attend.
- I'm sorry, but I have to miss this one.
- Let me think about it; when do you need to know?
- I can't take on a big role right now, but I can help you with....
- I appreciate you thinking of me, but I have to say no.
- I don't have any capacity to take on new projects.
- I'm trying to filter my commitments through my top values, and this is outside of my focus right now.
- I'm booked until _____, but check in with me after that.

---

[28] Iyanla Vanzant, "Iyanla Says...Claim Your Joy Now!", *ESSENCE Magazine*, January 3, 2013.
[29] Steve Jobs, Apple Worldwide Developers Conference, 1997.

- I can't help you, but you might want to ask _____; she mentioned wanting to get more involved.
- I promised my family that I wouldn't add anything to my calendar, so I have to say no.
- Thank you, but I have to pass on this.
- I wish I could be in two places at once; sorry I can't attend.
- I'm not the best fit for what you need; I suggest....
- I made a New Year's resolution to _____ and I need to honor that.
- We are maxed out and need to say no.
- I won't be much fun, so I'm going to say no.
- Unfortunately, it's not a good time.
- I love my time with you, but can't do late nights anymore. Could we meet for lunch?
- Committing to this will add too much stress, and I'm trying to take better care of myself.
- I can't do that right now.
- I only want to be away from home one night/day/weekend a week/month/year so I can't add another one.
- My heart just isn't in this anymore; it's time to hand it over to someone else.
- I'm really working on listening to myself and I don't feel like this is what I'm meant to do right now.
- I feel like I should give someone else this opportunity.
- This is something I need to let go of.
- I want to do it, but can't right now. Can we talk about it for next year?
- I'm not taking on any commitments until my kids go back to school/start kindergarten/graduate.
- I'm focused on _____ right now and have to say no.
- I want to help you, but we need to make sure it benefits both of us going forward.

- This isn't a good time for either of us; let's postpone until both of our schedules improve.
- My biggest priority right now is _____ and I want to honor that by saying no to this.
- I can't be there.
- I'm sorry, but no.
- I'm not available.
- I can't go.
- No.

UNDERSTAND TRUST

I've noticed in myself and my clients that growing in self-trust and trusting others is a really hard part of being human. Trust is comprised of three parts: safety, belonging, and mattering. When we think about trusting our partners, bosses, leaders, coworkers, teammates, and friends, it helps to think of these three elements as necessary in trusting the other person.

We trust someone when we can honestly say:

- I feel safe with you and feel that you would never intend to harm me.
- I feel that we belong together and we both recognize this relationship as important.
- I feel that I matter to you and believe you would consider my needs or feelings.

Think about the relationships in your life and explore this idea of trust based on feeling a sense of safety, belonging, and mattering. It might help to give language to what we are feeling when we struggle to trust someone.

These three elements can also help us explore trusting ourselves. Most of us find it challenging to trust that we can make good decisions, learn something new, keep our promises, fulfill our goals, be successful in our careers, stick to a health plan, pick the right partner, raise children well, and so many other things that creep into our brain as doubts.

How do these statements feel to you?

- I feel safe with myself and free from harsh inner criticism, which can be a form of self-harm.
- I feel like I belong in my body and am okay being alone with myself.
- I feel that I matter and will give myself the same level of care I give to others.

It might be good to spend some time exploring if being intentional about these things would help you develop a greater sense of self-trust. And, like always, make these statements your own. Put them into your own words. What would it take for you to feel like you are safe, belong, and matter to yourself?

We thrive in environments where we feel safe, we know we belong, and we can see that we matter. Make sure it feels like that inside your own brain. If it doesn't, explore the beliefs you have about yourself and what your thoughts are doing—they can always be adjusted and altered so that you can learn to trust yourself.

When we focus on developing self-trust, we can't help but notice an increase in confidence, resilience, empowerment, and worthiness. And, with a solid level of self-trust, you don't have to be afraid of trusting others—you've got your own back if they let you down!

Self-trust can be an antidote to anxious thinking—see if you can lessen your worries by saying: "no matter what happens, I can figure it out."

Trust yourself—you are more ready for your next step than you think you are.

TRY THIS

Take some time to consider where trust is most difficult for you. It may depend on the person or situation.
It might be a life-long struggle based on early circumstances that caused you to be skeptical of trust. Identify
where and why trust is hard. Then explore what you need.
Safety, belonging, and mattering are three elements of
trust, but there may be something else that comes up for
you. Imagine how you would feel if this were addressed
and improved. Learn to trust yourself first, then trusting
others will come a little easier—when you have your own
back, you know you can handle anything someone else
throws at you.

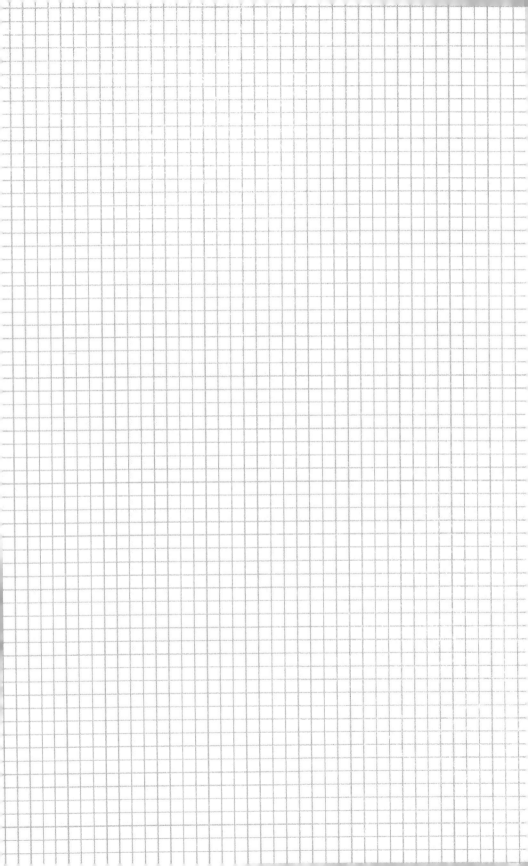

FIND MORE ENERGY

As human beings, we naturally have fluctuating energy levels, but we hold more power than we think we do to help our energy levels rise and fall. Sometimes we want more energy, sometimes we know we need to dial it back a bit.

The practices in this section are intended to help you regulate your energy levels and make the adjustments you need to feel the way you want to feel. Some of these ideas will sound familiar and some will be new to you. Different seasons of life require different energies. I hope you will come back to this section throughout your life and remind yourself that you can tap into more energy when you need it.

Energy is everything. We are all orbs of energy walking around this planet. Learning how to work with that energy, harness it, and manage it is one of our greatest tools for survival. And I believe that after we die, our energy continues—it just changes form. Instead of contained in a body, it is free to travel. I imagine my energy will help align things for my children, and then I might become a flower, then spend time as a tree, then make funny shapes in the clouds for children to notice, then I might be that orb that shows up in your beach sunset photos. Energy is never deleted, it just changes forms. I hope you can still notice the presence of those you love with you in a new form. My wish for you is that these practices help you live the energetic life you desire.

ADJUST YOUR
EMOTIONAL FREQUENCIES

Do you wake up with energy some days, while other days you feel zapped?

There are many factors that contribute to our energy levels. One of those factors is our emotions. Our feelings can cause an increase or a decrease in the energy we produce. The more positive our emotions, the more energy we generate. The more adverse the emotion, the lower our energy will be. As human beings, we are both contributing energy to others and affected by the energy of those around us.

Emotions are vibrations of energy. A way to think of it is: E-motion = Energy in Motion.

Every emotion has a vibrational frequency. It is like a radio station frequency—as you flip through stations, music is coming over radio waves into your car. There is country, pop, hip-hop, oldies, gospel—all on different radio frequencies we might enjoy. Think about different energies like these radio stations; there is a unique frequency for each emotion we feel. Some have a strong vibration and some have a low vibration. But all are a vibration of energy in our bodies.

Psychiatrist Dr. David Hawkins conducted a long-term study of energy fields and levels of consciousness from 1965 to 1994. He used scientific theories and hypotheses from the fields of kinesiology, psychology, spirituality, and quantum physics. His book *Power vs. Force* summarizes his methodology and findings. He created a "Map of Consciousness" to measure energy as it relates to our emotions, worldviews, images of God, and the effects of our energy on others.[30]

Dr. Hawkins found that the lowest-energy emotions are shame, guilt, apathy, grief, and fear. Shame was found to be the lowest energetic frequency in Hawkins's studies. Every human is going to experience these low-level emotions, yet we don't want to stay there or we'll begin to experience exhaustion, despair, and hopelessness. Many of you have experienced the heavy exhaustion of grief—Hawkins's research explains why grief is so exhausting. It literally is taking a toll on your body. It isn't that we are doing anything wrong, but we should notice how draining these emotions can be to our energy levels.

The highest-energy emotions are enlightenment, peace, joy, and love. In the middle of the chart is reason, acceptance, willingness, neutrality, courage, pride, anger, and desire. Desire and anger are higher vibrations than fear because they come with forward movement. When we have a desire, we are motivated to seek and grow. When we are angry, we have energy to process and fight. Those are higher-energy emotions than the stuckness that comes with shame, guilt, and fear.

Pay attention to what you notice about your own energy and the energy of people around you. If you are feeling low on energy, try to become more cognizant of your emotions. Strive to move yourself "up" the energetic spectrum into more life-giving emotions and notice the increase in energy you feel as a result.

There is a chicken and egg phenomenon here too. If you move your physical energy higher through nutrition, exercise, and sleep, then your emotions improve too. If you are aware of your emotions and work with your brain

---

[30] David Hawkins, *Power vs. Force* (California: Hay House, 2014).

to move emotionally toward love, peace, and joy, then your physical energy increases too.

In our relationships, energy works like a magnet. The higher you rise on the emotional energy spectrum, the more you will attract people into your presence who match your energetic vibration.

Experiment with tuning into your emotions and noticing how they affect your energy.

There is much more you could learn about these concepts in Dr. Hawkins's research, but for now, think about how your individual emotional energy might affect your relationships, your physical body, and your energy levels. Then think about how the collective energy of our country affects our politics, businesses, economy, society, religions, creativity, innovation, environment, and virtually everything we do. Dr. Hawkins found that the emotions of a group of people can drain energy from individuals and societies.

If we each start paying more attention, we can raise our collective consciousness. If we each rise toward compassion, kindness, love, joy, and peace, we not only help ourselves, but we also help everyone around us. Love begets love.

TRY THESE

1. Keep a log in the notes app of your phone or in your calendar of how you feel each day, emotionally and physically. See if you can notice the correlation of your emotions to energy. What were your emotions on the days when you felt high energy or low energy? How might you adjust your emotions to increase your energy? How are those around you affecting your emotions and energy levels? Are there adjustments you can make by minimizing exposure to certain people or changing your environment periodically?

2. Work with a professional to free yourself from feelings of shame and guilt. Process your fears with someone you trust. Heal old emotional wounds so that you can experience more joy, peace, and love in your life. You don't have to go it alone; seek out help in moving out of shame and into peace. You deserve to feel good on the inside and outside.

HALT WHEN YOU'RE FEELING OFF

"HALT" is an acronym a friend of mine shared with me after he learned it while in addiction recovery. It stands for: "Am I...Hungry, Angry, Lonely, or Tired?" And it's a great way to pause when you're upset to see if something else is going on—if what you think is the problem isn't the problem after all.

Many times when we're out of sorts, or snapping at people, or feeling yucky, or tempted to give in to something that's not healthy, what's really going on is HALT: we're hungry, or we're angry, or we're lonely, or we're tired.

Saying "HALT" to ourselves helps us to pause and tune into what we're feeling and needing at that moment. Once our needs are met, we can make more informed decisions and be more compassionate, kind, grace-giving, and patient with others (not to mention, more compassionate with ourselves, too.).

When you're feeling off, think "HALT" and ask yourself: "am I hungry, angry, lonely, or tired?" Check in with these four areas and do your best to take care of whatever needs come up. "HALT" is one of the most effective practices to keep in your toolbox of self-awareness.

It's also a great practice to use before you make a big decision or have a crucial conversation. Everything feels better when you've taken care of your own needs first.

TRY THESE

The next time you're feeling snappy, or easily frustrated, or otherwise not yourself, be proactive and think through each of the following "HALT" categories (to be extra proactive, write "HALT" on a note as a reminder and keep it nearby.).

1. Hungry:
   Do you have a headache, low energy, or low blood sugar because you need to eat something? It might be time to re-fuel to get through the rest of the day. You might also be emotionally hungry. Do you need to have a conversation with someone who brings you comfort? Are you bored and hungry for a project? Are you feeling empty and drained? Tune into these feelings and notice what you need to do to nourish yourself.

2. Angry:
   Are you stewing on something someone said? Is it ruining your day? Are you frustrated with something that feels outside of your control? Are you ruminating on something that is bothering you? Talk out your anger with a safe person. Move your body and burn off any anger-induced energy. Try to understand the source of your anger and then consider what fear might lie beneath. Many times, we are angry because we are afraid of something. What we think we are angry about may not be the real problem; it may be that a deeper fear has been triggered.

3. Lonely:
   Loneliness can creep in even when we are around other people; it's also an inner feeling of isolation. It

can be a feeling of not being included in something, a sense that you are an outsider to a group, or a feeling of not belonging. For some of us, feeling lonely causes us to be angry rather than sad. We could be angry with the people who are leaving us out. We all want to be seen, heard, and loved. If we feel lonely, it might be because we aren't feeling seen, heard, and loved. What do you need to do to move toward feeling more connected with someone?

4. Tired:

   Your brain, heart, and muscles are working all day long to propel you through life. It's understandable if you feel tired. There is a lot going on inside your body and in the world around you that is exhausting. Being tired is not a weakness; it's a signal from your body that you need to rest. Tiredness is our fuel gauge and we must learn to recognize when we need to pause and refill our tank. When you recognize tiredness, try a few minutes of meditation, a quick nap, or a brisk walk, or make a plan to go to bed earlier than normal. We can't think clearly when we are overtired. Pause and recharge.

SAVE YOUR BEST HOURS

Years ago, after I came home several days in a row zapped by fatigue and easily frustrated, my husband pulled me aside and said gently: "we want your best hours, but you seem to give those away to everyone else."

He was right. This was true, and I needed to hear it.

At that time, all my energy went into my clients from nine to five, but on the drive home, I would start to relax and realize how tired I was. Then I'd drag my tired self through the evening with my family; my most important people were getting my worst hours.

It's not something we do just to our people, either—we forget to give our best hours to the projects and activities that are most important to us, too. Our energy and enthusiasm naturally rise and dip, depending on the time of day.

And recognizing and honoring those rhythms is so important, not only for the health of our relationships, but for our own health, too. Taking time to reflect on how you spend your days can help you determine who or what is getting your highest levels of energy, optimism, and creativity, and give you the chance to make adjustments to honor your needs and the needs of those you love.

For example: if you want to write a book, what are your most creative hours?

Are you better when you first wake up? Is it in the evening when the house is quiet?

It's not always going to be easy—you might have to sacrifice something that doesn't feed you (i.e. that time we all waste on our phones)—but you'll better set yourself up for success if you recognize when you're at your best.

If your people are at work or in school during your best hours, then think of ways that you can try to conserve some energy for them, so that you can begin and end the day well with them.

The things you love doing deserve your best hours. The people you love deserve your best hours. Make some adjustments if you need to, and make the mundane tasks of life work around your best hours instead of stealing them away.

TRY THIS

Spend some time noticing where you feel the best energy during the day. During that block of time, devote yourself to something you love. Block the day into sections, and note how you feel during each. What's your energy level? How optimistic are you? Are you drained? Check in with yourself during the early morning, mid-morning, afternoon, early evening, and late evening. What do you notice? How might you be able to adapt your schedule to match up your best times with the people and passions that most deserve them?

MAKE YOUR CHECKLIST

A friend of mine has a note taped to the door leading out to her garage, with three questions: "Do you have your backpack? Do you have your lunch? Do you have your homework?" As the mom to three young kids, she needed a quick checklist to help them remember what to bring to school each day.

As adults, we could use a few quick checklists of our own, too. So often, we forget to check off our baseline needs and end up feeling not quite like ourselves.

Over and over, I hear the following statements from clients:

- "I'm tired of having low energy."
- "I feel like I am walking around in a fog."
- "Everything just seems off."

That's when I have them create a list of the basic things they need to remember to do to feel their best. They're the five or so things that should always take top priority to help prevent you from feeling off track or overwhelmed.

A checklist of your basic needs can help you tune into yourself, which will help you sustain clear thinking, loving relationships, and self-compassion, and live into your full potential. Think of it as your recipe for how to be your favorite self.

TRY THIS

When you feel out of sorts and not yourself, do a quick check of the following things. Add items of your own to this list and post it somewhere you will see often.

- Did I get any fresh air today?
- Have I been eating nourishing food?
- Did I talk to someone I love today?
- Am I getting enough quality sleep?
- What have I done to move and stretch my body today?
- Am I talking to myself kindly?
- Do I need to drink more water?
- What else do I need in order to have a good day?

SHIFT FROM "WANT TO" TO "WILL"

There's a practice I learned years ago from my coach, Sherry (yes, even coaches have coaches!), that's invaluable when it comes to achieving your goals. And it all comes down to getting the mysterious inner-workings of your brain in on the action. It's one of my very favorite ways to get unstuck.

When we want to meet a goal or achieve something that's important to us, we have desire. But that doesn't always translate into action. We tell ourselves things like: "I want to get a promotion" or "I want to be healthier." But what is more effective, what makes our brains sit up and listen, is when we say: "I will get a promotion" or "I will be healthier."

The difference between "want to" and "will" is the difference between desire and action. When our brain hears "will," it's wired to actively look for ways to help us meet those goals—to put connections together to propel us forward.

By shifting your "want to" statements to "will" statements, you are telling your brain: "I don't just want this, I'm going to make it happen." If you state your intent to act, your brain will jumpstart into action. It's like hiring your own personal helper that resides in your subconscious.

So if I switch from saying "I want to go on a walk today" to "I will go on a walk today," my brain will help me figure out when I'm going to do it, what

I'll wear, where I'll go, etc. It helps me by confirming the action, without me even realizing it's doing so.

Going from "want to" to "will" is a magical way to get unstuck and work toward meeting your personal goals. It's a small change that brings with it a powerful shift in commitment—one that brings hope, dedication, and, most importantly, action. Plus, what can it hurt to try it? Even if it's a big goal, your brain is right there, ready and waiting.

TRY THIS

What is something you want to do today? This week? This year? Say it out loud, but replace "want to" with "will." You'll hear your brain take on more power. Here are some examples to get you thinking:

- I *will* go for a walk today.
- I *will* be creative.
- I *will* travel more.
- I *will* figure out my purpose.
- I *will* pursue a new career.
- I *will* make new friends.
- I *will* make a big change.
- I *will* write a book.
- I *will* feel peaceful.

EAT FOR ENERGY

Did you know your brain burns about 300 calories a day to function properly? And your liver requires 200 calories a day, and your heart and kidneys need at least 440, not to mention all of the other organs, tissues, and muscles in your glorious body.

Another fun fact: when you sleep, you burn about 50 calories an hour. When you are just sitting, you burn 75 calories an hour. This is just an average—some of you are burning way more than that in your busy lives.

So, check this out—if you sleep for eight hours at 50 calories an hour, that is 400 calories overnight. If you sit still and don't do any major thinking for 16 hours a day, at 75 calories per hour, that would be 1200 calories. If you didn't move for 24 hours, just slept and sat, you would need 1600 calories to support your body's functions! Astonishing!

I went down this calorie rabbit hole with a teen client. She came into my office after school and I could tell she was having trouble focusing on our conversation. I excused myself, then brought in a basket of snacks and a water for her. She said she was starving and had skipped lunch. When I asked why, her answer was "prom" with a head tilt. I looked at her with loving, understanding, frustrated-at-our-society, been-there-myself eyes. I get it. We all do. Many of us have a messed-up relationship with food and our bodies.

While she was snacking and I was waiting for her brain to regain function, I googled "how many calories does your brain require to function?" I easily found sources from Harvard Medical, National Institutes of Health, and the UK all saying our bodies need at least 1,400 calories a day just for baseline organ function.[31]

I rattled off the numbers to her and we were both amazed. We had no idea what our bodies needed. I'm halfway through my life and have never considered what my brain, liver, heart, and kidneys actually need to keep me alive.

As she was on her third bag of trail mix, I could see her eyes brighten. I literally watched her cognitive function return. We spent the rest of the session talking about how she can thrive if she eats. I challenged her to triple the amount of protein she normally eats. I'm sharing this with you because she texted me a few days later, saying she felt more energy than she had in a long time. She said she was feeling like a zombie and now she felt alive again. I asked her permission to share this with you.

We deserve energy. Eat for fuel. Eat for your brain function. I want your organs to be fed so you can be the awesome person you are here to be. Eat, move, thrive!

TRY THIS

Here are some high-energy foods that will give you a boost this week: bananas, eggs, oatmeal, quinoa, sweet potatoes, fish, almonds, Greek yogurt, lentils, chicken, spinach, dark chocolate, shrimp, black beans, protein powder smoothies.

---

[31] Zimian Wang et al, "Specific metabolic rates of major organs and tissues across adulthood: evaluation by mechanistic model of resting energy expenditure," *The American Journal of Clinical Nutrition* 92, no. 6 (2010): 1369-77. doi:10.3945/ajcn.2010.29885.

You can google more ideas for lean protein and high-energy foods. Focus on eating for energy and see what you notice in your body and mind.

Make it a priority to fill your day with high-energy protein and notice your energy increase.

MOVE YOUR BODY

In the past, I haven't had a friendly relationship with exercise. I used to look at it only as an avenue for weight loss. It felt like punishment.

Then I read a fascinating book that talked about how moving your body is one of the most natural ways to alleviate symptoms of anxiety, depression, and loneliness. In *The Joy of Movement,* health psychologist and Stanford University lecturer Dr. Kelly McGonigal writes about the connection between health and well-being: "People who are regularly active have a stronger sense of purpose, and they experience more gratitude, love, and hope. They feel more connected to their communities, and are less likely to suffer from loneliness or become depressed." McGonigal teaches that hope, connection with others, and inner courage all increase when we move our bodies. [32]

Now, after learning about the innumerable benefits of movement, I look forward to the chance to be active, understanding that it helps me feel better—both physically and mentally.

I have a client who says that after his evening walk, he finds that his marriage is better. He admits that nothing changes over that time period other than the chance to spend some time outside, gain perspective, and generate

---

[32] Kelly McGonigal, *The Joy of Movement* (New York: Avery, 2021).

some endorphins. As a result, upon his return to his house, life always seems brighter. What he's experiencing is another one of Dr. McGonigal's research findings, that "neurochemistry of movement helps us bond and connect more with others."

Science proves that you literally feel better about your relationships after a session of movement: Exercise improves mental health by reducing anxiety, depression, and negative mood and by improving self-esteem and cognitive function. Exercise has also been found to alleviate symptoms such as low self-esteem and social withdrawal.[33]

There are so many ways to be active: going for a walk, dancing, cycling, riding horses, yoga, hiking, climbing, swimming, surfing, running, skiing, skating, playing a sport, lifting weights...the list goes on and on. See if you can pick an exercise you like to do to help change your relationship from "have to" to "get to." Can it be a form of joy for you? Can you see it as mental and physical medicine? Can you look at it as a way to become closer to others? Can you gift it to yourself? Could it become a spiritual practice?

We spend a lot of time in our heads thinking. But it's just as important to spend an equal amount of time in our bodies moving. If we remember to give our bodies some attention, gratitude, and love, they'll be even better at carrying our souls through life.

Movement is as essential to our bodies as sleep, food, water, and oxygen. Freedom, power, gratitude, hope, strength, grace, and connection—all of those feelings can come just from a little more time being active.

Ask your body what it needs today.

---

[33] Ashish Sharma et al, "Exercise for mental health," *Primary Care Companion to the Journal of Clinical Psychiatry* 8, no. 2 (2006): 106. doi:10.4088/pcc.v08n0208a.

TRY THIS

Find a place where you can be alone with no one watching you, to help you feel confident and comfortable. Close your eyes and tune into your body. What part of you feels like it wants to move? Maybe circle your hands, arms, hips, head, and legs. Do you want to twist, stretch, reach, kick, wiggle, or lightly dance? Move around in space. No judgment, just movement. Give yourself a few minutes to ease into this—it might feel strange and take you some time to relax. Allow your body to flow and move for as long as it wants to. If this feels good, try to do it again tomorrow. Maybe add music. See if you can loosen up mentally and physically as you listen to your body.

If you are unable to move freely due to physical limitations, move in a way that works for you. Here are some things to try when you can't make big movements: lower and raise your head slowly, open and close your jaw, furrow and release your forehead, smile a few times, touch your ear to your shoulder, make a fist and then open your fingers as wide as you can, circle your ankles, wiggle your toes. Get creative with the ways that your body can move. Small movements are enough to connect you to yourself and notice the benefits of movement.

THINK "GRACE. SPACE. PACE."

When I was in business school, I took a marketing class where the professor led us through several examples of famous ad slogans. One was used by Jaguar Cars in the 1960s: "Grace...Space...Pace." It did more than sell cars; it conveyed the automaker's values. The design and elegance of their cars communicated grace; the extra legroom and large trunk translated to plenty of space; and the supercharged motor was all about speed and power. Historically, the slogan is often regarded as one of the greatest in automotive marketing history.

Years later, as I was launching my business as a coach, that slogan popped into my head. I had been thinking specifically about pace: was the rate at which I was working sustainable? Something clicked, and I realized: that famous slogan is also a great practice for double-checking your work/life balance.

I now use those three words all the time to remind myself to be compassionate, to weigh my priorities, and to consider how well I'm balancing my life. I ask myself:

- Am I showing grace toward myself and others?
- Does my schedule have space for the people and things most important to me?
- Is my pace of work and activities sustainable?

When the pace of my work consumes me, I am not giving my family the space they deserve in my schedule. Not to mention, I'm likely to become short-tempered and low on patience, which means I start showing less grace to everyone around me, too.

For all of us, it's a healthy practice to periodically reconsider how we're spending our time and energy. We all know the consequences of stress in our lives: physical ailments, burnout, anxiety, depression, ruined relationships—the list goes on and on. That's why it's so important to check in with ourselves (and those we love) in case we need to make adjustments.

TRY THIS

When you're feeling stretched or out of balance, ask yourself the following questions:

1. Grace:
    Am I too intense right now to be patient with others or be kind to myself? Do I see the good in other people, or do I see everything that is wrong with them?

2. Space:
    Does my schedule allow for space every day to feed my soul, have fun with my favorite people, spend time on projects that make me feel alive, and/or be still and quiet?

3. Pace:
    Is my current pace too fast, too slow, or working well to achieve my goals while also meeting my needs for thriving, healthy, strong relationships and a sense of inner peace?

ALTER EXPECTATIONS

Around the holiday season, there's always an uptick in the stress level of my clients. One, Liz, came to me with anxiety that was through the roof and threatening to ruin the holidays altogether. As we worked on pinpointing the root cause, it finally came out: she was worried about a tablecloth.

She'd ordered the tablecloth to use for a special family dinner, and it hadn't arrived yet. But what that tablecloth really represented was all the high expectations she held—the ones that now threatened to come tumbling down. Without it, the dinner wouldn't be perfect. And if the dinner wasn't perfect, then the holidays wouldn't be perfect.

There are so many times when we place high expectations on something—a holiday, a family gathering, a new school year, a new job, you name it—only for them not to be met, leaving us angry and disappointed.

Expectations zap our energy and steal our joy. That's why it's important to drop those expectations, one by one, until you get down all the way to zero. If you have zero expectations for how things will go or how people will behave, then you're more likely to avoid disappointment, resentment, and frustration. The very things that drain our energy.

I had Liz write down every expectation she had for the holidays, no matter how big or small, on separate pieces of paper. Then, one by one, she crumpled them up and let them go, saying "zero expectations" each time.

Letting go of your expectations doesn't mean letting go of your optimism, hope, and enthusiasm....it means meeting people as they are in the moment, accepting the situation for what it is, and rolling with what happens as it happens.

And, sure: we're never truly going to have zero expectations, but it's a great mantra to use. If you keep repeating it, you'll remind yourself to keep letting go.

Everything else will fall into place.

TRY THIS

When you're feeling stretched or out of balance, ask yourself the following questions:

1. Do you have an event coming up that's causing you stress? What expectations do you have that might be driving that stress? Write them out one by one on strips of paper. When you're done, go back through them and read each one aloud. Then, let them go, one by one, throwing them away and repeating "zero expectations" every time.

2. If you still find yourself feeling anxious, take a deep breath, place your hand on your heart, and say something encouraging to yourself. A phrase I like to use? "Good enough is truly good enough."

BURN THE PASTURE

One of my favorite places on the planet is the Flint Hills of Kansas, where my parents have a cattle and horse ranch. Every April, they burn the grassland so that in May the grass is more nutritious for cattle who "summer" in the Hills.

This spring ritual of burning grassland began with Native Americans who lived in the Midwestern Plains. They noticed that after a grass fire caused by a lightning strike, within a few days, green, dense, nutritious bluestem grass would cover the land. Bison herds gravitated to the new grass, as did other wildlife. Thus, Native Americans began the original practice of what is today called "controlled burning" or "prescribed burning."

This type of burning helps to reduce wildfires that spread quickly in areas of dead grass and wild cedar trees. It also removes the underbrush that blocks sunlight from allowing new grass to grow. And, in naturally removing weeds, burning reduces the use of pesticides.

Wild animals and cattle who will summer on the land benefit from the nutritious bluestem, which has deep roots and thus grows quickly and evenly after a burn. About two weeks after burning, new life begins to show and the land has a cast of bright green again.

This got me thinking about what we may need to burn away in our own lives:

- old ways of thinking
- chronic self-doubt
- biases and judgments
- places we feel silenced
- clutter in our homes and minds
- patterns of self-sabotage
- worries and fears
- things that no longer serve us
- regrets, guilt, resentment, and shame

Let it burn.

It may feel empty and charred for a bit, but when there is space for light to reach the soil, the glory begins.

And then the light comes in.

And new life returns.

TRY THIS

What can you burn away and where might you trust that new life will spring from the ashes? What is it time to let go of? Picture those old thoughts, ways of behaving, regrets, and shame stories burning away until there is nothing left but rich black soil. Now, what do you want to grow in this new wide-open space?

Let it go...then let it grow.

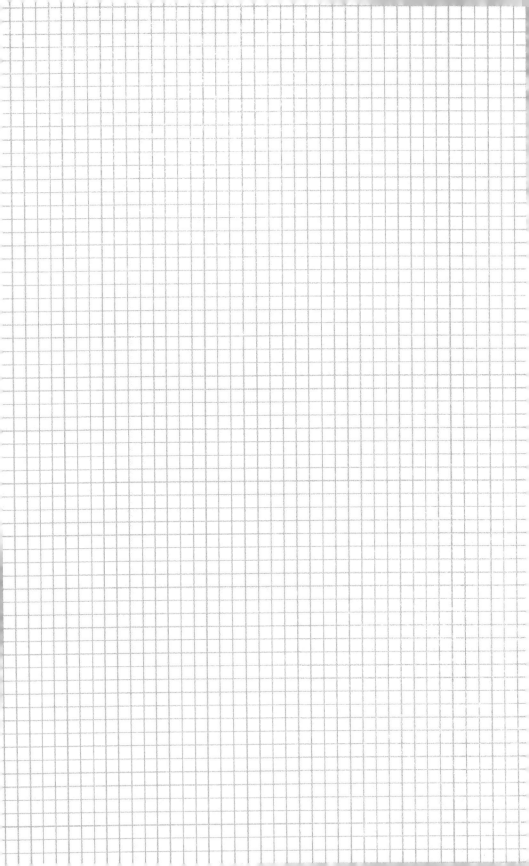

PRACTICE
SELF-COMPASSION

I stumbled upon the clinical research on self-compassion in 2015 when I was in the middle of my seminary education. I had a paper and sermon due on the unconditional love of God and I realized I struggled with receiving unconditional love. In my head, I was never doing, giving, or being enough. There was always something more I expected out of myself...and deep down I realized that I thought God felt that way about me too. In a rabbit hole of research on this topic, I found the work of Kristen Neff at the University of Texas, Austin. She has over two decades of research posted on her website on the topic of self-compassion. As I dove into these studies, I quickly realized how foreign the concept of self-compassion was to my brain.

Be kind to myself? Isn't being hard on myself what makes me successful? Isn't self-criticism what motivates me to get on the treadmill? Isn't telling myself that I'm a bad person making me somehow into a good person? I realize now how ridiculous that all sounds. But at the time, it made sense to me. I was loving on the outside, but crucifying myself on the inside.

Kirsten Neff introduced me to a new way of thinking. My seminary paper took on a whole new spin. I offered that maybe Jesus was talking about self-compassion when he said "love others as you love yourself." I theorized that Jesus was saying: "learn to be compassionate with yourself, you are a child of God after all, and once you realize your own worthiness you will easily see the inherent worthiness of every other human being—and that is how we build the Kingdom of God." I think I got an A on that one.

Then I became passionate about this topic and found the work of Chris Germer at Harvard. Then Dacher Keltner at the University of California, Berkeley. Then Stanford's Center for Compassion and Altruism Research and Education. And the list goes on and on. In this section, I bring you my favorite practices for building a sense of compassion toward yourself. This section builds on the practices in "Befriend Yourself" and "Trust Yourself," so be sure to spend time with those sections too.

May you see yourself, and everyone else, through a lens of compassion.

OBSERVE WITHOUT JUDGMENT

In a yoga class once, I remember trying to touch my toes and hearing the teacher say: "remember to observe without judgment; notice how far you can go, but don't judge your flexibility."

Maybe she could read my thoughts, which were something along the lines of: "I shouldn't be in yoga because I can't touch my toes." Observe without judgment? That was such a foreign idea to me. Everything I did seemed to come with a judgment of myself. At the time, I thought: isn't that how you improve?

Receiving the guidance to "observe without judgment" felt like permission for me to let myself off the hook in a loving way. Hearing that instruction was a relief and an invitation into a new way of living. For the rest of the yoga class, and the rest of that week, I kept pondering this thought.

To learn to observe myself without judgment was a powerful shift. After that shift, I started enjoying yoga, instead of feeling inferior to the flexibility of others. I would notice I could go a little further. I would notice that some days were better than others. I would still notice that others could do the poses beautifully, but the judgment of myself started to dissolve.

I started applying it to other areas of my life: instead of telling myself "you're not being productive enough," I shifted to "you need downtime." Or, instead of "you are being too impatient with the kids," I shifted to "you are tired and need something to eat." It was liberating to notice something without adding an editorial thought.

It was like being given a free pass from inner criticism in my life. I didn't have to be my own judge and jury. I didn't have to draw a conclusion. I didn't have to have an opinion. I could observe, but release any judgment. This was a powerful lesson for me.

Mother Teresa said: "if you judge people, you have no time to love them." That applies to judging—and loving—ourselves, too.[34]

Judgment indicates potential separations between you and others, you and your higher power, you and your soul. We are all human and going through this lifetime together. As we dissolve our judgments, we feel more connected. As we show compassion to ourselves, we are more likely to show compassion to others.

TRY THESE

1. Ask yourself to think about these phrases so you become aware of your subtle judgments throughout the day. Once aware, you can choose to observe without judgment.

    First thing in the morning:
    A common observation I make of myself is _____,
    which leads to the judgment_____.
    Now I will observe this quality without judgment.

---

[34] Gwen Costello, *Spiritual Gems from Mother Theresa* (Twenty-Third Publications, 2008).

While driving:
A common observation of other drivers is _____,
which leads to the judgment _____.
Now I will observe other drivers without judgment.

At work:
A common observation of my coworkers is _____,
which leads to a judgment _____.
Now I will observe my coworkers without judgment.

At home:
An observation I make about the people I live with is
_____, which leads to a judgment_____.
Now I will observe them without judgment.

As I reflect on my day:
An observation I make of myself is _____, which
leads to a judgment _____.
Now I will observe my day without judgment.

2. Focus on one area (work, parenting, partnership, body image, or any other) and be intentional each week about being kinder to yourself. This allows you to show greater love to others. Becoming the observer rather than the judge leads to a more peaceful existence for you and those around you.

Note: If these practices have made you think of yourself as a judgmental person, remember to observe rather than judge. Observe your thoughts and behaviors, then adjust toward what you want them to be. This is inner work we have to do every day. That's why it's called "a practice."

STOP THE SECOND ARROW

Life sends painful arrows at us sometimes. We all know the sharp pangs of grief, illness, loss, break-ups, failures, setbacks, disappointments, mistakes, betrayals...most of us will experience these things multiple times in our life-times. Being human means we face getting hit with arrows from time to time.

But as I experience the pain of a life arrow, am I also shooting myself with a second arrow?

Second arrows are thoughts in our head that sound like this: you're so stupid, what were you thinking, how could you have done that, you deserve what is happening, you always mess up, this is happening because you did _____, everyone is going to leave you now, only bad things happen to you, God must be mad at you, you shouldn't have done _____, if you had done _____ this wouldn't be happening now, there is no way out of this.

That is painful to read, isn't it? Some of those second arrows are even more painful than the first ones. I would bet that at some time in your life you shot yourself with a second, third, or maybe fourth arrow. Instead of tending to our pain, most of us hit ourselves again with the blow of self-denial or self-be-trayal. We think punishing ourselves may help us not make the same mistake again. It doesn't—it only makes you angry, isolated, and anxious. We think getting ill or being sad is a sign of weakness and we need to toughen ourselves up. It doesn't work—it only makes you feel more alone, sad, and hopeless.

This wisdom comes originally from the Buddha, who taught about compassion using the image of two arrows. Hilary McBride offers a beautiful description of it in her book *The Wisdom of Your Body*. Here is Hilary's introduction to this concept:

> *"Life shoots the first arrow: something difficult happens. We get an injury, we get sick, we face a loss, we struggle with a disease, and that is the first arrow. But we are the ones who shoot the second arrow. The second arrow is shot when we add to our own pain and suffering by how we talk to ourselves and others about what is happening with us."*[35]

We can practice changing the way we talk to ourselves. After some practice, it becomes more automatic to be gentle with yourself when you are in pain. Notice where life arrows are hitting you right now. Notice if you have any second arrows flying around in your thoughts. Then replace those second arrows with self-talk that is more loving and encouraging to yourself.

Here are a few examples and alternatives to the second arrows.

- You get fired. Second arrows might sound like: "you screwed up, they never liked you, you are never going to make that much money again." Instead, try some of these phrases: "this is hard, this hurts, this is a big disappointment, this is scary but you will figure it out, what would help you have some hope today?"
- You get a diagnosis. Second arrows might sound like: "something is wrong with you, this is happening because of too much stress and you should have left that stressful job long ago, you didn't eat the right foods, this is bad and you might not recover." Instead, try: "this feels unreal, I can't get my mind around this yet, I'm giving myself time before I talk about it, I love my body and I will help it heal, I'm not alone and I will find the right people to help me."

---

[35] Hilary McBride, *The Wisdom of Your Body* (Michigan: Brazos Press, 2021).

- Someone leaves you. Second arrows might sound like: "you aren't lovable, you always mess up relationships, you will never find someone again, you aren't worth staying around for." Instead, try: "this is breaking your heart, you love them and this really hurts, you are lovable, you are worthy of love."

If you are concerned that talking to yourself like this will make you sadder, madder, or lonelier—it won't. It might make you emotional at first to show yourself tenderness if you normally don't, but it brings profound healing and diffuses the pain of the first arrow greatly. Trust me, this was a foreign concept to me ten years ago. I thought being tough on myself made me better. But then in graduate school, I found over 20 years of clinical research at UT Austin, Harvard, Stanford, and UC Berkeley that proved there was transformative power in being kind to yourself. So I tried it for the first time in my life in my 40s. The researchers are right. Life is so much better when you stop shooting arrows at yourself.

We are all learning together what it means to be a human right now, so let's not make it harder than it already is. No more second arrows.

TRY THIS

When you are in pain, emotional or physical, can you notice the second arrows you might be sending to yourself? Maybe find a word or phrase like "stop" or "don't do that to yourself" or "that is self-torture" that you can say out loud to yourself to avoid the tendency to hit yourself with the second arrow. You are hurting enough, no need to pile it on right now. Give yourself time to heal from the first arrow. Put down the additional arrows. They only make the pain go deeper.

VISUALIZE YOUR LIFE AS A MOVIE

Have you seen the awe-inspiring movie CODA, which won the Academy Award for Best Picture in 2022? The movie is centered around Ruby, a teenage girl who is the only member of her family with the ability to hear (CODA is an acronym for "Children of Deaf Adults").

We watch as Ruby is forced to make an extraordinarily difficult choice concerning her family, and, as people with families ourselves, we understand the complexities of her decision making. As viewers, we root for Ruby, feel love for her, and watch with compassion as she navigates both her fears and desires.

Watching CODA reminded me of a practice I've used in my own life and a practice I like to teach to my clients: one that can help us observe ourselves through a compassionate lens, just like we do with Ruby.

I ask clients to try visualizing their own lives as a movie. To look back at the decisions they've made throughout their lives and watch them as though they were watching the main character of a great movie. Root for them. Have compassion for them. Notice with admiration the strength that went into every decision. Understand why they did what they did.

This practice can help us depersonalize events in our lives and is a helpful way to overcome regret, guilt, and shame in how you view your own decisions.

Select a scene that you may have filed away as a "mistake" in your life. If this happened to a character in a movie, would you have a broader perspective on the situation? Would you see additional sides to the story? Are you more likely to consider the roles others played in your decision? Would you understand the circumstances and have more compassion for the character than you do for yourself?

When I think of the tough decisions I've had to make in my own life, I don't always have the same level of compassion for myself that I have for the characters I love in movies. Visualizing my life as a movie has helped me observe my inner strength, see my loving heart, and forgive myself for the times I felt like I messed up or should have known better.

When we watch a great movie, we might cringe a bit when we see someone we're rooting for make a bad decision. But we can also see why she's doing what she's doing; we can observe her from afar. We can see the bigger picture.

When a memory comes up that triggers a feeling of shame or self-blame, see if you can watch that scene and see it differently this time. You can also use this as a practice to help your decision making for the future by zooming out and observing yourself from afar to help gain greater clarity.

TRY THIS

Close your eyes and think of an event or a situation in the past that brings you feelings of guilt, shame, or regret. Play that scene back and ask yourself a few questions:

- Can I look back at this scene with perspective? Can I see it in a different way?
- Might it have led to a lesson or growth?
- Was it not completely my fault? Was it out of my hands?
- Might there be more to the story?

- Can I view the scene now with compassion rather than judgment?

REMEMBER OUR SAME-NESS

One of the hardest things I experienced when I was a new parent was that unshakeable feeling you get in the middle of the night, when you're trying to soothe your newborn: "I am the only one up right now with a crying baby." The reality is, there were thousands of moms—likely millions—around the world who were up at the same time, feeling the exact same way I was.

It's easy when we feel alone to turn to self-pity, which makes us believe that we are the only person suffering. But actually, there are always millions of other people on this planet who are feeling the same fears, uncertainty, sadness, or longing that we're feeling, right in that very same moment.

No matter what we're going through, if we can pause for a moment to consider how many others are in the same boat as us, that's all it takes to remember that we're never alone. Sometimes, we just need to be reminded of our same-ness.

Being reminded of our same-ness helps self-pity turn to self-compassion; we become more aware that others are feeling what we feel. We can find peace knowing that we're all on this Earth together living the same human experiences.

Our world gets smaller when our perspective gets bigger; we understand each other more when we remember that we're all the same. Our shared humanity makes us all feel more connected.

Finding same-ness means taking the time to send compassion to others in your boat. That might sound something like: "may all mothers who are exhausted feel peace." Or: "may all of us who are struggling with our jobs feel peace." Or: "may all of us facing surgery feel peace."

When you stop to remember our same-ness, you teach your brain to default to compassion, which will end up bringing you peace, again and again and again.

TRY THIS

Take time to consider a few things you've been struggling with lately. Imagine how many other people around the world might be facing the same struggle. What's a compassionate message you could send to them to help them find peace? Can you find self-compassion by sending that same message inward? Repeat this exercise every time your thoughts veer into "I'm the only one" territory, and see if you can't start retraining your brain to veer instead to "I'm not alone."

Find your own way to remind yourself that you aren't the only one suffering at this moment. The way I remind myself is to say: "Ginger, there are seven million other people on the planet feeling the same way you do right now. There is a woman in South Africa having this struggle, and a woman in China, and one in France, and India, and Thailand, and Iran, and Canada, and Brazil. You are all feeling exactly the same way in this moment." It really helps me picture those women in each culture struggling with being human, just like I am right now. Then I feel more connected with all of humanity and with people who know my struggle—we can carry it together.

TRY SELF-SOOTHING

As babies, we have an innate awareness of what will make us feel better. We cry out for someone to hold us. We reach for a pacifier. We rub the corner of a special blanket. We hug a sacred stuffed animal tightly. We know how to find comfort.

As adults, we struggle with helping ourselves feel better—or worse, we skip it altogether. Unfortunately, our society doesn't teach coping mechanisms well; we tend to rely on quick fixes to avoid suffering. We rush to ignore our problems, medicate them away, or pretend they don't exist in our desperate attempts to solve them. We are simply not comfortable with being uncomfortable.

But there are ways to sit with and face our problems without increasing our suffering, and that's where self-soothing comes in. Just like when we were babies, self-soothing gives us a much-needed dose of comfort when we are upset.

We can learn to self-soothe in a healthy way; it just takes some practice. It means being intentional about naming what brings you comfort in healthy ways. And even though you're soothing yourself, it's a practice that serves your loved ones, too: when you soothe yourself first, you're giving yourself the chance to be your best self for others.

It is so important to show ourselves compassion. There will be hard days, days that will try you, situations that will trigger you. Be gentle with yourself.

Be kind to yourself.

The next time you feel anxious or some other negative emotion, pause and ask yourself: "what would help me feel a little better right now?" Find what soothes you. When you do that, not only are you showing yourself kindness, you naturally become kinder to everyone around you.

TRY THESE

1. Make a list of things you can easily do at home to soothe yourself. Keep this list close for the next time you could use some comfort. Here are some examples:

   - Sit in the sun.
   - Wrap up in a favorite blanket.
   - Drink a warm soothing beverage.
   - Flip through vacation photos.
   - Play with a pet.
   - Go for a walk.
   - Listen to nature sounds.
   - Watch the flame of a candle or fireplace.
   - Listen to your favorite song.
   - Watch a favorite TV show.
   - Take a hot bath or shower.
   - Look at the stars.
   - Put clean sheets on your bed.
   - Close your eyes and take a few deep breaths.

2. Now consider what resources you can tap into that always make you feel better, no matter where you are, and add those to the list. Here are some resources to consider:

- Websites you enjoy
- Games you like to play
- Songs that warm your heart
- Friends to call or text or email
- Mentors who provide perspective
- Videos that make you laugh

3. Ask yourself: "what are some things I can remember to tell myself that will help me feel better?" Add those to the list and refer to them when you could use some comfort. Here are some suggestions:

- "I am safe in this moment."
- "I am stronger than I think I am."
- "This is a hard time."
- "I have permission to be disappointed."
- "It is okay to be sad."
- "This is only temporary."
- "I am not alone."
- "I am learning to trust myself."
- "I am loving, lovable, and loved."
- "There is no right way to feel."
- "I am doing the best I can."
- "I will take this one day at a time."
- "I can and will do this."

EXPERIMENT WITH "MAYBE"

Some time ago, a friend shared with me that, like many times in the past, she was struggling with anxious feelings before going to an event with new people. Before the event, she was noticing the same self-critical thoughts that always showed up, things like "I don't have anything interesting to talk about" and "they might not like me" (what I know to be true about this woman is that she is super interesting, and that everyone likes her).

She then told me that she'd become so tired of those thoughts, she decided to try something new: she'd challenge each one by flipping it and tacking on a "maybe" to the beginning: "maybe I do have interesting things to talk about. Maybe they will like me."

What she'd really done was use some neuroscience on herself: she'd given her brain a healthy dose of hope just by using the word "maybe." When we include the possibility of "maybe," we reframe our thinking; we give ourselves agency and potential.

Hope has been widely researched as a feeling that results in a release of dopamine, a feel-good hormone that then paves the way to healing, optimism, and, ultimately, happiness. Plus, according to Dr. John Medina, a researcher at the University of Washington School of Medicine, optimism and hope can even increase your lifespan by nearly eight years.[36]

Hope is a simple feeling: it's the belief that things will get better than they are right now. But it doesn't always come naturally to our brains, which is why it's worth adding in a practice like "maybe" to help challenge your thoughts, reframe your thinking, and even add a few years onto your life.

TRY THESE

1. Get in the habit of adding "maybe" to any uncertain or anxious thoughts that show up this week. Some examples:

   - I'm not strong enough for this. / Maybe I am strong enough for this.
   - This is going to be miserable. / Maybe this won't be miserable.
   - That was a bad decision. / Maybe that wasn't a bad decision.
   - I can't do this. / Maybe I can do this.

2. Think of something coming up that's been giving you feelings of anxiety. What thoughts come to mind? Take a piece of paper and make two columns: in the first, write down the uncertain or self-critical thoughts. In the second column, try flipping each one and adding a "maybe." Reference this list as needed in the days and weeks to come, to give your brain an extra dose of optimism and dopamine.

---

[36] Carmine Gallo, "Brain Science Reveals the Striking Power of Optimism," *Forbes*, November 2017. Retrieved from https://www.forbes.com/sites/carminegallo/2017/11/19/brain-science-reveals-the-striking-power-of-optimism/?sh=61337c2f71aa.

GIVE YOURSELF PERMISSION
TO DO NOTHING

Recently, I spoke on the subject of self-compassion for the employees of a charity that houses families who have children in a nearby hospital. I was struck by how many of them were beating themselves up for "not accomplishing more" when they got home at night.

I wanted to help them become comfortable with doing nothing after a day of pouring all they had into helping emotional families, so I said, "You have permission to go home, ignore the mess in the kitchen, and lie on the couch." "You have permission to watch four hours of TV and turn your brain off." Their faces indicated surprise and relief. To hear it from someone else somehow made it a little more official.

But here's the really magical thing: when you give yourself permission—when you hear it from yourself—not only do you make it official, you stop being the one who's holding yourself back.

Often, it feels selfish to give ourselves permission to do nothing—in today's productivity culture, we're supposed to grind and hustle and work hard and be busy busy busy. It can feel as though our lives should always feel heavy and hard.

This practice is not selfish, it's just the opposite. By allowing yourself to have permission to do nothing, you're giving yourself the chance to feel peace, rest, renewal, and all manner of positive things. Then you show back up to your loved ones with a new sense of energy and inspiration.

Pinpoint what you're longing for, then say to yourself, "you have permission to..." or "you're allowed to...." To our brain, those phrases make it feel official, like someone else is giving us permission. Saying it to ourselves actually sounds like it's coming from an outside authority.

Start giving yourself permission to do nothing, and see what magic starts to develop from a more relaxed and reset state of being.

TRY THIS

Choose a time where you usually expect yourself to be productive and instead give yourself permission to do nothing during this time. It might be an evening or weekend where you are away from work and typically expect yourself to catch up on things at home. Write a permission statement on a piece of paper that says your first name, then: you have permission to do nothing today. Notice how it feels to do this exercise. What resistance do you notice? Can you push through the discomfort and truly do nothing?

THANK THE COSMIC 2X4

My friend and I use the term "cosmic 2x4" to capture a phenomenon in our lives. We have noticed that when we don't listen to the whisper of our souls saying "something is off" and ignore the signs that we need to make a shift, the universe hits us with a cosmic 2x4 to help us get the message. Picture a lumber-store 2x4 board being swung toward you—that's a cosmic 2x4.

This gives us language and imagery to help us see that things need to change. This friend and I have both had a few cosmic 2x4 moments in our lives, and we've watched people we love get hit by them too. You can likely relate to this also. We've all faced versions of these situations: we've ignored dysfunction in an organization and then were super hurt by a toxic leader, or ignored the early symptoms of disease and then heard a big diagnosis, or ignored speed limits and had a rollover accident, or ignored relationship red flags and had a messy divorce, or ignored comments about how much we drank and then ended up in rehab, or didn't pay bills on time and then a poor credit score halted the home purchase, or got defensive when a family member commented on our working too much and later crashed from burnout.

We hear the whispers, ignore them (or don't want to face them), then something big happens to get our attention—the cosmic 2x4. One time when I was a business consultant, I was struggling with the ethics of an organization I was trying to help. I was blowing the whistle that they were hurting people and the corporate leadership wanted to ignore it. I said to my friend: "it feels like the bad guys won." She said: "I don't see it that way at all, I see that this was the cosmic 2x4 to get you out of there, away from the bad guys. God has other big stuff for you to do, but not there." I could feel the shift in that moment. With that awareness, I could move away from an attitude of "this bad thing happened to me" and into "this happened FOR me so that I would leave." And years later, I can say she was exactly right.

The cosmic 2x4 hurts upon impact, but it is actually prompting us to wake up and make a change. Think of the crappy things that have happened in your own life. Could you see that instead of these things happening to you, they were happening for you?

Cosmic 2x4s help us make a change, move on, pay attention, wake up, surrender, get the message, do something differently, leave, reset, expand, slow down, get still, notice things, and appreciate life.

So why does it have to hurt? Because sometimes that is the only way we wake up. But we can avoid the deep pain if we learn to listen more closely and take action earlier. The whispers are your intuition speaking to you—listen to it.

Oprah Winfrey describes it this way:

> "Life whispers to you all the time. It whispers, and if you don't get the whisper, the whisper gets louder. If you don't get the whisper when it gets louder, I call it like a little pebble—a little thump—upside the head. The pebble or the thump upside the head usually means it's gone into a problem. If you don't pay attention to the problem, the pebble then becomes like a brick. The brick upside your head is a crisis, and if you don't pay attention to the brick upside your head, the crisis turns into a disaster and the whole house— brick wall—comes falling down."[37]

Let's pay attention to the whispers and avoid the disaster.

---

[37] Oprah Winfrey, "Oprah's Lifeclass," *Own*. Retrieved from https://www.oprah.com/app/oprahs-lifeclass.html.

TRY THIS

What whispers are you hearing in your life right now that may need your attention? Try speaking to them by saying: "I see you, I hear the warning, I am paying attention, I can't take action right now, but thank you for helping me see the warning sign." Then make a plan for what you will do with this new level of awareness. It might be an exit strategy that you develop, or you might delegate something to someone, or make an if-then statement. If-then statements sound like: "if [*this happens*], then [*I will do this*]." You heard the whisper and you are watching to see what happens next. If it turns into, as Oprah says, a "brick upside your head" then you will take action.

And if you don't hear the whispers, thumps, or bricks and you get hit by the 2x4, be grateful for it—it is the pain that helps you make a shift and sometimes we have to be hit hard with reality before we can see it. That's okay too. It was the way it needed to happen. Now, move forward to the next thing because better days are ahead!

CONSIDER WHO YOU ADMIRE

If I asked you to name five people you admire, who comes to mind?

They can be living or deceased. You can know them personally or not. They can be real people or fictional characters. You don't have to know a lot about them, just what you admire from what you know.

To admire someone means to respect, think fondly of, hold in high regard, revere, be in awe of, approve of, marvel at, or appreciate. Who do you watch from afar and think highly of? Who inspires you? Who do you think of and wonder "What would they do, how did they survive, or what advice would they have for me?" Who reminds you that what you desire is possible?

The order in which they come to mind doesn't matter. Don't critique yourself if someone came to mind before someone else. Allow your brain to go where it goes, unfiltered.

Pause now and do this practice before you read further, because I'm going to share with you what you can learn about yourself in doing this practice.

List your five and think about why you admire them. What is it about them you admire?

1. I admire _____ because _____.

2. I admire _____ because _____.

3. I admire _____ because _____.

4. I admire _____ because _____.

5. I admire _____ because _____.

Do you notice any patterns among the traits of these five people?

Are there key words that stand out to you as you review your descriptions of why you admire them?

Is there a theme that emerges as you think of these five people you admire?

Here is the really cool thing....

The people you admire have qualities you have too.

That's right, the people you admire are very similar to you at the core of your being. That is why you admire them. Your subconscious sees the potential of what you can be. What you admire is often what you long to become or already are. You are what they are. You are what you admire in them.

The people you admire are mirrors to your soul. Celebrate these parts of yourself that are worthy of admiration. See that you already have the things you seek. You are already on the path by setting your sights on these five people. You can decide to continue toward becoming what they are: the thing that made you write their name down, the feeling you get when you think about them, the thing they've done that you long to do.

You are on your way to it too. The truth is, you already possess it.

TRY THESE

Allow yourself to see that you share things in common with the people you admire. Celebrate those parts of you. Honor that you already have it. It is in you. That thing you admire, it is true of you too.

Have this conversation with people. Ask them who they admire and why. Listen to what they admire in the person they are describing. Help them see that they share those same qualities with the person they admire. As you help them see the mirror reflected in whom they admire, it will lead you to trust it for yourself too.

How would you live today if you trusted that you share the inherent qualities in the people you admire? How do you show up in the world if you already have it? Do you carry yourself differently into the day? Do you make decisions differently? Do you trust yourself more? Does it help you on the path to loving yourself and who you truly are inside? Spend some time with this and soak in the self-compassion it brings to your mind and heart.

WINTER GENTLY

Wintering is a verb introduced to me by author Katherine May. Prior to reading May's work, my verb for winter was "hating winter." As a Midwesterner, I enjoy four definite seasons. However, winter is my least favorite and often a time of heaviness in my soul. Thanks to May's book *Wintering*, I see it differently now. Here are some of her words:

> *"When I started to feel the drag of winter, I began to treat myself like a favored child, with kindness and love. I assumed my needs were reasonable and that my feelings were signals of something important. I kept myself well fed, and I made sure I was getting enough sleep. I took myself for walks in the fresh air and spent time doing things that soothed me. I asked myself, what is this winter all about? I asked myself, what change is coming?"* [38]

Instead of fighting winter, now I find that I can enjoy it. I watch nature (which I had previously thought of as "winter dead") be in a season of rest, not death. I see the bare trees as an invitation to rest, not a depressed sense of gloom. I enjoy weekends cuddling with my favorite blankets, people, and dogs on the couch. I do puzzles with a cup of hot tea and an audiobook play-

---

[38] Katherine May, *Wintering* (New York: Penguin Random House, 2020).

ing in the background. Before, winters were a time of expecting myself to organize closets, take on new work projects, and accomplish things. Now, winter is about recovering from the busy year and resetting before spring, when I love to come alive again.

I hope you will think about loving yourself through your wintering months. Katherine May also describes wintering as a time when it might actually be summer but you are in a season of grief. These are times where we feel isolated and alone. Wintering is a time of being really gentle with ourselves before we go out into the world again. This is one of my favorite paragraphs in her book:

> *"Sometimes the best response to our howls of anguish is the honest one. We need friends who wince along with our pain, who tolerate our gloom, and who allow us to be weak for a while, while we're finding our feet again. We need people who acknowledge that we can't always hang on. That sometimes everything breaks. Short of that, we need to perform those functions for ourselves: to give ourselves a break when we need it and to be kind, to find our own grit in our own time."[38]*

You might go back and read that again, it is so beautiful. One, we need people in our lives with whom we can be real. Two, we must be loving to ourselves. Those two things—compassionate friends and self-compassion—make being human so much easier.

I hope you are wintering well this year, wherever you are. If you live in a hot climate, your version of wintering might be in July and August when you stay near air conditioning and go slower. Or wintering may come when we least expect it, with grief or disruption to our plans. Whenever it is, be gentle with yourself while the days are darker. Spring will always return.

TRY THESE

1. Notice which season of the year is the hardest for you emotionally. Explore that a little deeper and see if you can identify why it is hard for you. Are there things you can do to make it better? As it approaches, can you make a plan for something you look forward to? What would bring you comfort during this season? Can you change the narrative about this time of year into a new story? What good could come of it for you? What do you need? How could this time be different than before?

2. Find someone who is in a winter season like you are and go through it together. There is always someone who is struggling at the same time you are. My friend Wendee and I discovered that we both hate winter. We now check in with each other during the winter, send each other funny social media memes, talk about how miserable the weather is and what we are going to do to make it through. Last winter she gave me a blanket to wrap up in and when I do, it feels like a hug from her. It has helped so much to know she's feeling exactly the same way I am. Then we celebrate spring together! Find someone to go through the tough stuff with you. We don't have to do it all alone. Share what you are feeling and someone out there will say "me too." That's your person.

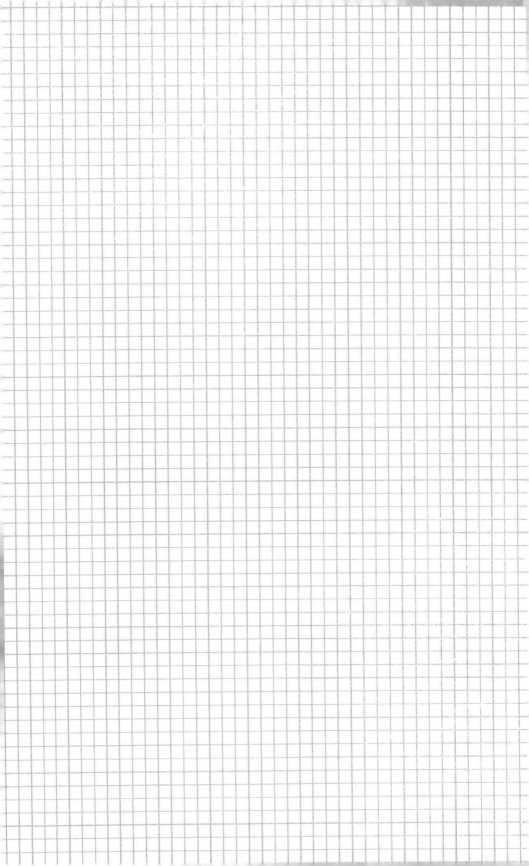

KNOW
YOUR PURPOSE

Having a sense of purpose and knowing you are making a meaningful contribution helps you feel more rooted in life. When we know why we are here, we feel more stable in the storms of life. There is a bigger picture to our life and that helps us feel like we matter. Many studies show that life expectancy, well-being, and happiness improve when we can report that we have a sense of purpose in our life. [39]

I feel like I searched for purpose for my first 40 years of life. I wanted to be a physician, then a businesswoman, then an interior designer, then a teacher—and through it all I felt this inner churn that I still had not found my thing. I knew there was something I was here on Earth to do, but I couldn't figure out what it was. I have three Master's degrees to prove that I kept searching for answers. It was when I started really checking in with my soul that the search began to show me some answers.

---

[39] Eric Kim et al, "Sense of Purpose in Life and Subsequent Physical, Behavioral, and Psychosocial Health: An Outcome-Wide Approach," *American Journal of Health Promotion 36*, no. 1 (2022): 127-147. doi:10.1177/08901171211038545.

I am walking proof that the journey can be winding and take a long time, but eventually I found the work that fills my soul. I teach about self-compassion and compassion for others, I write about how we can make this human experience a little easier, I work with people to help them move forward, I speak to groups about living their collective potential...I finally found my lane and it feels so good. The practices in this section are practices that helped me throughout my purpose-finding process. I feel passionate about every human being knowing they have a purpose. I hope these practices help you discover yours.

TEACH WHAT YOU KNOW

Many people are stumped by the question: "what is my purpose?"

It seems like an enormously challenging question to tackle, when in reality, the answer is usually right in our lap. It's as simple as this: what could you teach someone to do?

When I pose that question to clients, they often have no problem coming up with at least one thing. We all know something that others want to learn. What comes easy to you is amazing to someone else—and passing that knowledge along can indeed be a worthwhile and important purpose.

There are many things you know how to do well enough to teach. You already have within you what it takes to have purpose. You are already here for a reason.

Here are some other great questions to consider along the same lines:

- What did you once struggle with? You could teach someone that.
- What do people ask you to help them with? That's a clue.
- What problems are you able to solve easily? Those count, too.

These are all clues that can help point you toward your path of teaching others. Going through a list of questions like those can help you see all of the ways you could help others—then you get to decide which one feels the best.

Finding our purpose can feel so big, when really, it's right in our lap. All we need to remember is that we were put on this Earth to pass on what we've learned so that we might make someone else's journey easier.

TRY THIS

Here are some prompts to think about as you ponder how you can pass along what you've learned to others:

- What do you love to do?
- What can you help with?
- What can you teach someone how to do?
- How have you mentored others in the past, formally or informally?
- What have you been trained to do?
- For what do people come to you for help?
- What did you once struggle with?
- What have you overcome?
- As a child, what did you pretend to do?
- How do people describe what you do for them?
- What problems can you solve?

ZOOM OUT

I had a client once, Jamie, who felt lost and without purpose. She was so mired in everyday tasks that she hadn't stopped to think bigger. So I took her through an exercise I like to call "zooming out." I asked her to zoom way out and look at her life: what had she struggled with? What had she overcome? Then I asked her: "might there be others facing those struggles?" Could she see the big picture, and connect what she'd been through with those who could use her help?

Years before, Jamie's son had been diagnosed with autism. She'd dedicated herself to navigating what the diagnosis meant and how to advocate for her son. Zooming out made her realize that there were other parents just starting on that path who might feel as overwhelmed as she once did. She lit up and felt hopeful that her purpose could be to help those other parents. Not long after, she founded a support group, which she continues to lead today.

Like Jamie learned, it's easy to get caught up in the cycle of mundane daily tasks. Often, we find ourselves going through the motions on repeat, until one day, a voice inside us says: "wait a minute, this can't be all there is! What am I on this Earth for?"

We fall into a trap of keeping our head down and focusing on the day-to-day, when what we need to do instead is zoom out. Think of yourself as having eagle vision: if you could look at life on Earth from above, what do you see people struggling with? How could you help them?

When you zoom out, you might see a number of needs that you could help to meet:

- Being kind
- Caring for someone
- Using your voice
- Sharing your story
- Reducing suffering
- Giving hope
- Parenting
- Teaching
- Leading
- Guiding
- Writing
- Providing
- Inspiring
- Encouraging
- Helping

TRY THIS

Write a summary of your life's journey, and consider who else might be going through similar experiences. How could you help those people? Consider the following:

- What you've survived
- What you've celebrated
- What you've regretted
- What you've learned
- What you wish you would've known
- What you've researched

- What you've struggled with
- What you've been diagnosed with
- What you've been taught
- What you didn't know before
- What you know now

LIGHT UP

What makes your eyes sparkle?
What do you love to talk about?
When do you notice energy rise in your body?

When life seems aimless, it's important to think about what lights us up. When you're excited about something, you feel like you have purpose. When you carry light, the darkness lessens.

Can you imagine a world where we're all more lit up and excited about our days? It might sound idyllic, but what if we could move the needle forward a few notches? What would our encounters during the day be like? Might we walk around less angry, agitated, and frustrated?

Might we feel like we're honoring ourselves? Might we allow for and accept the things that give us joy? Might we know what we're here to do?

There will always be times we feel uncertain or in search of answers, but if you're more intentional about naming and pursuing what lights you up, you can make your days better. You can ease your burdens, welcome in joy, and feel more at peace with the path you're on.

Many of us aren't sure what lights us up because we spend our days with our heads down, taking care of others, working, and doing all the mundane tasks that come with making a life.

But naming—and pursuing more of—what fills you with energy is a key ingredient in finding a sense of purpose. Your purpose is to follow what you are excited about.

You are here to do what lights you up.

TRY THESE

1. Take some time to consider: What excites you in this season of life? Write down everything that you can think of. How can you add more of those things to tomorrow? To every day? To your life? What feels most like a path that you can follow?

2. If you're unsure, or are curious to hear what others might think (often, others can pinpoint things about us more quickly than we can), ask some friends and family for their observations:

   - What do you notice that I do well and enjoy doing?
   - When do you notice I light up or have a sparkle in my eye?
   - What contribution do you think I make to our family/friendship/workplace?

REMEMBER "ON MY WAY"

On my 50th birthday, my friend said: "when the front number changes, it is significant!" This one felt significant. I notice that in the second half of my life, I'm more clear about what I want and don't want. I love that aging brings clarity and wisdom. There are things I thought I would have accomplished by 50 that I'm still working on, and there are things that can fall off the list of goals because they just aren't as important now as they were before. I was writing a letter to myself about what my 50th birthday meant to me and noticed I was using a practice I wanted to share with you. It is a twist on affirmations that you and I can both practice at any age, to help ourselves feel hope that we are on our path toward our goals.

You likely have heard of affirmation practices where you are supposed to look in the mirror and say "I am" statements such as: I am beautiful, I am successful, I am an expert, I am worthy. Often those don't feel fully true to us when we look in the mirror. Here is a small adjustment I suggest:

- I am on my way to feeling beautiful.
- I am on my way toward success.
- I am on my way to becoming an expert.
- I am on my way to feeling worthy.

When you feel disappointed that you aren't further along in your journey by now, reframe that thought by adding "I'm on my way to..." and it feels like a hug to your brain. We are growing and learning every day and things take longer than we want them to, but we are headed in the right direction.

You are on your way to finding that person.
You are on your way to learning that skill.
You are on your way to making that change.
You are on your way to saying what you need to say.
You are on your way to quitting that unhealthy habit.
You are on your way to trusting yourself.
You are on your way to feeling peaceful.
You are on your way.

And so am I.

I'm grateful we get to grow together.

TRY THESE

1. What "I am" statements do you wish were true for you? See if you can adjust them with "I'm on my way to..."

2. What do you want in life? What are your big dreams? What do you want to become? List it all, even the things that you may judge yourself for. Now, realize you are on your way toward those things. It starts with wanting them. If you want it, then it might be meant for you. By naming it, you are on your way toward it. What can you do each day, week, month, quarter, and year to move closer to it? Make an "on my way" plan for how you will get there. Then every day, remind yourself that you are indeed on your way.

CRAFT A PURPOSE STATEMENT

A few of my clients come to seek coaching after they retire. Tori had been an executive who worked 60-hour weeks and hadn't had time to volunteer. Now that she had the time, though, she couldn't figure out how or where to start. She knew she wanted to help, but having had no hobbies to help guide her, she was a blank slate.

I knew of a practice we could use to help Tori: we could craft a purpose statement for her. A purpose statement is a simple formula to help figure you out and remind you of your helping purpose, and it goes like this:

I help _____ with _____ so that _____ .

Here's how it went with Tori. First, I asked her: what do you love doing for people? She thought for a few minutes. "Having people over," she said. "Cooking for them." When I asked her why, she talked about the bonds and connections people seem to make when they share food. She liked being a part of that. She also felt like cooking was her way of caring for others. From those answers, we had our purpose statement:

I help people with being fed so that they feel taken care of.

We had a starting point. From there, the next step was to figure out how she could do this on a bigger scale. How could she help more people? After we crafted her purpose statement and Tori had time to think more on it, she ended up working in a hunger ministry at a church and now has a volunteer position that she loves: delivering hot meals to the unhoused.

We are hardwired for compassion. We naturally want to help others. But sometimes, it's difficult to figure out how best to do that. When you wonder who you should be helping, or when you lose sight of how you are helping, a purpose statement can help be your North Star. You can return to it anytime you yearn for purpose.

If it's hard for you to figure out your purpose statement, don't despair. It will come to you. In the meantime, when you don't know what else to be, be love. Your first thought in the morning can be: "today, I will be love." Use that day simply to show someone some love. Love is a lot of things: a smile, a warm expression, an encouraging conversation, a listening presence, forgiving someone, giving a compliment, sharing enthusiasm, or facilitating a peaceful pause—that's all. Your confusion about your purpose can be solved, just like that.

TRY THIS

Place your name at the top of a blank piece of paper and write the answers to the following questions, allowing thoughts to flow freely and without judgment; just observe all of your complexity. Ask yourself:

- Who do I help?
- With what or how do I help them?
- So that they can/feel/find/fix/be what?

Then, summarize your findings into a statement like one of these: "I help _____ with _____ by _____." This is simply a guide to help you remember that you are helping and it matters. Revisit these questions periodically; our purpose evolves as we age and experience life.

FIGURE OUT YOUR ASSIGNMENT

There are innumerable causes out there that could use our support—people and communities in need, crises that arise, natural disasters—things that make us feel stirred to action. Things that make us feel like we should do something. That we should help in a big way.

Figuring out what, exactly, we should do can feel overwhelming, though. And that's where we often can get stuck. We're quick to talk ourselves out of action by saying "I don't have what it takes," or "someone is already doing it." Thanks to self-doubt, we take away the opportunity to find purpose through helping.

We all think we need to have this giant purpose, that we have to swoop in and be a Hero. But in reality, it's much smaller and simpler than that. It's as easy as asking yourself: "what is mine to do?"

Question yourself when you feel a stirring: is there some small assignment that feels like you're being chosen to do? A baby step toward your calling? Often, your purpose uncovers itself in small ways, and what you need shows up without you realizing it.

We will never feel ready or fully equipped for our callings. We will always doubt our abilities, timing, credentials, power, and resources. That's all part of a calling. If we say yes to our assignment, though, we help others and lift ourselves up at the same time.

Assignments feel like they come from a higher power. They feel like an epiphany about how you can help humanity suffer less or find hope. Your assignment feels like a nudge. It's a stir to take even the smallest of actions, which can end up making a very big difference. If you feel that stir, it's yours to do. You've figured out your assignment. It is a divine assignment.

We are each being called to different actions. That thing that breaks your heart, that issue you've been enraged about, those people in need who you can't stop thinking about, that idea for a solution that's come to you, unbidden—those are divine inspirations, signs of a calling. Go with them. Explore them.

Each and every one of us will hear callings throughout our lives. We all have a part in making the world a more compassionate place. Life has more meaning and purpose when we say yes to those nudges and callings.

So listen to that voice deep down inside. Figure out what feels like your assignment and take a small step toward it. It is yours to do.

TRY THESE

To help figure out what your assignment could be, ask yourself the following questions:

1. Who do you want to advocate for? Here are a few examples, to get you started:

    - Children?
    - Animals?
    - Adolescents?
    - The unhoused?
    - Those living with illness?
    - People of a certain age?

2. What breaks your heart in the world? Where do you feel like a difference needs to be made? Here are a few examples, to get you started:

    - Hunger?
    - Domestic violence?
    - Foster care?
    - Poverty?
    - False incarceration?
    - Equality?
    - Human rights?
    - The environment?

3. Look at the things you do all day for people. What forms of helping bring you joy? Think about how you could build on those forms to help more people.

4. What's your current capacity to help, time-wise and resource-wise?

5. Write on the top of a piece of paper: "what is mine to do?" Now pray, meditate, sit in silence, connect to your higher power and ask: "what would you have me do? Whom would you have me serve? Where would you have me go?" Then sit in silence and see what comes to you. You may have to do this a few times, but hints, nudges, and ideas will arrive and you will begin to see what is yours to do.

ASK YOURSELF
THREE BIG QUESTIONS

In her memoir *Inheritance*, author Dani Shapiro writes about the identity crisis she faced when a genetic test indicated that her deceased father was not her biological father.[40] While struggling through her grief and feeling lost, she went to an acupuncturist who asked her, mid-session, if she was familiar with "the three great spiritual questions":

1. "Who am I?"

2. "Why am I here?"

3. "How shall I live?"

While reading Dani's beautiful story, those three questions kept looping through my brain. I wanted to be able to answer those three big questions myself, which sent me on my own journey to find out. I worked at it. I thought about these questions during walks, captured pages of my thoughts on paper, and eventually realized I had developed my answers to those three questions. It felt good to be able to answer those with clarity and confidence, but it took some work to get myself there. To me it felt like a new level of peace, a deeper sense of knowing myself, and clarity on what was truly important to me.

----

[40] Dani Shapiro, *Inheritance* (New York: Knopf Doubleday, 2019).

I talk with people every day of all ages who are searching for those same huge, existential answers. If you can't answer them, you are not alone. And I have found that my own answers continue to evolve as I age and have more life experiences. Our identity, purpose, and values change over our many chapters of life.

This is a practice of pondering that I hope you will return to periodically to renew your sense of who you are, what your purpose is, and how you align your life according to your values.

I'll share a bit of my answers with the hope that it might inspire you to spend some time developing your own.

- Who am I? I am a loving soul. I am a mother, wife, and daughter. I am a teacher of love and compassion. I am someone who is connected to a higher power that I call God. I am someone who is doing their best. I am someone having a human experience, which means I'm learning from my mistakes and hoping to grow every day.
- Why am I here? I am here to be the love in the room. My purpose is to make people feel loved, seen, heard, understood, and worthy. My contribution to humanity right now is to help people feel less alone in struggles, provide tools and resources to help them feel better, and to be a source of hope and inspiration.
- How shall I live? At this time in life, I value learning, integrity, connection, family, health, and fun. I want my days to feel meaningful. I want to remember to play. I want to laugh. I want to emit joy and love. Sometimes, when I'm overwhelmed or need to center myself, I run through the whole list. Sometimes I just need to repeat to myself one of these phrases to regain perspective and find courage.

Before this work, I used to place my identity on successfully meeting the expectations of everyone around me. But doing that caused me to lose myself in the process. Now, finding the essence of who I think I am (at this moment in time) has allowed me to be more authentic, vulnerable, and confident. I wish this for all of us.

TRY THESE

1. Place your name in the middle of a blank piece of paper and write words that describe you all over the page. Let yourself free-write; don't edit or overthink, just write down what comes to mind. Keep going until you fill the page.

2. Write down all the things that come to mind when you ponder this question: If your lifetime resulted in one improvement for humanity, what is it? Or if that doesn't resonate, try it this way: My wish for all people is to...

3. What three things/people/projects are most important to you at this moment? Are you living in alignment with the way you spend your time and those items?

4. Craft some "I am..." statements. Craft some "My purpose is..." statements. Craft some "I will live...." statements. When you feel lost or out of alignment, return to these statements as a reminder of your core identity and the essence of who you are right now. Then return to this exercise and update as life continues to unfold.

FOLLOW YOUR CURIOSITY

When I turned 40, my life came to a screeching halt. My kids had just started kindergarten and first grade, and without them at home, I felt lost. I found myself thinking: "who am I? What now?"

Not only was I struggling to find a vocation, I was also struggling with a lot of spiritual questions, like: "what am I supposed to do? How can I serve others and create meaning in my life? Do I have a calling?" I longed for the answers to appear on a billboard in neon letters so I would be sure to see it along the highway of life.

Unfortunately, I don't think any of us will ever get those answers in neon letters. I do think we can find the path we're meant to travel, though. We just have to follow our curiosity.

For me, it was a Bible study I was taking part in that provided the clues I was so desperately seeking. I realized how much I liked the academic part of the study, and that I wanted more of it. My quest for a deeper dive led me to consider attending seminary, and eventually, I found my way there—where, instead of a vocation, I went on a spiritual journey and found my purpose instead: to help people and be an instrument of love.

I wasn't sure where seminary would lead me, but I knew I wanted to study theology and allow the next thing to unfold. We don't always have to be sure of why we are doing something; just follow your curiosity and see where it leads you.

Those big questions we so often ask ourselves—things like "what was I put on Earth for?"—can feel so daunting. Why not try to make it easier on yourself? Ask: "what am I curious about?" and see where that takes you. It might just put you on the path to finding your purpose.

Once you find a few clues, go a step further: how could you go deeper into that topic or interest? Figuring that out can help lead you to something clicking in your brain: that moment where you say, "oh, maybe that's what I'm supposed to do." You can use your interests and help people at the same time—that can be your path. That can be your purpose.

TRY THESE

1. To help you answer the question "what am I curious about?" consider the following:

   - What have you always wanted to learn more about?
   - If you go to a bookstore, what are you drawn to?
   - What accounts do you follow on social media?
   - What environments make you happy?
   - What are you doing when you lose track of time?

2. Now that you have a few ideas, could you learn more by joining a group or taking a class? Do some research to see how you might continue following your curiosity—how you might be able to dig deeper and find the way to what you're meant to do.

CHECK IN WITH YOUR SOUL

A client once came to me, struggling to figure out his next move. He was unhappy at his job and considering a big career change, but was hesitant to step into the uncertainty that would come with it.

I asked him one of my very favorite questions: "what's your soul telling you?"

He sat quietly for a minute before admitting that he didn't quite know what I meant. "What, exactly," he asked, "is my soul?"

For a lot of people, the concept of a soul is a hard thing to wrap your head around. There's not one exact, universal definition of a soul; it's a lot of things to a lot of people. The important thing, though, is to remember that you have one. It's deep within you, and it can help you find the answers you seek.

In an online class that I lead, we spent a few sessions talking about our souls. I asked the participants to define what their soul meant to them, and they offered up a number of descriptions:

- "My center"
- "My inner spirit"
- "My true self"
- "The part that's authentically me"
- "My core"

- "The part of me that no one sees"
- "My compass"
- "Spiritual energy"
- "A light inside"
- "A stripping away of fear"
- "An inner guide"
- "A wide-open space"
- "Lightness"
- "Creativity"
- "A deep knowing"

Whatever definition you land on—and you can try on a few until you get to one that feels right—know that your soul is just as big a part of you as your physical being. And calling on and connecting with that part of you deep within is one of the most important practices there is for finding the answers you seek.

A great way to start doing that is to simply check in with your soul. Get as quiet and still as possible, and just listen. Open your mind and heart, then patiently wait for the inner wisdom that will come forth. Connecting with your innermost self—the one who knows your deepest desires—can help you find your way.

What does it feel like to connect with your soul? Here's how those same class participants described it:

- "A peace that surpasses all understanding"
- "Surrender"
- "Noticing"
- "Paying attention"
- "Realizing it was there all along"
- "A feeling of 'Oh, here I am!'"
- "Hope"
- "Flow"
- "Being tuned in"

- "A buzz of happiness"
- "Like the end of a deep exhale"

Those beautiful descriptions might give you the inspiration to try sitting with your soul and seeing what it feels like for you.

Whether you're seeking an answer or not, connecting with your soul is a gift you give yourself. The more you do it, the more easily you'll hear it.

We often don't know what we want, but that is usually because we're not listening. Your soul can be your greatest guide. Welcome it. Connect with it. Check in with it. Sit with it.

TRY THIS

1. Find a quiet place and sit comfortably. Set a timer if you want, but start small; even two minutes is enough to begin getting comfortable with this practice.

2. Take a few deep breaths, close your eyes if it helps you to focus, and ask your soul: "what would you have me know today?" Pause and listen. If you can't hear anything, that's okay. Just taking time to sit and ask yourself this question is still a great way to get your innermost being working on the answer.

3. After you get comfortable trying this practice a few times, experiment with asking questions for the answers you seek. Notice if you feel more at ease, peaceful, or connected.

4. Be patient with yourself; this can be a challenging practice if you're new to it. Take a deep breath and just be. That is enough.

FIND YOUR RAISON D'ÊTRE

My daughter asked me to quiz her on the conjugation of 50 French verbs as she prepared for a test. I haven't taken a French course for over 25 years, but helping her study brought back to mind one of my favorite French phrases, "raison d'être."

Raison d'être translates into English as "reason for being."

What is your reason for being?

When the world is in chaos and our hearts are troubled, it helps to have a sense of purpose so that we may feel grounded and rooted amidst the chaos.

There are many reasons for your being:

- You bring love and kindness everywhere you go.
- You care for loved ones.
- You create new things.
- You serve and give.
- You smile.
- You guide and nurture.
- You remind people they are not alone.
- You help and comfort.
- You are the love in the room.

Ponder your raison d'être. When you feel overwhelmed, return to your simple yet profound purpose. You are here for a reason. Many reasons.

TRY THIS

For some of us it is already clear, but others may still be searching for a sense of purpose. We all share the purpose of being an instrument of love in the world. But sometimes we wonder what else we are supposed to be doing. Searching for purpose is a topic that often arises with my clients. Especially now, when so many areas of our country are hurting, I hear many people asking: "how can I help?"

We need frontline responders, teachers, guides, experimenters, visionaries, healers, disrupters, caregivers, builders, connectors, risk-takers, innovators, organizers, networkers, messengers, dreamers, generators, implementors, developers, nurturers, creators, artists, storytellers, counselors, advisers, servers, and many others.

Do any of these words resonate with your soul? Consider what you naturally gravitate toward and what comes easily to you. Making an impact doesn't have to be hard work; follow what comes easily to you and it will seem like magic to someone else.

If you landed on a role that resonates with you, then repeat this mission to yourself every morning. Take this on as your superpower. You are here to contribute. We need you to fulfill this role to the best of your ability.

Finding a sense of purpose adds meaning to our lives and can even extend them. Harvard researchers found that a sense of purpose improves our physical health and life expectancy.[41] Knowing your purpose fulfills you and serves others at the same time. Revise your purpose statement until it feels true and powerful to you. Then go out into the world and be that.

[41] Kelly Bilodeau, "Will a purpose-driven life help you live longer?" *Harvard Health Publishing,* November 2019. Retrieved from https://www.health.harvard.edu/blog/will-a-purpose-driven-life-help-you-live-longer-2019112818378.

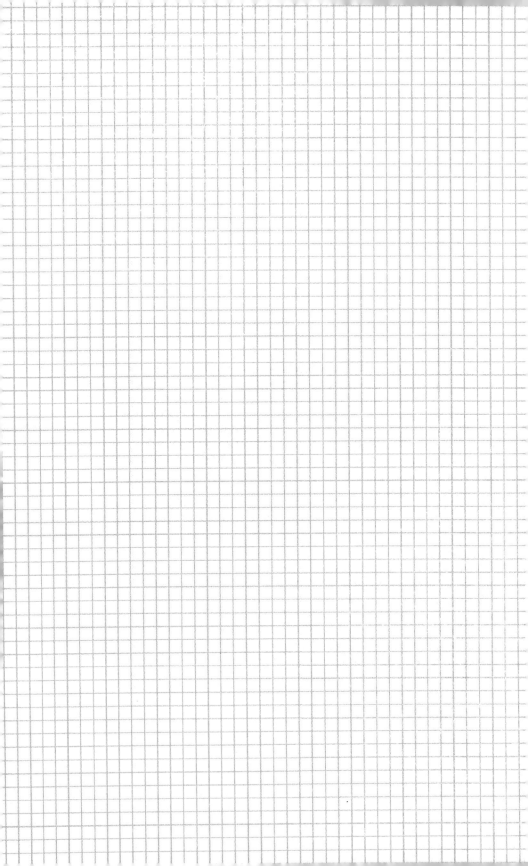

STAY PRESENT

Learning to stay in the present moment comes up a lot in my client sessions, from a young salesman who loses focus during boring meetings, to a mother who is bored playing dolls, to a grandfather who reads the news on his phone while the family reunion is happening. Staying in the Now is something we know we should do, but seldom are we taught how to do it.

Our brain is hardwired to think ahead because its job is to keep us safe from danger. So we are working against our wiring when we try to stay in the present moment. This section is comprised of practices to help your brain stop wandering and return to the present moment.

In the book of Proverbs, there is a line about carefully considering the path of your feet. I have heard it loosely translated to "be where your feet are." This can be a helpful mindfulness practice. I use it sometimes to remind myself to bring my mind back to where my body is. My mind is often miles ahead of my body. Bringing them back together helps me feel more present. Where my feet are, my mind should be also. That sounds kind of proverbial, doesn't it? Let's try it. I hope you find the practices in this section helpful in training your mind to not be distracted and instead enjoy the wonders right in front of you.

RIGHT HERE, RIGHT NOW

Does your mind ever wander? Of course it does, you are a human being with a busy brain! It can be a glorious thing to let our minds wander, but it can also cause us to not be present in the moment.

A client shared that when she's playing trains with her son, she thinks about all she should be doing instead. Then her son senses her distance and rising stress. He gets frustrated with her and says: "Mommy! You're not playing!" She tries to re-focus, but can't seem to stop her wandering mind. I think we can all relate to her in some way.

There's the spouse we aren't listening to, the show we have to rewind, the page we read again and again, the scrolling while having a conversation. We are very distracted human beings in this century of human existence.

Here is a practice for us all to try this week: return to the present moment by saying to yourself: "right here, right now." Here are some examples:

- Right here, right now, I am drinking my coffee.
- Right here, right now, I am brushing my teeth.
- Right here, right now, I am noticing the water in my shower.
- Right here, right now, I am eating this meal.
- Right here, right now, I am driving on this road.
- Right here, right now, I am sitting in this meeting.

- Right here, right now, I am at this table with these people.
- Right here, right now, I notice my heart beating.
- Right here, right now, I am playing trains with my son.
- Right here, right now, I am fully listening to this person.
- Right here, right now, I am noticing my breath go in and out.

As busy human beings, our minds and our bodies are often separated. Our body is in one place and our mind is in another. These beautiful brains of ours are hardwired to keep us safe and they are really good at thinking ahead. However, in our noisy society, we have to help our brains feel safe and turn off the alarm system. Technology has evolved much faster than the human brain. At this point in human evolution, we have to be very intentional about helping our brains find peace, which is why mindfulness practices have sky-rocketed in popularity. We are longing for practices to bring peace to our busy minds.

Mindfulness practices (like this one of being aware of your drifting mind and returning to the present moment) have been clinically shown to reduce heart disease and improve memory function, immune system responses, and brain health.[42] I notice that I am much more peaceful when I am practicing "right here, right now" throughout my day. I feel like I listen more carefully, think more clearly, and react more thoughtfully when I am intentional about staying in the present moment.

Right here, right now I am sending you love and peace. This practice always makes me smile because the Jesus Jones song "Right Here Right Now" was a college anthem for me in the early 90s. Look it up, it's a good one!

---

[42] David Creswell et al, "Mindfulness Training and Physical Health: Mechanisms and Outcomes," *Psychosomatic Medicine* 8, no. 3 (2019): 224-232. doi:10.1097/PSY.0000000000000675.

TRY THIS

Where do you notice getting distracted throughout your day? Why do you think that happens? Are you bored, uninterested, frustrated, escaping something, tired, procrastinating, trying to be productive and thinking of all you need to do, or do you even notice you are distracted? Become more aware of these moments. Listen to what people are telling you: "Dad, put your phone down." There is truth in that, your people deserve your attention. You make people feel loved when you are fully present. And life is full of amazing things if we just take time to notice what is happening right here, right now.

TAKE A MINUTE TO ARRIVE

Many of us live on autopilot day to day. On our commutes to work and while doing mundane tasks, our brains are often thinking miles ahead of our bodies.

To help us stay present and pay attention, there is a simple practice to be mindful and arrive fully at each and every moment.

The practice is known as "a minute to arrive," and it works like magic during those times you're transitioning between the many things packed into your day. Before a meeting starts, or when you get into your car, or head into the next place you need to be, take a deep breath and spend a minute naming the things around you. Narrating what you notice will help you stay in the moment with yourself instead of spiraling back into the past or jumping ahead into the future.

A friend who is a physician told me that she noticed she was always running late and rushing into her patients' rooms, out of breath and distracted. Now, she uses her own version of the "arrive" practice. Before she enters a room, she stands at the door and takes a deep breath. She says the patient's name and the phrase "be present" to herself before she opens the door. She's noticed a significant difference in how much calmer and more attentive she is after taking that moment to arrive.

Several large companies—like Google, Verizon, Target, and Intel—even offer their employees a minute to do a version of this meditation, taking a breath and centering themselves, before starting team meetings. As a result, the meetings are more productive, people feel more connected, and overall levels of efficiency tend to increase.[43]

Just by being intentional for a few seconds and matching our minds to where our bodies are, we end up making fewer mistakes, being less distracted, and becoming more aware and present. Even better, we also find ourselves becoming kinder and more compassionate along the way.

Over and over again, we move through our days at a brisk speed into new settings and sometimes never truly arrive. But just by taking that one crucial minute, we can find a way to stop, breathe, and arrive into a life that feels so much better.

TRY THESE

Here are a number of ways you can take a minute to arrive, depending on where you are.

1. When you arrive somewhere, set an intention to arrive mindfully: allow yourself a few seconds to sit still, notice what's around you, be aware of the people in the room, and remind yourself why you are there.

2. When you get in your car, pause and think: "I'm in my car. Where am I headed and how will I get there? Do I want to listen to music, a podcast, or silence? I will put my phone away so that I'm not tempted to look at it. I will drive carefully with full attention."

---

[43] James Duffy, "10 Big Companies that Promote Employee Meditation," *More Than Accountants*, January 2020. Retrieved from https://www.morethanaccountants.co.uk/10-big-companies-promote-| employee-meditation/.

3. When you get to your desk at work, pause and think: "I have arrived at work. This is my desk. I feel my chair supporting me. I'm here to help others. I will focus on this task before switching to another one."

4. When you go into a meeting, pause and think: "I am here at this table. I can feel my body in this chair. I'm taking a deep breath. We are meeting about... I hope to contribute by..."

5. When you have lunch, pause and think: "it's time to take a break for lunch. What do I feel like eating? What does my body need? I will eat mindfully and pay attention to each bite. I will enjoy this food and the energy it gives to me."

6. When you're with a group of people, pause and look around. Notice each person. Think about their names. What colors are they wearing? Send them kind thoughts. Can you sense what someone is feeling? Is there something you want to say to any of them?

7. When you get home at the end of the day, think: "I have arrived at home. I am safe here. I notice tension in my shoulders and neck. I will allow that part of me to relax. I'm taking a deep breath. I will enjoy my family and maybe some quiet time alone tonight."

MAKE IF-THEN STATEMENTS

One of the reasons it is hard to stay in the present moment is because we are hardwired to be thinking about the future. Our brain is always looking ahead to keep us safe. What threats are looming out there? What do we need to stay safe? What should we be prepared for? What's coming next? What do I need to be thinking about?

But this forward thinking can rob us of fully enjoying this moment—this present moment, right now. I notice this with women especially: we are miles ahead, thinking of everything that needs to be done. I have clients in their 80s who remind me not to miss the moments because I'm thinking about the future. They share that if they could go back and soak it all up, they would pay more attention to what is right in front of them.

If-then statements are something that helps me stay in the moment. I think through the things I'm worried about in the future and make a plan for how I will handle them. If [*this happens*], then I [*will do this*].

I picked up this practice when I was working for a large consulting firm. I was in change management, which meant helping people get used to the new systems we were installing. My friends were on the systems side, coding new software for people to use. They built it, I trained the people on it.

One night there was a glitch in the programming and we all stayed late supporting the team and fixing the glitch. My friends kept reviewing "if-then" statements in the coding language. "If the user enters xyz, then abc happens." I heard this over and over again as we went line by line through the computer code.

In my personal life, I was in the process of moving to a new city. I was afraid of all that could go wrong. But I liked this idea of if-then statements and while the team was puzzle-solving, I started playing with my own if-then statements:

If I don't like it after six months, then I will move back.
If I picked the wrong place to live, then I will find a new place.
If I get lost in the city, then I will ask for help.
If I miss my family, then I'll fly back to see them.
If I don't make friends, then I'll take art classes.
If I am lonely, then I'll get a cat.

They fixed the computer program, but more importantly, I felt less afraid of moving to a new city. It was like a weight of worry lifted off of my shoulders. I had a plan for all of the things I feared. 20 years later, I know there is neuroscience to explain why I felt better. Our amygdala in the center of our brain sounds the alarms when we are afraid. But the amygdala calms down when our prefrontal-cortex (at the front of the brain) makes a plan. If-then statements make our brains feel like we have a plan in place and thus our fear diminishes. And when our fear diminishes, we can enjoy the present moment more.

TRY THIS

What are you currently worrying about? Are there future events that feel out of your control? How could you apply if-then statements to your worries? I have used this practice a lot with clients waiting on medical test results. I write all the "if" statements on the whiteboard and then we work through our "then" plan. Instead of spiraling down the path of worry, we make a plan for everything we can think of and our brain settles down. In a world where so much is out of our control, this practice helps us feel like we can control our next steps. And truly, that is all we can do anyway. If [*this happens*], then [*I will do this*]. You've got this!

ANTICIPATE THE GOOD

Staying present in the moment is something we talk about a lot, and rightfully so: it's a helpful and effective way to slow us down when our brains are racing. But there's a whole lot to be said about looking forward, too. Looking forward can bring us hope when we need it the most.

Hope is the idea that in the future, life will be better than it is at this moment. And looking forward helps us to see the good coming in our future. There's science behind what looking forward does for us, too: studies show that not only does it give us a mental boost, it can lessen our worried thinking, irritability, and sadness.[44]

I often talk about the importance of looking forward with my teen clients. When one of them was feeling particularly hopeless, we did an exercise where we imagined their future and all of the things they had to look forward to. They remembered how excited they were to go to college. Another client was reminded how much they were looking forward to a school trip. Keeping those kinds of things in mind can do so much for our mental well-being.

Whether it's something big, like a trip, or something small, like ice cream

---

[44] Holly Burns, "To Enjoy Life More, Embrace Anticipation," *New York Times*, May 2022. Retrieved from https://www.nytimes.com/2022/05/31/well/mind/anticipation-happiness.html.

after dinner, it's important to plan things you can look forward to. Having something on the calendar builds anticipation, and anticipation is one of the central pillars of hope.

Allowing yourself to look forward is also an act of self-compassion. Sometimes we experience challenging times, but we can still give ourselves hope. By looking forward to brighter days, we can feed our souls when life is difficult.

There's a well-known passage in *The House at Pooh Corner* where Winnie the Pooh discovers the magic of looking forward:

> *"What do you like doing best in the world, Pooh?"*
>
> *"Well," said Pooh, "what I like best—" and then he had to stop and think.*
>
> *Because although Eating Honey was a very good thing to do, there was a moment just before you began to eat it which was better than when you were, but he didn't know what it was called.* [45]

Anticipation is what that feeling is called. Looking forward. And Pooh is right: the moment before the experience is sometimes even sweeter.

TRY THIS

Make a list of things you are looking forward to. Consider "can't wait" desires, such as the following:

- I can't wait to go...
- I can't wait to see...
- I can't wait to hug...
- I can't wait to eat...
- I can't wait to be...

---

[45] A.A. Milne, *The House at Pooh Corner* (London: Puffin Books, 1992).

Next, write down the feelings you will have when you experience each item.

Finally, reflect on your answers. Think about fostering anticipation every day as a practice to help you look forward and foster hope. Based on your answers, what do you most value? How do these things help you see what freedoms you most appreciate? How might this exercise help you prioritize the ways in which you spend your time?

LISTEN WELL

One of our deepest desires as humans is to feel seen, heard, and understood. And it's just as important to recognize those needs in others.

In our own quest to be known, we often forget to give others the space to do the same. We interrupt, or turn the conversation back toward ourselves, or we listen from a selfish standpoint: "how does this apply to me? Do I agree with what they're saying? What will I say next? How can I impress them?" We listen for cues to make the next move, instead of making the other person feel seen, heard, and understood.

As a child, I was outgoing and talkative around others. My mother would gently remind me to practice listening more and speaking less, saying: "you already know what you know. Listen to what someone else has to say. Then, you'll know even more."

We can do that through the practice of not just listening, but listening well.

Listening well is an act of compassion, kindness, and love. Plus, being a good listener is an easy way to endear yourself to others; everyone loves a good listener because everyone loves to be heard.

Listening well isn't always easy, though. If left unattended, our minds often begin to wander. When you feel yourself start to lose interest in what someone is saying, bring yourself back into the present moment with one of these tricks:

- Picture the setting and context of what they're describing to you like you're watching a movie.
- Look into their eyes and match the tone of their story with thoughts of love, compassion, excitement, joy, sadness, ache, or peace.
- Replay their sentences in your mind like you're taking notes or transcribing exactly what they're saying.

In our noisy world, it's more important than ever to hone the skill of listening for deeper meaning: our relationships deepen, the world opens wider than ever before with possibilities, and we all grow toward unity and oneness with our shared human experiences. And when we get better at listening to others, we also improve our ability to listen to our own souls. We end up seeing, hearing, and knowing ourselves better, too.

If you want someone to trust you, listen well. If you want to grow closer to someone, listen well. If you want your kids to tell you more, listen well. If you want to better give and receive love, listen well.

TRY THESE

1. Here are some questions to ask to practice listening well:

    - What is this person feeling right now?
    - What does this person need from me to feel understood?
    - What is the story beneath the story?

2. When you feel the urge to interrupt or comment, train your mind like you're training a puppy to stay: "wait...wait...wait...." In that time of pause, consider:

- Am I interrupting because my ego wants to talk? If yes, wait longer before talking.
- Is my comment about me or them? If it's about me, wait longer before talking.
- Is my advice/opinion being requested? If not, listen a little longer.

TOLERATE DISCOMFORT

Discomfort is something we all want to avoid. We feel it when something is happening that we don't want to happen or when there is a gap between the way something is and the way we want it to be.

Our society is built on selling ways to bring you comfort. Products and services are invented to increase comfort: insurance, medicine, technology, religion, education, banking, clothing, furniture, restaurants, groceries, utilities, homes—almost everything can be traced back to a way to help you avoid discomfort in life.

The downside to advancements in those industries is that we are getting less comfortable with being uncomfortable.

Our society is experiencing an uptick in divisiveness, hate crimes, movements to limit human rights—all things which indicate growing levels of intolerance. We are losing our ability to tolerate things that are not as we want them to be.

Our brains are getting used to having what we want at our fingertips—we have all of the information we need within a few clicks, we can have things delivered to us within minutes, we can scroll past anything we aren't interested in. Our society is losing its ability to be patient and tolerant. We see this playing out in how easily irritated people become when they have to wait a little longer or choose an alternate product.

This is not going to sound like fun to you, but I want you to try tolerating something you do not like to tolerate.

Here is a four-step method for beginning to build tolerance:

1. Awareness: Notice the feeling you are having about the circumstance.

2. Curiosity: "Why is this bothering me so much today? What else is going on inside me that this situation triggered today?"

3. Perspective: "Can I see it another way? Might they have an explanation for doing what they did? What if this situation actually benefits me in some way?"

4. Release: "I release my need to control this situation. I will take a deep breath and realize that I actually can tolerate this sense of discomfort."

We release inner angst by increasing our tolerance for discomfort. It might feel counter intuitive, but it really works. The more you can allow things to be as they are, even when you don't like them, the less angst you will feel inside. And when we reduce our levels of inner angst, we are less triggered by being wronged. It creates a positive cycle toward inner peace.

Here are some things to practice building tolerance:

- I can tolerate a long wait in line.
- I can tolerate an unplanned delay.
- I can tolerate not hearing a response from someone.
- I can tolerate annoyances.
- I can tolerate this uncomfortable feeling.
- I can tolerate disagreement.
- I can tolerate this feeling of hunger a little longer.
- I can tolerate denying the urge to do that unhealthy thing.
- I can tolerate people not liking me.
- I can tolerate rejection.

- I can tolerate not getting exactly what I want.
- I can tolerate uncertainty.
- I can tolerate that this person parked over the line and took up two spots (anyone else struggle with this one?!?!).

Tolerance is a muscle we have to intentionally build. This is an exercise in brain training. Your brain likes to throw tantrums when things don't go as we want them to.

As the driver of your brain (remember, you have agency in controlling where your brain goes), we need to help it calm down in times of discomfort. Our brain's tantrum leads to anger, road rage, high blood pressure, unhealthy cortisol levels, hurting the feelings of people we love, and later regretting our angry explosions.

If you build your muscles of tolerance, life gets much easier to endure. If we each build our muscles of tolerance, we become a little more peaceful inside, and then we naturally emit more peace into the world. Right now, we can certainly benefit from a collective contribution of peace in our world.

TRY THIS

Notice when you get agitated by something that brings you discomfort. Sometimes it is hard to notice this at first, because it seems like we are right to be angry with the situation. But the truth is, we are angry because we want to control the situation and we can't. So, when that happens, help yourself tolerate the moment by taking a deep breath (or a few), relax your shoulders and jaw tension, and say something comforting to yourself like: "this is frustrating, but I can tolerate it" or "I don't like this at all, but I can make it through this moment." Coach yourself through it like you would help a friend go through a tough moment. It is a hard moment, but you can do hard moments. Do you notice your body and mind calm a bit when you practice this? The situation may be stressful, but you don't have to be stress-full.

BE IN THIS HOUR

Last year, I was feeling sorry for myself because it was a dreary Midwestern January day, I was in holiday recovery mode, and I seriously dislike winter. I kept noticing a loop of this thought in my brain: "if I lived on the beach, I would be so much happier right now." As I was pouting around my office with post-holiday-back-to-work blues and lamenting all the reasons I don't live on the beach, I picked up a stack of old papers and a post-it note fell out of the stack with these words on it:

Happiness, not in another place...
not for another hour,
but for this hour.

In my messy handwriting, I jotted down these words of poet Walt Whitman and underlined the word "this" twice.

As I picked up the note and read the quote, it really hit me. I don't remember why it resonated when I wrote it down, I don't remember why I captured it on a post-it note. But what I do know is that day was the day when I really needed Whitman's wisdom.

THIS hour.
Right here, right now.

In the dreary winter, in the dark days, we can find happiness in this place, in this hour.

After my wake-up moment with the post-it note, I asked myself: "what would you do if you were on the beach right now, Ginger?" My answers included: "I would go for a walk. I would sit in the sun. I would swim. I would listen to the birds. I would see palm trees and flowers. I would spend the day outside being happy."

I realized that a lot of that can happen in the Midwest in January too.

So that afternoon, I did go for a walk in the dreary mist. I did listen to birds. I did spend time outside. And after my walk, I was happier. Not Ginger-in-the-ocean-happy, but happier than I was before the walk. I can long for happiness, or I can create it. I think that is what Whitman's timeless wisdom meant for me that day.

Let's all try to find happiness in this place, in this hour. Not in resolutions, or what-could-be, or if-I-had, or if-I-accomplish-this-I'll-be-happy. Let's find happiness in this very moment right now, where we are, just as we are today.

TRY THIS

What do you wish was different about your life right now? Make a list; you can crumple it up and throw it away or burn it after this, so be honest and trust that no one will see it.

Now, review that list. Next to each item, write why you want it to be different than it is. Spend some time with yourself exploring if there are ways you can address those things without radical change. Can you bring that future happiness you imagine into your life today?

You may see that there are things on the list that do need to radically change. Make a plan for those to happen. You deserve to live the life you want to.

Until then, can you find happiness in this hour, this place? See if that feels a little better than wishing it to be different than it is. This hour. This place.

PRACTICE SOUL SITTING

I am a big fan of Soul Strolls, but I also love Soul Sits. These offer us another way to connect with our souls on a hot, tired, or less active day. But first, let's explore what we are connecting to when we connect to our soul.

How would you describe your soul? In an online class that I lead, these were some of the words from the participants: center, inner spirit, true self, authentically me, my core, part of me that no one sees, eternal, compass, spiritual energy, light inside, unashamed, where I hear God, inner guide, wide open space, the part of me closest to God, laughter, dance, connection, lightness, creativity, music, tears, a deep knowing.

How does it feel when you are connected to your soul? Here are some of the responses to that question: a peace that surpasses all understanding, surrender, noticing, paying attention, the feeling of "oh there it is," I realize it was there all along, oh I'm here, hope, flow, God is with me, anything is possible, watching, opening, chills, tears, expect to see something now that I'm tuned in, a buzz of happiness, it feels like the end of a deep exhale.

Those beautiful words from the women in that class might give you the inspiration to find your own way of describing your soul. Give yourself the gift of pause right now to describe what soul means to you.

Soul Sitting is about noticing the soul of things around you and being reminded of your soul's connection to everything that exists.

Begin with noticing the living things you see: plants, animals, people. From where you sit, what do you notice?

If you are in nature or can see it through a window, consider that the center of a flower is the soul of that flower. Notice the flower's petals as you have never seen them before. See how the stems lean toward the sun. Notice colors, buds, and stages of blooming. Consider the bark on the trees and how many storms that bark has weathered. Consider that the trunk of the tree is rough on the outside and soft on the inside. Notice that the scars have stories. In leaves, appreciate the intricacies of the veining. See individual blades of grass form a lawn by each making their own contribution. Imagine the roots of the plants you see going into the ground to provide stability and nourishment. Take it all in with fresh eyes of awe and wonder.

As you spend time sitting with your soul, ask Nature: "what would you have me know today?" Pause and listen.

As you close your Soul Sitting practice, you may feel more at ease, peaceful, or connected. Notice, with gratitude, the miracles all around you. I believe God created it all and that Nature is our greatest teacher. The trees, flowers, oceans, mountains, and grasslands can teach us more than any human can offer. Listen to them.

Your soul, the essence of who you are, is connected to all forms of life. Spend some time remembering and reflecting. Take a deep breath and just be. That is enough.

TRY THIS

Review this practice again. Then lay your book down and close your eyes. Take a deep breath. When you feel a sense of calm, open your eyes. What do you see? Look at it like you have never seen it before. Be in awe. What might you miss when you are rushing through your day?

What is nature offering you today? What lesson does it
have to offer to you? What wisdom is it communicating?
What does it want you to know?

EXPLORE FUN AND EASY

First, think of a task you dread. Here's a list to get you started:

- Washing dishes
- Doing laundry
- Exercising
- Public speaking
- Doctor and dentist appointments
- Waiting in line
- Waking up early
- A long commute
- Social events
- A yard or home project

When you think about this task, do you notice that you feel a sense of yuck, heaviness, and low motivation?

Now, ask yourself: could this be fun and easy?

I know this seems ridiculous at first. But, stick with me.

We tend to make things heavy and hard that aren't really that hard.

We begin to imagine how miserable we will be, but actually it is our choice to be miserable. Often, our sense of dread causes us to suffer through the task. A simple reframe can kick out those negative thoughts and the task suddenly becomes much less miserable.

Next time you feel dread, stuck, obligated, or frustrated, ask yourself if this could be fun and easy. You can feel your brain light up immediately. A spark of hope registers in your brain and your attitude shifts.

You might be rolling your eyes right now in disbelief, but try it out.

Yes, there are things that are never fun and easy—but in that case, alter the question to be: "how could I make this a little easier for myself?" I do this with bill paying because it is never fun. However, listening to music or watching a movie or sitting outside while bill paying really helps make that not-fun task a little less miserable.

This is a great practice to help us get through the daily tasks of being human. Many things are easier than we think they will be. This is a helpful way to lighten up and not take things so seriously. There is enough big stuff to worry about, let's make the small stuff more fun!

Here's to life being more fun and easy!

TRY THIS

Try out this practice on:

- Homework
- Cleaning
- Projects
- Exercise
- Eating well
- Relationships
- Aging
- Business

- Conversations
- Finances
- Changes

How can you approach these things with ease instead of making them hard? How can you make them fun? If fun is too much of a stretch, how can you make them less miserable?

Living with ease is living in harmony with life. Allow it to flow. Release the resistance. Stop the habit of making things hard. Life can be easier if you approach it with ease and see what happens.

CONSIDER TEA

The tricky part of staying present is often that we have so many balls in the air, we are afraid they will drop if we stop worrying about them. Or we are afraid that we will forget something. Or run out of time to finish the project. So we are often distracted with thinking of what we need do next and not focused on the task at hand.

When I feel overwhelmed, I use the acronym TEA (time, energy, attention) as a reset button:
What is getting my time, energy, and attention right now?
What do I want to be giving my time, energy, and attention to?
Who and/or what deserves my time, energy, and attention?

TEA is a helpful acronym to help us stay in alignment with our priorities, values, and goals.

It is also a helpful practice as an energy barometer—if your energy is low, consider what you are giving your time, energy, and attention to...then make some adjustments.

We get to choose and control how we spend our time, when we share our energy, and what we give our attention to.

Decide with whom and on what you will share your precious TEA.

TRY THIS

1. There are 168 hours in a week. Track how you spend your time for one week. Note everything in 15- or 30-minute increments.* Then reflect on how you spent your time. Is it what you intended? Does it reflect your most important people and work? Create a fictional ideal week for yourself by blocking the time the way you wish you could spend it. How do they compare? What adjustments are needed?

2. Think about the things and people that drain your energy. Now think about the things and people that fill you up with good energy. Can you seek out the things and people that give you energy and minimize the things and people that drain you? Or, if you can't avoid the energy drainers, can you protect yourself by imagining a clear bubble around you holding your good energy in and keeping the heavy energy out?

3. Where do you want your attention to go? Are there projects you want to finish? Are there things you want to learn to do? Are there people you want to spend more time with? What do you want to give attention to in this chapter of your life? How can you carve that out for yourself?

---

* A free worksheet on this exercise is available at lauravanderkam.com

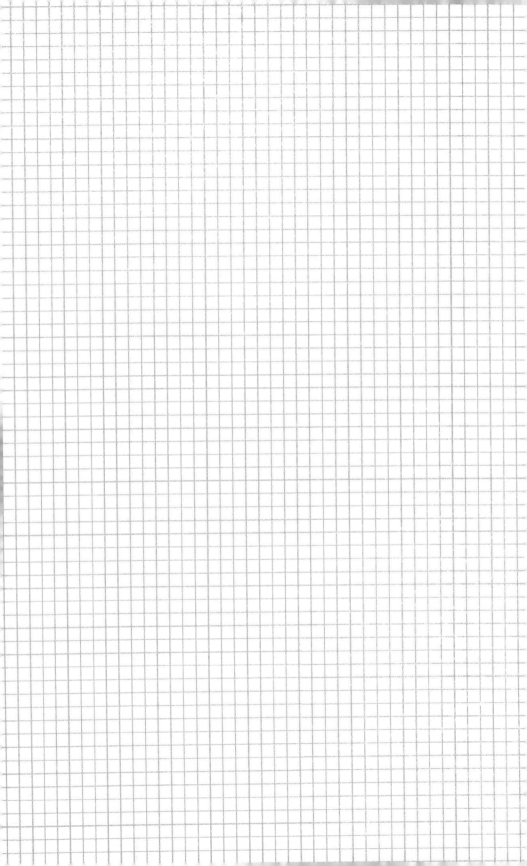

CREATE JOY

In the "Find More Energy" section of this book, I shared the research of Dr. Hawkins, who found joy to be one of the highest energy vibrational emotions human beings can experience. So, I dedicated this section of the book to help us practice creating joy.

Joy is something we create—actually, I like the word allow even more than create. We allow ourselves to feel joy. We remember that life can be fun, funny, amazing, thrilling, awe-inspiring, imaginative, and meaningful.

I hope you will read through these practices to get a feel for them and then return to this section when you notice that your life could use a dose of joy. Looking up videos of babies laughing at an adult popping bubble-wrap or kittens playing in a barn or baby goats jumping over each other usually does it for me. What makes you laugh? Seek out more of that.

When you are filled with joy, you inspire others to seek more joy.

DECLARE A CAKE DAY

I've always had a thing for what I call "math dates." Those days that stand out numerically—like 2/22/22 or 5/5/23. All my friends know that I love them, so I often post about them on social media, declaring that we should all celebrate with cake.

Over time, these posts evolved into what my friends would call "Cake Days." They would remind me of upcoming Cake Days or point out the ones I missed. This became a fun practice of noticing something small and celebrating it together.

Cake Days always bring a small dose of joy into my life—they remind me to celebrate the small things, instead of waiting only for the big occasions.

There are all kinds of little, everyday things we can and should celebrate, like finishing a work project, checking something off the to-do list, a sunny day, having friends and family we love—the list goes on and on. Those are all special occasions, too! When you declare that something is cause for a Cake Day, you're giving yourself a reason to feel joy. And when you feel joy, you exude joyful energy to others.

Cake Days are also good for when you need a lift. When you're struggling through a difficult week, why not think of a reason to have cake? To celebrate some small thing, to help you remember that there's still a lot of good in your life?

If you're feeling a little "meh" and want a way to lift your spirits, virtually every day of the year is some sort of holiday. And, therefore, there is always a perfectly good reason to celebrate with cake. Like Nothing Day (January 16), International Joke Day (July 1), or World Kindness Day (November 13)—why not start by being kind to yourself?

Cake Days can help us mark all the everyday reasons we have to honor this great, big, magic ride we are on together.

When we celebrate the little things, we send ripples of joy out into the world. Those ripples create a contribution to humanity that matters. And move us all toward a world filled with joy.

TRY THIS

Spend some time this week noticing the things that feel like little causes for celebration. What makes you feel good? What makes you feel grateful? What small things feel like special occasions? Make a plan to celebrate one of those things with cake. Or stop by a store and pick up some cake for no reason at all. You're here, and you're loved—and that's always worth celebrating!

FIND THE MIRACLES

There's a quote often attributed to Albert Einstein that I've always loved: "There are only two ways to live your life. One is as though nothing is a miracle. The other is as though everything is a miracle."

Einstein was onto something. There are indeed two ways to live, and one can help pull you through when life gets tough. Little miracles are everywhere, and the practice of looking for them is one of the most effective ways to bring ourselves hope.

Here's what I have noticed in the practice of noticing miracles: if I'm in awe of the miracles around me, then the minutiae of my worries starts to dissolve. If I stop to consider the miracle of gravity that's keeping me on this Earth, or the beautiful flower growing out of a crack in the sidewalk, or even the computer in my pocket that I can use to hear the voices of my loved ones, then I notice more and more miracles.

When we feel hopeless or in a dark place, it seems like everything is bad. That's when our mind goes into high gear, telling us things like: "it's never going to work out for me" or "bad things always happen to me."

The practice of finding miracles opens up the possibility that everything in fact isn't horrible, that there are amazing things beyond explanation happening all around us.

We can begin to challenge our negative thoughts by saying: "hey, I'm a part of this world full of miracles, and amazing things are happening in my life too." By signaling to your brain that you're looking for tangible evidence of good things—the everyday miracles that are beyond our imagination—you train it to keep looking. This is how we help ourselves find hope. Then we notice that things start to feel better.

Sometimes our anxiety, stress, pain, and grief distract us from the miracles around us. The daily pressures of life can keep us moving at a pace where we forget to notice all the numerous miracles that cross our paths.

Often we just need a reminder that we can still see miracles. Which means we still have hope.

When waves of stress overwhelm you, take a deep breath and notice the miracles of nature all around us: our complicated, amazing human bodies, the gravity that never fails us, the air we breathe. We are surrounded by miracles. It is up to us to pay attention, and let them work their magic.

TRY THIS

Take some time to look around you today. Can you find examples of small miracles—things that have occurred without a logical explanation? Maybe you even try making a list of those miracles to come back to during times when you need a reminder that there's always hope. Here are some examples:

- Your heart beating
- The sunrise and sunset
- The talents and gifts people were born with
- The food we eat
- The beauty of artwork
- The technologies that make life easier

- Flowers and plants
- The sound of birds
- All the colors around us
- The friends we've met
- The children we create
- The love we have experienced

GET YOUR THREE STEPS IN

There are a lot of mornings where I want to put my head under the covers and never come out. I love my work, but sometimes, first thing in the morning, it is easy to forget that. My brain lets dread take over, telling me that I have a long and difficult day ahead.

I have started experimenting with a quick three-step practice before I get out of bed, and I'm amazed at how well it works. I have noticed how my brain knows to override that dread-filled voice and move instead toward hope for the day ahead. I call this "getting my three steps in" and it takes me less than a minute.

1. Smile.
   This may sound silly, but it works: a smile tells your brain that you're safe, everything is going to be okay, and that you feel happy. It seems like it should be the opposite—that smiling is the result of feeling happy rather than the cause—but actually, we can tell our brain what to think and feel. Plus, research has shown that smiling releases dopamine and serotonin[46] (both feel-good hormones) and boosts our immune systems, making it

---

[46] Nicole Spector, "Smiling Can Trick Your Brain Into Happiness--and Boost Your Health," *NBC News*, November 2017. Retrieved from https://www.nbcnews.com/better/health/smiling-can-trick-your-brain-happiness-boost-your-health-ncna822591.

an easy way to take care of your emotional—and physical—health and remind your brain that this day has the potential to be great.

2. Tell your body "thank you."
    One by one, thank your organs, muscles, and bones. This is not only a way to appreciate all the miraculous ways your body functions, but a step toward more deeply appreciating yourself, too.

3. Decide one thing you can do to have a good day. Ask yourself: "how can I have a good day?" Pick one thing that will cheer you up that's entirely within your control—a special coffee drink, or a 10-minute walk outdoors, for example—and resolve to make that happen. Realizing how much agency you actually have over your days is a great way to help lessen dread and move toward a place of hope and lightness.

It's incredible how far those three little steps can take you on your journey out of heaviness into hope. They are also as effective any other part of the day—before you go to bed at night or if you need a mid-day boost. The next time you feel that sneaky sense of dread starting to creep in, remind yourself: "I have to get my three steps in."

TRY THIS

Put a note beside your bed that says "three steps." Even better, put it right by your alarm clock, so it's the first thing you see (and if you use your phone to wake up, try naming your alarm "three steps"). Try it every morning when you wake up—or when you go to bed, which also works great—for at least a week, and see if you notice a more hopeful feeling when it's time to start or end your day.

PURSUE MEANINGFUL DAYS

I was doing some research and found a number of studies on hope in people with terminal illnesses. One study talks about the importance of hoping for a "meaningful quality of life," a phrase that really stuck with me.[47]

What makes a life meaningful? It's different for each of us. One thing that holds true, though, is that a meaningful life is made up of meaningful days, which is a great place to start.

Meaning can come from anywhere: it can come from nature, or loved ones, or your job, or your hobbies, or helping out those in need—there are a million ways to find meaning, and it's different for everyone. Taking time to figure out what brings meaning to you is a practice that will serve you well the rest of your life. Days add up, and without intentionality, we might lose our chance of finding hope, and peace, and joy.

If we make each day meaningful, then we make our entire lives meaningful. And by doing so, not only do we foster hope within ourselves, we do the same for others: we can inspire them to pursue meaningful lives, too.

---

[47] Adam Kadlac, "Fostering Hope in the Face of Death," *Clinical Ethics* 15, no. 4 (2020): 167-174. doi:10.1177/1477750920927167.

TRY THIS

Think about what makes up a meaningful day for you. It could be anything from "standing in the sun" to "listening to music" to "spending time with someone I love." Make a list of those things—maybe even keep a small notebook to add to them from time to time. Check back on that list often and tell yourself what you'll do to make sure your day has meaning. Here are some examples:

- I'm going to listen to the birds today.
- I'm going to read today.
- I'm going to buy myself flowers today.
- I'm going to make food I love today.
- I'm going to take a walk today.
- I'm going to send a message to someone I love.
- I'm going to watch something that makes me laugh.

NOTICE CONTAGIOUS HAPPINESS

Years ago, I used to go to dinner every month with a former colleague, Marie. Even though we no longer worked together, we'd grown to be friends and still made it a habit to see each other on a regular basis.

One night, when I got home from dinner with Marie, my husband brought up the fact that I always seemed to be in a bad mood after I'd spent time with her. I hadn't realized it—but he was right. Marie always seemed to be angry about something, and often spent the entire dinner talking about all the things going wrong in her life. After a few hours of being her sounding board, I'd come home under my own little dark cloud.

What I know now from years of experience is this: the company you keep can have a major effect on your emotions. Studies have shown that emotions—whether positive or negative—are actually contagious.

This phenomenon is called "emotional contagion" and has been studied extensively both at Emory University and Yale University.[48] Emotional contagion is why I always came home feeling bummed out after time spent with Marie. I couldn't help it. I absorbed her negativity.

---

[48] Allison Aubrey, "*Happiness: It Really Is Contagious*," NPR, December 2008. Retrieved from https://www.npr.org/2008/12/05/97831171/happiness-it-really-is-contagious#:~:text=Happiness%3A%20It%20Really%20Is%20Contagious%20A%20new%20study%20finds%20that,network%20%E2%80%94%20reaching%20friends%20of%20friends.

Now, I am intentional about spending time with my happy friends, the ones who always seem to be lit up. Not only because I enjoy being with them, but because I know that they'll leave me feeling better. Even when going through hard times, these people can face it with strength, humor, and hope.

If you want to let more happiness into your life, you just need to look for the happy people. The ones who give off positivity. The ones who leave you feeling good after you've spent time with them. Scientifically, they're spreading happiness to you—which means you can turn around and spread it to someone else. And before you know it, you've made the whole world a little happier.

TRY THESE

1. Take a field trip this week to a place where you know happy people will be, like a park or an ice cream shop. Spend some time hanging out there, and see if you don't leave feeling just a little happier.

2. Think about who some of your happiest friends and loved ones are. Pick one and connect with them by either sending them a message or setting up a chance to see them. Challenge yourself to start keeping in closer touch with the happy people in your life.

PUT IMAGINATION TO WORK

As kids, we were great at using our imaginations. We played house, performed on pretend stages, lived in pillow forts, and had imaginary friends. We didn't hesitate to dream up all kinds of scenarios and put ourselves right in the middle of them.

As adults, we tend to neglect our imagination or worse, forget to use it altogether. The good news is: we can still resurrect our imaginations, regardless of age.

Our imaginations hold so much power; they can actually help move us to where we want to be. To places of opportunity and hope.

Let's say you're a kid, and you're pretending to be a teacher. By using your imagination, you're making it a real possibility that you might one day be a teacher. When we imagine, our subconscious actually tells our brain to file the idea away, so that it will know to look for it. You're filing away the thought: "I can be a teacher if I want to," and giving your brain a chance to help you make that happen.

As an adult, you can still use your imagination to work in similar ways. Here's an example that comes from one of my clients: she came to me frustrated because she hadn't found the right partner. Together, we imagined what her life would be like with the exact type of partner she wanted. She visualized things like visiting Colorado with him and going on hikes. By using her imagination to visualize that future, she gave herself hope by clearly naming what she wanted. It felt more like a real possibility, one that her subconscious could file away and take steps toward.

If you find yourself hoping for something, try imagining that scenario in detail. By doing that, you're giving yourself a dose of hope, which will allow you to hang on in that moment and believe that the future could be better. Plus, you're training your brain not to worry so much—to stay calm and pull yourself out of despair.

Try using your imagination more every day: imagine your days filled with things that you love to do. What would those things be? Feel the shift into hope when you see them—what you're really seeing is the potential.

TRY THIS

Use the following questions as a way to unlock how the imagination you used as a kid might be able to still serve you as an adult.

What did you pretend as a child in your home or yard? List as many things as you can think of.

Did the environments you created in your imagination have similarities to the environment in which you live today? Do you have a spirit of adventure that was evident in how you pretended as a child? Do you care for people now as you did in your pretend play? Think a little more deeply about the things you imagined as a child. You may find they help you become more self-aware.

How might using your imagination today help you with creativity, decision making, or finding hope?

How could a return to pretending help you as an adult? Experiment with role-playing how you would like a conversation to go. Explore how you might do the job you dream of. Pretend you're on a date with the partner of your dreams. Pretend you're walking the beaches, streets, or landscape of the place you want to visit. Pretend you already have what you most long for.

Notice what you feel when you pretend as an adult. You might feel resistance at first; you might feel silly or too idealistic. Move into that discomfort a little further to make the most of this experience. Acknowledge those feelings, and place those feelings of resistance on a shelf. Allow your inner child to pretend again. The power of pretending is a path toward hope for the future you desire. What we imagine often becomes our reality.

SEEK OUT MINI THRILLS

Take a moment and think about the tiny things that make you happy. Things like putting on your favorite socks, or using a body wash you love, or the way your dog's tail wags when you come home.

I like to call these "mini thrills," which is any small thing that brings you a surge of excitement or pleasure. Reading a good book, eating an ice cream cone, napping, watching a good movie, buying yourself flowers, laughing with someone you love, starting a new hobby, rearranging furniture in a room...all of these are great examples. And often, they happen without us even noticing the thrill.

A simple practice to try if you want to bring more joy into your life is to seek out at least one mini thrill a day. To go a step further, you can even tell yourself: "I'm excited about watching a movie tonight." What we know about our subconscious mind is that it is a storehouse of beliefs—if I'm naming what I'm excited about, my subconscious brain files a belief that today is going to be a good day. I'm fascinated by how easy this is and how much it helps; we just have to remember to do it.

Often, life is a lot better than we think it is. To keep us safe, the amygdala in our brain likes to remind us of all that can go wrong. The amygdala's job is to keep us alive and watch for danger. But sometimes, we need to turn off our alarm system so that we can experience peace, joy, and love.

If we're living in fear, we forget to notice the good stuff. And there is so much good stuff that we miss by worrying. Many of us steal joy away from ourselves by worrying about things that will likely never occur. Seeking and noticing mini thrills is a great way to change that habit.

Every day, challenge yourself to pursue at least one mini thrill. Think of things that you are looking forward to, things that make you smile, people who are easy to be with, and projects that feed your soul. Take time to pause and notice the good feeling—that surge of excitement or pleasure.

When you get intentional about filling your days with these things, you move toward a more joyful life.

TRY THESE

1. Before you go to bed tonight, plan what mini thrill you'll have tomorrow. Allow yourself to be excited about it by saying: "I'm excited about _____ to-morrow!" It's amazing how this shifts your outlook on the next day. And remind yourself again in the morning to help your outlook shift even more.

2. Share a mini thrill each day or week on social media. A beloved client of mine, Amy, did this and used the hashtag #minithrill. I loved watching her delight in little things all summer. Her delight brought me delight. If we all use this hashtag we can see what small things thrill us and get ideas from each other.

FIND HAPPINESS
THROUGH GIVING

One of my teen clients decided she wanted to share her struggles with anxiety more publicly. She started by sharing her story of struggle when she saw someone struggling. She became generous by sharing her experience with anxiety. When she saw someone sitting alone at lunch, she joined them and asked them if they were okay and told them her story. When she saw someone who was reading a poem aloud in class freeze with anxiety, she shared some practices that helped her through those moments. While she hoped she'd made those others feel better, she was stunned by how much better she felt after sharing her story.

What she experienced is something science has already told us: that there's a reason why you feel better when you give.

In 2017, the University of Zurich in Switzerland published a study that evaluated the brain activity in a person as it correlated with generosity. 50 people were each given $100 and split into two groups: one group was told to spend the money on themselves, while the other group was instructed to spend the money on other people.

The participants' brains were then studied, using MRI scans to evaluate the areas of the brain associated with social behavior and generosity. Those areas in the brains of the group who gave the money away were noticeably more affected than those who had spent the money on themselves. Feelings of happiness were reported to be higher in the charitable group, too.[49]

This study may seem obvious, but the MRI data showed that areas of the brain associated with joy and happiness light up in the brains of those who gave gifts to others as opposed to those who kept the money for themselves.

Whether it's through your stories, your time, or your resources, giving to others can be a direct line to your own joy and happiness. If you find yourself feeling down or in search of a lift, think about what you might have to offer someone. You'll be giving yourself something just as valuable, too.

TRY THIS

Think about what resources you have today, this week, or this month and make a giving plan. Here are some suggestions:

- Sharing your story
- Smiling at everyone you encounter
- Offering help if you see someone struggling
- Wishing someone at the gas station a good day
- Making food for someone
- Offering to run an errand
- Giving someone a gift card
- Anonymously doing something nice for someone

---

[49] Soyoung Park et al, "A Neural Link Between Generosity and Happiness," *Nature Communications,* July 2017. doi:10.1038/ncomms15964.

USE THE POWER
OF YOUR THOUGHTS

My friend Shirley has a son named Josh. Recently, I asked her how he was doing. "He's doing great!" she said. "As he likes to say, every meal is his favorite meal, every person he's with is his favorite person, and every day is the best day ever!"

Josh lives with autism and faces challenges every day, but his soul knows the secret to creating joy—the secret so many of us are searching for.

Here it is, and it couldn't be simpler: we can create joy with just the power of our thinking.

Josh chooses to embrace each moment as the best one ever. He may not realize he's making that choice, but it's his way of existing in the world. And it's a way of being where joy comes easily to him.

Since that conversation with Shirley, I've thought a lot about Josh when I eat a meal, spend time with family, reflect on my day, and even when I'm doing mundane tasks. I can choose to see it all through a lens of hard, heaviness, and dread, or I can choose to see it through a lens of wonder, enthusiasm, and joy.

Some days it's easier to find joy than others, but making this an intentional practice has helped me re-frame my perspective and find joy more easily than I used to.

We should all follow Josh's lead and decide that everything is our favorite thing. It's hard to believe that it could be this simple, but it actually can be. It might not change your circumstances, but it can add lightness to your spirit and lift the heaviness a bit.

Using the power of your thoughts to create joy can have lasting power, too. You are training your brain to look for the good, which will soon become your default way of thinking.

When you always look for the good, chances are, you'll always find it.

TRY THIS

Number a sheet of paper from 1 to 10. Challenge yourself to create joy by listing ten things you experience throughout the day that make you feel lightness, wonder, or enthusiasm. What are the little, everyday things that bring you happiness? What favorite things cross your path more often than you realize? To train your brain even more, repeat this exercise for several days in a row.

MAKE TIME FOR AWE

The University of California Berkeley's Greater Good Science Center has been studying the art and science of awe for over 15 years. I've been following their work and am intrigued that they are proving clinically what we all instinctively know to be true: feeling a sense of awe makes us feel good.

Awe is a positive emotion that's triggered by the awareness of something larger than one's self. It's a complex emotion that's sometimes not immediately understandable, but can feel similar to wonder, amazement, vastness, reverence, and insignificance. The simplified definition is that awe is what comes from viewing something that's beyond words or beyond explanation.

What I'm in awe of is different than what you're in awe of: it's a personal thing. It can surprise us, too—while we expect to feel awe in the presence of something grand, sometimes it's a tiny thing. Often, no matter what it is, we're caught off guard and spellbound for a moment.

Think of a time when you felt in awe of something or someone—it might have been when you looked at the stars, or visited the Grand Canyon, or kissed the head of a baby. It might have been seeing a butterfly leave a chrysalis or witnessing a hummingbird's hum, or in the quiet moments watching a sunset.

There is so much peace and joy to be found when you get intentional about making time for awe. By being aware of it, and looking for things that are beyond logic, we can put things into perspective and see things from high above. It gives us "eagle vision": what you'd see while soaring above the Earth.

Awe can be a powerful spiritual teacher that helps us see the big picture. When you're down in the weeds, there's so much around you that you can't see. When we zoom out and notice all of the amazing things happening on Earth, we learn to focus on all the good happening around us. By being intentional about seeking awe, we lift ourselves up and give ourselves the chance to take it all in.

TRY THESE

1. Go for an "awe walk": head outside and focus only on the amazing details of nature. On your walk, you might select a color and watch for things in nature of that color.

2. Practice "awe seeing": look at yourself and other people through eyes of awe.

   - Notice the essence, soul, or spirit that resides inside you and every person.
   - See yourself and others as children who want to be loved and celebrated.
   - Think about the heartbeat inside your chest. Realize the person you are talking to also has a heart working hard for them inside their body.
   - See a life story in someone's eyes and, when you look in a mirror, see your own life story in your eyes.
   - Notice the scars from life experiences. Consider what this person has survived or experienced.

3. Be in awe of what it means to be human and realize that we share this human experience with every other person on Earth.

4. Take some time throughout the day to notice all the daily miracles around you:

   - When you wake up: start your day by saying "wow," followed by something positive. Here are some phrases to get you started:
     Wow, I get to do _____ today!
     Wow, I slept really well!
     Wow, I really love my bed!
     Wow, I get to see _____ today!
     Wow, I can't wait to have a cup of coffee!
   - On your drive: pause while you are traveling to work, school, or elsewhere, look out your window for a minute, and find a "wow" phrase:
     Wow, look at the sky today!
     Wow, my car is an amazing machine!
     Wow, public transportation gets me where I need to be!
     Wow, all of these people are going to work just like me!
     Wow, I feel good about _____ today!
   - Evening activities: as you get tired throughout the day, it's easy to see what's wrong instead of right. But you can change this and restore your energy by focusing on the good things. Here are some phrases to try:
     Wow, look at the sunset!
     Wow, I love coming home!
     Wow, my/our dog/cat/etc. gives me unconditional love!

Wow, I accomplished _____ at work/school today!

Wow, I love this dinner!

- Going to bed: Ending the day with a sense of "wow" prepares you to fall asleep with positive thoughts:

Wow, this was a good day!

Wow, I am grateful for this bed!

Wow, my body supported and powered me through the day!

Wow, I am hopeful for tomorrow!

Wow, I have family and friends I love!

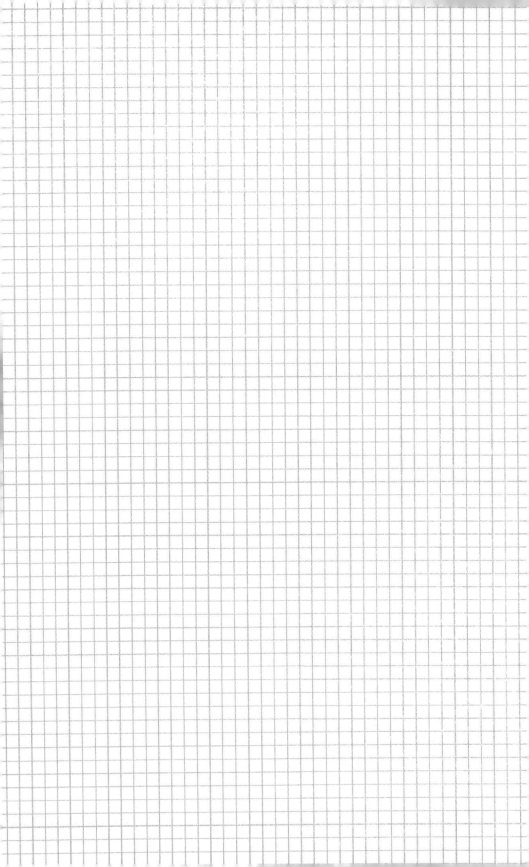

CONNECT WITH
COMPASSION

In one of his last works, The Descent of Man, Charles Darwin said that natural selection would favor those with compassion and that the "most sympathetic members, would flourish best, and rear the greatest number of offspring." You might recall that Darwin didn't believe in God until late in his life. After all of his research on evolution and human behavior, he landed on the belief that people are compassionate by nature and there is a God that is beyond human imagination.[50]

I found this research while I was in seminary and dove deeper into the topic of the compassionate nature of people. That led to me ultimately leave organized religion and become someone who taught and researched compassion. Compassion is what I saw Jesus teaching people. Compassion is what I have found in the teachings of Judaism, Islam, Hinduism, Buddhism, Native American theology,

---

[50] Paul Ekman, "Darwin's Compassionate View of Human Nature," *JAMA* 303, no. 6 (2010): 557-558.doi:10.1001/jama.2010.101.

and African religions. At their core, these world religions are teaching compassion.

So if that is truly the core of every faith, why don't we see more compassion in our human behaviors? This continues to boggle my mind. But in the meantime, this section offers practices to grow our compassionate hearts and minds even wider than they already are. My hope is that if you and I do this work, then we'll create a ripple effect in the lives of those we encounter. If we are kind, then they are kind, then the person they are kind to is kind to the next person, and maybe we'll begin to see the cosmic needle arc a little more toward compassion. It starts with you and me. We can do this together and watch the magic unfold.

ENERGETIC CORDS

Both of my teenagers traveled to Scotland to act in a play at the International Fringe Festival. It was the opportunity of a lifetime for them, but hard for my husband and I to be away from them for two weeks. They traveled with ten students and two teachers. My teens asked us to stay home because they really wanted to do this on their own to prove to themselves they could travel internationally for two weeks without mom and dad. I got it, but it felt like our whole world was in that airplane over the sea. Everyone did great and came home safely. Likely, you also know the experience of being separated from someone you love.

When we are apart from those we love, it is helpful to remember that there are energetic cords that connect us. Though we were on separate continents, it helped me to imagine an energetic cord connecting me to my children. As a mom, I felt helpless and far away, but I could send them love even though there was an ocean between us.

Your love for another person creates an energetic cord that connects your heart to theirs.

If you are separated from someone you love, try this visualization today. Read through it first and then close your eyes, take a deep breath, and imagine this connection.

Bring your beloved person to mind, see them wherever they may be at this moment. Picture a golden glowing cord extending from your heart. See that cord traveling over land and sea until it connects to your loved one's heart. Now send the energy of love through that cord—see it flowing from your heart to theirs.

When you feel far away or helpless, this visualization can bring you peace and send a gift of loving energy to the person you love.

An energetic cord exists between any two people who have an emotional connection to one another.

That means that there may be cords no longer serving us. We may need to remove an energetic cord if the relationship is draining our energy. When it feels like a cord is siphoning energy out of you, then it is time to cut that cord.

Here is a visualization you can practice to detach from an energetic cord: Bring to mind the person with whom you wish to release the connection. Imagine a cord connecting the two of you. Picture a pair of scissors cutting through that cord. You might imagine that person now floating away from your life. They are no longer tethered to you. You are free of their energy. Allow them to drift away with gratitude. Repeat this process until it feels like the energy has been released.

You can love someone and cut the energetic cord at the same time. Your love for them remains, but their energy is free of yours. There may be family members or friends who you want in your life, but you need to release the energetic bond between you. After you cut the energetic cord, you will likely notice a more peaceful feeling when you are in their presence. You can be with them, but not drained by them.

This may feel strange to you, but humans have explored this phenomenon for thousands of years. Ancient sacred texts, mindfulness teachings, and research in psychology all speak of a feeling of connection to another person beyond explanation. We know this feeling because we have all experienced it. Because it isn't something we can prove or see, though, our logical minds create doubt and resistance.

Let your senses feel it and give yourself permission to know it is real. You are still connected to anyone who has touched your heart even when they are far away, estranged, or deceased. If someone you love has died, imagine this golden cord connecting your spirits together. This is a peace-giving practice.

You and I have an energetic connection as you read these words. I wrote this book for you and you are reading it. We are connected now through this book and I love thinking about how it bonds our souls.

TRY THIS

Spend time with the visualizations above. It may feel uneasy at first, but keep doing it. Your brain might resist it a bit, but your soul longs for this kind of practice. Imagine energetic cords running all over the Earth to the people we love. You can even send a cord to someone you don't yet know. Maybe it is a partner you want to bring into your life. Imagine that your heart is sending a cord out to the perfect match for you and visualize the cord connecting to that person. Maybe you want to connect to someone who is hurting. Imagine sending a golden cord from your heart to a mother who just lost a child in another country. Picture your energetic cord traveling across the ocean into the city where she lives and into the hospital or home where she is grieving. Send your love and compassion wherever you feel called to send it. This can be a profound practice of loving kindness—for you and them.

PRACTICE UBUNTU

Ubuntu (pronounced *ooh-bun-too*) is an African philosophy that captures our common humanity and shared human experiences; it highlights our interconnectedness. As this idea has spread throughout humanity, ubuntu teachings have been translated in a number of ways, such as:

- I am because you are.
- We are bound together beyond what we can see.
- I grow because you grow.
- One finger cannot pick up a grain.
- A person is a person through other people.

I first discovered the concept of ubuntu in seminary while studying African indigenous religions and quickly fell in love with the wisdom it offers. The more I thought about ubuntu, the more it helped to shape me into a compassionate person.

At its most basic, ubuntu promotes human kindness—the concept that we need to cooperate with fellow humans in order to survive. Ubuntu reinforces that the whole village thrives when we teach, protect, care, feed, heal, and help one another.

Archbishop Desmond Tutu once wrote:

"You might have much of the world's riches, and you might hold a portion of authority, but if you have no ubuntu, you do not amount to much. Ubuntu is what it means to be truly human, to know that you are bound up with others in the bundle of life."[51]

Where can you and I work to make ubuntu the guiding action in our lives? What happens if we apply more ubuntu thinking throughout our days? Maybe it means we release a competitive spirit, a scarcity mentality, or our tendency toward self-centeredness. Maybe it means we don't need to win, get ahead, or do more than someone else. Maybe it means we don't need to be right. We focus instead on being kind.

As a global community in the 21st century, we have the opportunity to come together—to spread human kindness, to care for one another, and to show respect for all living things. If we lead with ubuntu, we can all thrive and contribute to the change we long to see in the world.

TRY THESE

1. Consider the list of often-marginalized groups below (this list is not meant to be comprehensive). Choose a group of people you would like to learn more about. Is there a group you relate to the most? Is there a group whose struggle has always been a cause of concern for you? Notice if one of these groups makes you feel uncomfortable; maybe that is a group to consider learning more about.

---

[51] Archbishop Desmond Tutu, *God Has a Dream: A Vision of Hope for Our Time* (New York: Doubleday, 2003).

- Immigrants, refugees, and migrants
- Women and girls
- Victims of human trafficking
- Those battling mental illness
- Children and youth
- The LGBTQ+ community
- People of differing religions
- The developmentally delayed
- The physically disabled
- The incarcerated (and their loved ones)
- People released from incarceration
- People of low socioeconomic status
- The unemployed
- People without housing
- The aging population
- People of a particular ethnicity/country of origin

2. Find ways to educate yourself on the current issues facing this group of people. Read a book about them, or explore other ways you could learn more from trusted sources. Seek out the stories of individual people as much as possible and aim for a better understanding of what it is like to be them.

3. Consider contributing your time, resources, and love to this group of people. Search for agencies that support this group of people. Two good places to start are volunteermatch.org and charitynavigator.org.

4. In your social circles, share what you are learning. You may find that people in your circles want to learn more, too.

SEEK LIKE-HEARTED PEOPLE

We often hear of being "like-minded" with others, but in a nation where we are divided on a lot of topics, I think it is helpful to think about finding "like-hearted" people.

Think about the people who are kind like you are. Consider those with whom you share a passion. Think about the people who are excited about the same things you are. Consider those who love things like you do.

Think about the compassionate people you know who have hearts like yours. When we know we share like hearts, we can hold space for disagreement. We can look beyond our opinions and see the love we carry inside.

We don't have to think alike, as long as we love alike. I realized this when I began hiring coaches for my team to help me meet the high demand for our method of compassionate coaching. As I was in conversations with candidates, I was looking for like-hearted people. I wanted to find coaches who will love our clients like I do, take a compassionate approach to giving advice, and create a judgment-free space. I knew they were all teachable and could learn my methodology, but it was important to me to find the right hearts.

My office is now filled with new energy from those beautiful hearts serving people in beautiful ways. I have learned that like-hearted is more important than like-minded. I welcome their different perspectives, life experiences, and skills. We all bring different gifts into our coaching sessions. What matters is that our hearts are aligned.

As you encounter people this week, notice who feels like-hearted to you. Those are your people. It has been said: "we are who we spend time with." Surrounding yourself with big-hearted people helps us grow our hearts even bigger. Love begets love.

TRY THIS

Think through the like-hearted people in your life. It may be friends, family, or people you want to get to know better. Notice that you might be different, but your hearts want the same things. When you encounter someone new, see if you can determine if they are like-hearted. Observe without judgment. Just notice who has a heart like yours. Seek out deeper connections with those people.

TAKE A COMPASSIONATE PAUSE

I was leading a workshop with a group of healthcare providers when one of the participants said: "I'm afraid I'm losing the compassion that called me into this line of work. I feel like I'm getting more hard-hearted and angrier by the minute."

I don't think he's alone in feeling this way; life is hard, and especially tough for those on the frontlines of healthcare. They are often overworked and under-appreciated, leading many to feel like finding compassion is a struggle.

Studies have shown that just by giving ourselves five minutes of compassion, it increases the compassion we have for others, too. In one healthcare-specific study, they found that after doctors took time to practice self-kindness, their patients reported having a more positive experience.[52]

It's the airplane oxygen mask theory: before you can take care of others, you have to start with yourself. You can't pour out what you haven't filled up on—and that includes compassion.

In a workshop with emergency department residents, we focused on self-

---

[52] L. Carol Ritchie, "Does Taking Time for Compassion Make Doctors Better at Their Jobs?" *NPR*, April 2019. Retrieved from https://www.npr.org/sections/health-shots/2019/04/26/717272708/does-taking-time-for-com passion-make-doctors-better-at-their-jobs#:~:text=Cavan%20Images%20RF-,Studies%20show%20that%20 when%20doctors%20practice%20compassion,%20patients%20 fare%20better,and%20doctors%20experience%20 less%20burnout.&text=For%20most%20of%20his%20career,%20Dr.

compassion practices in order to learn, as one person put it, "how to keep from drowning." One of them is a practice I call "compassionate pause."

A compassionate pause is an intentional moment of pause to notice what you are feeling and say something encouraging to yourself. A physician might stop in the hallway and close their eyes for a few seconds and say to themselves, "that was a tough patient, but you are a good human."

The focus is to soften the irritation that might be causing an inner struggle with compassion. This isn't a free pass to let bad behavior off the hook or turn you into a doormat. Think of it instead as a practice to save your own health: the cortisol released when we're stressed and feeling hard-hearted isn't good for us. If we can practice softening just one notch, we can interrupt that cortisol release and save ourselves from the damage a stress cycle can cause.

A compassionate pause helps your emotional health and the emotional health of those around you. You'll find that when you talk to yourself more kindly, you end up talking to others more kindly, too.

To be the compassionate people we want to be in this world, we have to practice taking a compassionate pause for ourselves.

TRY THIS

Here are a number of questions to ask yourself the next time you're struggling to find compassion for yourself or for others:

- Would taking a compassionate pause for a few seconds help me feel more calm? (A compassionate pause might be just a few deep breaths with your hand on your heart, silently encouraging yourself.)
- What if I took that angry thought and just softened it down one notch?

- Could I think about that person who irritates me, honor my feelings, and then encourage myself to move on and not keep thinking about the irritation?
- When I am frustrated with someone in my family, could I leave the room for a compassionate pause to honor my frustration and then return with a more caring and curious mindset?
- To those who consider themselves perfectionists: what if you softened one notch in your expectations of yourself? Just consider what one notch softer would feel like. Would it grant a little relief?
- To those who struggle with balance: what if you paused and allowed yourself a little break, or gave yourself permission to do nothing?
- To those irritated at work: during your workday, can you remind yourself to take a compassionate pause between meetings or tasks?

IDENTIFY EXPANDERS

A few years ago, my friend Kara called me an "Expander" in her life. Kara is a super cool human being who is always teaching me new things. As soon as her word "Expander" hit my brain, it felt good and I wanted to know more. She explained that one of her spiritual teachers coined the term to mean someone in your life who helps you expand into your potential.

She described an Expander as someone you identify with who is what you want to become or is doing what you want to do. They embody what you want. They give you the inspiration that, if they have it, then you can too.

Kara said that I am an Expander to her "of faith, strength, self-compassion, knowingness, individuality, joy, and fun." I immediately loved this new job title and made it my mission to become even more of that for the people in my life.

Kara is an Expander to me too. She suggests things that I haven't thought of yet. She confirms my intuition and encourages me to follow it. She was the one who encouraged my first ideas for my business, Compassion Fix, and the work I do today. When we are together we talk about our dreams, share our wonderings, and help each other see how it can all be possible. She expands my heart and mind.

Who are the Karas in your life? And who can you be a Kara for?

Find those people who help you expand. I'm always watching for people who expand my thinking, help me learn, and encourage my potential. I feel more alive and happy when I'm with my Expanders. I am more authentic, energized and hopeful around them. If, as you read this, your inner critic is whispering: "that sounds a little selfish," open your curiosity about this topic and tell that inner critic to be quiet for a few minutes while you read the rest of this section.

If we are all living in an expanded manner, we inspire others to do the same. It isn't selfish, it is world-serving.

The opposite of expansion is constraint. This happens when we get defensive instead of open to learning something new. It happens when we play small and dim our lights. Constraint occurs around certain people who are jealous or questioning our talents. We constrict when we live in fear. Constraint occurs when we surround ourselves with only people who agree with us.

Expansion comes when we open up to being a little uncomfortable, seeing a new point of view, and exploring new ideas. There is so much to learn in our lifetime; open up to it, and allow yourself to expand.

TRY THIS

Expand this week. Expand the love you have for others by reaching out a little further. See if you can expand the love you have for yourself this week too. Take a deep breath and notice the expansion of your lungs. Drive a new route to work. Try food from another culture. Read about a topic you have always wanted to explore. Stretch yourself in new ways. Expand beyond your comfort zone just a notch and see how it feels.

Find your Expanders and be an Expander.

RECOGNIZE YOURSELF IN OTHERS

At some time in our lives, we all have had a coworker who was tough to get along with. I remember one who was competitive, and often seemed to undermine those of us who worked alongside her. She came off as abrasive and quick to interrupt others.

One day, instead of continuing to harbor resentment toward her, I decided to try a different tactic: I tried to see myself in her. She was afraid of not mattering. I was too. She wanted to be heard. I felt the same way. She was learning and trying to find her way, just like I was—and everyone else around us, too.

As humans, we're all new here on Earth, and we're all constantly trying to find our way. Together, we share that experience. Our interconnectedness is amazing, when you think about it—we all want to be known and loved. We are all the same on the inside, with the same organs and basic human functions.

Research has consistently shown that to be compassionate with others and with ourselves, we must be able to recognize a shared experience among all of us.[53] We know what it's like to be human, by the very fact that we are humans ourselves.

---

[53] Dreisoerner, A., Junker, N. M., & van Dick, R. (2020). The relationship among the components of self-compassion: A pilot study using a compassionate writing intervention to enhance self-kindness, common humanity, and mindfulness. Journal of Happiness Studies, 1-27.

But this is easy to forget when we're frustrated with someone, or hold different political views, or get cut off in traffic. When we stop to remember our similarities—to see ourselves in others—it becomes a lot easier to cool off. Then it is easier to find compassion for one another. And to remember that we're all just trying to navigate our way through this same human experience we all get to share.

Every human being longs for the same things: to feel safe, to be loved, to feel a sense of achievement, and to know that they matter to someone. We have so much in common because we know how hard life can be. We all want to know we are lovable. We all want to know we can accomplish something. We all want to feel safe. We all want freedom and opportunity. We all want to feel significant. We all laugh, cry, wonder, forget, worry, doubt, fear, grieve, and hope.

The next time you find yourself really irritated with someone, practice looking at them and recognizing yourself. Imagine that their heart is beating, just like yours. Their lungs are expanding with each breath, just like yours. They have a complex and complicated brain, just like yours. They're worried about their kids, or trying to figure out what to have for dinner, or how to manage their busy schedules—any or all of that, just like you.

Being human is hard. And right now, there are eight billion others on this planet having a shared experience right alongside you. Practice recognizing yourself in everyone who crosses your path, and see how much softer and more peaceful this human experience can be for you.

TRY THESE

1. While out in public (in traffic, at the store, or anywhere else), notice someone near you. Remind yourself that they're having a human experience, just like you are, and see if you can imagine answers to the following questions:

- What are they worried about today?
- Who have they lost in their life?
- What disappointments have they faced?
- What do they feel unsure about?
- What big questions do they have?
- How are they navigating this experience in the same ways that you are?

2. Now think of someone who's made you angry, or just has a way of getting under your skin. As you think about them, consider what you have in common while you ask yourself the following questions:

- What are they worried about today?
- Who have they lost in their life?
- What disappointments have they faced?
- What do they feel unsure about?
- What big questions do they have?
- How are they navigating this experience in the same ways that you are?

JUDGE SOFTLY

Something magical happens the first time your child has a tantrum in public or your baby starts crying on a flight. From that moment on, you will forever feel for someone you see in the same situation. You know it's hard. You've been there.

You learn firsthand the meaning of the well-known adage: "before you judge a man, walk a mile in his shoes." That wisdom is said to have originated from "Judge Softly," a poem written in 1895 by Mary T. Lathrap. Mary was a reformer, suffragist, and preacher whose timeless works of poetry spoke to social justice and human equality.

Is there any image that speaks more to social justice and equality than the concept of walking in another's shoes? The more we put ourselves in the shoes of others, the more we understand what it is like to be them. The more we understand, the more connected we feel. The more connected we feel to others, the less isolated we become.

Compassion connects us and reminds us that we're all sharing a human experience. Judging others separates us and leads to feelings of isolation. If we stay in our shoes, so to speak, we isolate ourselves and we risk feeling alone.

The next time you notice yourself judging another person, try a simple mindset shift toward compassion: imagine you are that person. You're the parent with the screaming baby. You're the person driving slower than everyone else on the highway. You're the person who's distracted at work. You are a human just like they are. We're all trying our best to navigate this world, and we are doing it with billions of others.

The more you put yourself in others' shoes, the more you'll grow in compassion, be reminded that we're all sharing this human experience, and soften your judgments of yourself, too.

TRY THIS

Follow the prompts below to give you an idea of how this might work in your life. Notice the judgment, then imagine what the other person might be experiencing.

"That parent shouldn't let that child throw a fit."
Here I am frustrated and tired, with a toddler melting down in the grocery aisle. I wish people would quit staring.

"That person is really out of shape."
Here I am feeling heavy and out of breath after climbing the stairs. I wish I was motivated to get fit. This embarrasses me.

"He made a really bad financial investment."
Here I am falling for something too good to be true, hoping I could make more money for my family. I knew it wasn't smart, but I was desperate.

"She is so materialistic."
Here I am buying things that I hope will make me feel better about myself, because I am struggling with my self-worth.

"Those kids are spoiled rotten."
Here I am, trying to make my kids happy and longing for them to love me. I thought giving them everything they wanted would work.

"That was a really dumb thing to say."
Here I am feeling insecure and trying to contribute to the conversation without thinking it through all the way.

"That guy doesn't belong in this club."
Here I am, feeling out of my league and unaccepted here, trying to convince myself that I belong.

"Those kids must have bad parents."
Here we are, trying to be good devoted parents. Yet despite our parenting, our kids are making poor choices.

"That woman thinks she's more talented than she is."
Here I am putting myself out there; I feel scared and vulnerable.

CONNECT INSTEAD OF CORRECT

Sometimes when we gather with family and friends, we encounter some sensitive moments around divisive topics, differing opinions, or past hurts. In our country right now there are a lot of things to talk about, and we all want to be right. But as compassionate people, we can make more progress in getting people to listen to us if they first feel loved and safe. When someone feels under attack, their brain cannot receive your opinion or contribution to the conversation. If all brains around the table feel safe, the conversations can be thoughtful and kind.

An easy way to stay thoughtful and kind is to think about connecting with someone rather than correcting their thinking.

When we feel safe, we are more likely to be curious and explore new ideas. Before your gathering, think through what topics will likely be raised and how you want to handle them. Having a plan ahead of the event helps you manage your brain and move out of the fear center and into the calm, thoughtful center. When you are afraid, your brain sounds the alarms at any indication that conflict is beginning to occur. When you have a plan for how you want to handle the conflict, you move out of your amygdala (fear center) and into your frontal cortex, which allows you to be rational, logical, and clear thinking. With a plan, you can be your calmest self and not react based on fear.

Start your gathering by setting a tone of love and respect for every person there. See the good within each person. Think about what pains and scares them. When we remember that we are all walking around concerned and worried, then we are more likely to have compassion for one another. Often, the more someone is living in fear, the more irritable they are. Instead of arguing with that person, see if you can approach them gently like you would approach a child who was afraid.

Here are some prompts to help you move the conversation toward connection rather than topics that tempt us toward correction. Have a couple of these in your pocket to ask an individual or use them to prompt everyone to share around the table.

- Who's had the greatest impact on your life?
- Where is the most beautiful place you've ever been?
- What are some of your happiest family memories?
- If you could travel anywhere, where would you go?
- What has being a member of this family taught you?
- What's a typical day like for you?
- What are you looking forward to in the coming months?
- What do you love to do so much that it makes you lose track of time?

These questions will help you learn more about those you love and may lead to new insights about those around the table.

I understand that we all have that one person who can push our buttons, and it's hard to always take the high road. Give yourself permission to disappear for a few moments of self-compassion. Take a quick walk, sit in a quiet corner, or seek out the kindest person in the room. Remember that you are a good person and talk to yourself with loving encouragement.

Gatherings can be lovely and gatherings can be hard. We are all trying to find our way. Follow where your heart leads you and take the path of love—that can never be wrong.

TRY THESE

1. Before the next gathering where you know people will have differing views from yours, jot down some ideas for conversation topics besides the controversial ones. What would be fun to talk about with these people? What would you truly like to know more about in their lives? What could you offer as a conversation starter? Also, make a plan for what you will say if the conversation goes a direction you don't want it to go. Have an exit strategy ready so that you can change the topic or leave the conversation if it gets too intense. Focus on connecting, not correcting. Love wins.

2. In parenting it can be very helpful to remember "connect, not correct." Children want to feel a loving ,supportive connection with their parents, not always be corrected. It is tempting to see parenting as a duty to correct a child's behavior or thinking. Instead, think of your duty as being a loving, safe adult for this child. Connect first, then you can have a loving conversation to guide them.

ALLOW MELANCHOLY

A few years ago, my family was visiting the Lincoln Museum in Springfield, Illinois, when I was struck by the quotes from Abraham Lincoln speaking openly about his struggles with melancholy, a word used in the 1800s to define a lingering sadness.

In his many letters on display, he also wrote to encourage others who are suffering. To his best friend, Joshua Speed, he wrote: "remember in the depth and even the agony of despondency, that very shortly you are to feel well again." And to a woman who lost her young husband in battle: "you are sure to be happy again. Knowing this, truly believing it, will make you less miserable now. I have had enough experience to make this statement."

That message rings true today just like it did back then: there will be better days. So many of us fight against being sad or down; we don't like having bad days. We grow frustrated with ourselves, and want to get out of those bad days as soon as possible.

I often hear clients beat themselves up over this; they say: "I shouldn't be sad... I have everything I need. I should be grateful." They don't know why they feel like they do, and punish themselves if they can't figure it out.

But it doesn't work like that—being sad is just part of being human. It's not something we can will away, no matter how hard we try. And the more we grow frustrated with ourselves, the deeper we can go into that hole.

What does work is to normalize feeling sad, to remember that it's temporary and cyclical. You will feel better again. A bad day won't last forever. A better day will soon take its place.

When you find yourself feeling down and you can't pinpoint why, it's important to let yourself feel sad instead of beating yourself up. Show yourself some self-compassion. Tell yourself: "this is just a bad day. It will pass." Remind yourself: "I don't have to figure this out or fix this. I can just let myself be sad."

Be kind to yourself and do whatever it takes to find comfort—whatever small thing that might soothe you—until a better day comes along. When we can do this for ourselves, we get better at doing it for others. Holding space for someone who is sad, without suggesting what they should do, is one of the greatest gifts you can give to a melancholy friend.

TRY THESE

1. Write a note as a reminder: "bad days don't last forever." Keep it somewhere that you can see the next time you're feeling down.

2. Make a "bad day" list of small things that bring you comfort: something special you like to eat, taking a bath, reading a book, or watching a favorite TV show. Show yourself some self-compassion by choosing something from that list the next time you're feeling down.

3. If you're having a bad day today, put both hands on your heart, close your eyes, and say to yourself: "I'm feeling down, and that's okay. I don't have to fix it or figure it out. This is just a bad day. It will pass."

4. When you encounter someone who is having a bad or sad day, allow space for them to feel what they feel. Avoid the temptation to change the emotion, fix it, or rush them out of it. Just meet them where they are. Hold space for the emotional day they are having. Allow melancholy when it arrives. We don't have to be afraid of it. It connects us more deeply to that person. They trust you enough to be vulnerable around you—that is holy sacred ground.

SHARE YOUR STORIES

When my children were in middle school, one of their most beloved teachers died suddenly. He was vibrant, young, and fun-loving—they felt the loss of him deeply. At ages 12 and 14, they struggled to wrap their minds around how someone could be so alive in their classroom and then gone in an instant.

After several tear-filled days, I asked them to tell me about some of their favorite times with Mr. Gannon. The tears turned to smiles as they shared their memories, things like the random tennis ball he kept on his desk, and how much he liked outdoor adventures. The stories continued as they grieved, and gave them a way to keep the memory of him alive.

Matt Gannon taught my children more than middle-school history. He taught them that our lives matter. Every day matters. Matt's 26 years mattered a lot. His death taught his students that life is fragile, but love remains. Watching his family and friends grieve, taught his students that we can come together in tragic loss with love and compassion. Years later, his students still talk about the impact Mr. Gannon had upon them. His story lives on through the telling of stories about him.

Grief can take us through a number of emotions. Sometimes, it wants to talk. Then be quiet. Then talk again. Invite and allow all of that; grieving is a time when we must handle ourselves with care.

When someone dies, they live on in our stories. If you are grieving and feel like talking, share your stories. Talk through your memories with others, without worrying about making them uncomfortable. Sharing is a way for you to become closer to others, as you honor someone's memory. Stories are how we connect with one another.

If you have a loved one who's grieving, ask them for stories about the one they lost. Don't be afraid that you will make them sad by bringing it up; instead, you'll gift them with the opportunity to share their memories with you. You're showing up for them, and giving their grief the chance to talk when it wants to.

TRY THESE

1. If you're grieving, above all else, handle yourself with care. Give yourself extra love. You have permission to proceed the way you need to.

2. Reach out to those who support you, and ask for their stories of your loved one. Share your own, if your grief wants to talk. Consider writing down a few of the stories that you share or hear, so that you can return to them whenever your heart needs to hear them.

3. When someone is grieving a lost loved one, ask them to tell you their stories about them. Don't be afraid of making them more sad, gift them with the opportunity to to keep that person alive in their heart. Listen well as they tell you about them. We live on in the stories told about us. Share your stories.

CONCLUDING REMARKS

I once heard the acronym L.I.F.E. as Love Instead of Fear and Ego. It stuck with me and I think that might sum up our life's mission – to strive to live each day with love instead of ruled by fear and ego. I hope these practices will help you live your life with more love and less fear. I hope you will learn how to manage your complex, brilliant brain by utilizing these practices. Mostly, I hope this book brings you hope that there are things you can do and that life doesn't have to be lived alone. When you feel lonely, open to these pages and hear me speaking to you with encouragement and empowering you to find solutions.

Talk about these practices with the people you love. Select a friend, coworker, family member, or beloved teenager and start a book club of two. The two of you sharing what you are learning about yourself and others. Share how you have made these practices your own. How you have tweaked them, put them into action, and integrated them into your own life. I would love to hear about that too. Send me some of your notes of these book-club-of-two discussions. I'm imagining you in coffee shops, on benches in parks, in beach chairs, hiking a trail, and at weathered kitchen tables with a cup of tea. I want to do this being-human journey with you. We are all trying to find our way and we can do it together. My email is Ginger@GingerRothhaas.com.

I hope these practices become part of your human journey and you use this book as a quick reference guide when you need a tool. As Pierre Teilhard de Chardin taught, "We are not human beings having a spiritual experience. We are spiritual beings having a human experience." I hope these practices make your human experience a little easier.

.

ACKNOWLEDGEMENTS

To my beloved Compassion Fix Community, thank you for cheering me on. You were wind in my sails every week as you asked: how is it coming along, when will it be finished, where will it go on my bookshelf, will I be in it, what will my made-up name be, do you need pre-readers, did you remember to include this, and are you taking care of yourself like you tell us to? You kept me laughing and you filled my soul with love as you encouraged me to create this offering of my heart for the world. It is a joy and honor to do life with all of you.

To my cover and layout designer extraordinaire, Olivia Feathers, our paths crossed at the right divine moment. Your artistic eye, gracious being, and keen attention to detail were exactly what I needed for this project. You deeply understood and appreciated how this book could help people and that helped me believe in it too. Working with you was a delight every time we met. Thank you for being meticulous and having a great sense of style. More books to come my dear Olivia, we are just getting started!

To my proofreader and citation guru, Anne Accardi, you calmed my anxiety and I sleep better knowing your skilled eyes and brilliant brain were part of this project. Your patient demeanor and reassuring tone were exactly what I needed as we crossed the finish line together. I want you involved in everything I do now. Thank you for helping me make this book better every time you read through it.

To my early editor, Tina Neidlein, thank you for saying you liked my weekly emails and you could help me put them into a book. I am forever grateful that you listened to me talk-out what was in my brain and said, "oh that's really good, you should write about that!" You helped me move forward and beyond "someday I'll write a book." I'm still getting a C- on closing tabs on my laptop, but you taught me a lot of other great things about getting my thoughts organized and I'm grateful for our time together.

ABOUT THE AUTHOR

Ginger Hedrick Rothhaas is the founder of Compassion Fix®, a provider of coaches and therapists working together to help make being human a little easier. Ginger holds master's degrees in business, theology, and divinity. She studied at the University of Kansas, Xavier University, and Saint Paul School of Theology. She has been a management consultant, adjunct professor, professional speaker, and business owner, but her favorite role is that of a mom launching two funny and smart teenagers into the world. She lives with those teens in Kansas City with her husband and two enthusiastically loving dogs. You can follow her work @gingerrothhaas and @compassionfix, as well as gingerrothhas.com and compassionfix.com.